GOVERNING CARBON MARKETS WITH DISTRIBUTED LEDGER TECHNOLOGY

Carbon markets involve complex governance challenges, such as ensuring transparency of emissions, facilitating as well as recording transactions, overseeing market activity and preventing abuse. Conventionally, these have been addressed with a combination of regulatory, procedural and technical structures that impose significant burdens on market participants and administrators while remaining vulnerable to system shocks and illicit practices. Distributed ledger technology (DLT) has the potential to address these problems. This volume offers the first book-length exploration of how carbon markets can be governed using DLT, offering conceptual and theoretical analysis, practical case studies and a roadmap for implementation of a DLT-based architecture in major existing and emerging carbon markets. It surveys existing expertise on DLT, provides progress updates from industry professionals and shows how this technology could offer a cost-effective and sustainable solution to double counting and other governance concerns identified as major challenges in the implementation of carbon markets.

Alastair Marke is the Director-General of the Blockchain & Climate Institute (BCI). He is an expert supporting the drafting of the ISO 14097 climate finance standard and a UK representative on the ISO 22739 blockchain and DLT standard (use case, smart contract and governance) working groups. He has edited another pioneering book in this field – *Transforming Climate Finance and Investments with Blockchains* (Academic Press 2018).

Michael A. Mehling is a Professor at the University of Strathclyde Law School and Deputy Director of the Center for Energy and Environmental Policy Research at the Massachusetts Institute of Technology (MIT). He is a member of the BCI Advisory Board.

Fabiano de Andrade Correa is the Director of Legal Research at the BCI Secretariat. He is a lawyer and international consultant with more than fifteen years' experience across the private, public and international sectors, and serves as deputy chair of the Climate Change Law Specialists Group within the IUCN World Commission on Environmental Law.

Governing Carbon Markets with Distributed Ledger Technology

Edited by

ALASTAIR MARKE

Blockchain & Climate Institute

MICHAEL A. MEHLING

Massachusetts Institute of Technology

FABIANO DE ANDRADE CORREA

Blockchain & Climate Institute

CAMBRIDGE UNIVERSITY PRESS

CAMBRIDGE
UNIVERSITY PRESS

University Printing House, Cambridge CB2 8BS, United Kingdom

One Liberty Plaza, 20th Floor, New York, NY 10006, USA

477 Williamstown Road, Port Melbourne, VIC 3207, Australia

314–321, 3rd Floor, Plot 3, Splendor Forum, Jasola District Centre, New Delhi – 110025, India

103 Penang Road, #05–06/07, Visioncrest Commercial, Singapore 238467

Cambridge University Press is part of the University of Cambridge.

It furthers the University's mission by disseminating knowledge in the pursuit of education, learning, and research at the highest international levels of excellence.

www.cambridge.org
Information on this title: www.cambridge.org/9781108843560
DOI: 10.1017/9781108919166

First published 2022

A catalogue record for this publication is available from the British Library.

Library of Congress Cataloging-in-Publication Data
NAMES: Marke, Alastair, editor. | Mehling, Michael, editor. | Corrêa, Fabiano de Andrade, 1982– editor.
TITLE: Governing carbon markets with distributed ledger technology / edited by Alastair Marke, Blockchain and Climate Institute; Michael Mehling, Massachusetts Institute of Technology; Fabiano de Andrade Correa, Blockchain and Climate Institute.
DESCRIPTION: Cambridge, United Kingdom ; New York, NY : Cambridge University Press, 2022. | Includes bibliographical references and index.
IDENTIFIERS: LCCN 2021063086 (print) | LCCN 2021063087 (ebook) | ISBN 9781108843560 (hardback) | ISBN 9781108919166 (ebook)
SUBJECTS: LCSH: Emissions trading – Law and legislation. | Carbon offsetting – Law and legislation. | Blockchains (Databases) – Law and legislation.
CLASSIFICATION: LCC K3593.5.C37 G68 2022 (print) | LCC K3593.5.C37 (ebook) | DDC 344.04/6342–dc23/eng/20220430
LC record available at https://lccn.loc.gov/2021063086
LC ebook record available at https://lccn.loc.gov/2021063087

ISBN 978-1-108-84356-0 Hardback

Contents

Figures

Tables

Notes on Contributors

LEAD AUTHORS

Alastair Marke

Alastair Marke is the Director-General of the Blockchain & Climate Institute (BCI), a think tank supporting governments in the deployment of blockchain and emerging digital technologies to achieve climate change policy goals. He is a co-drafter of the ISO 14097 climate finance standard and a UK representative on the ISO 22739 blockchain and distributed ledger technologies standard (use case, smart contract and governance) working groups. In the UK, Alastair serves as an ad hoc expert adviser to the All-Party Parliamentary Group on Blockchain.

Alastair is a seasoned climate change and innovation policy adviser in the field of international development. Seeing the dire need to accelerate global efforts to fill the current climate finance gap, Alastair co-founded the BCI comprising more than eighty experts from thirty countries in 2017. The group produced the world's first book on blockchain and climate change issues – *Transforming Climate Finance and Green Investment with Blockchains* – in July 2018. Alastair is a recognised speaker and strategist of a series of innovation projects that apply blockchain to renewable energy, green finance, disaster risk insurance and so on.

Michael A. Mehling

Professor Michael A. Mehling is the Deputy Director of the Center for Energy and Environmental Policy Research (CEEPR) at the Massachusetts Institute of Technology (MIT) and a Professor at the University of Strathclyde Law School. Michael serves on the boards of the BCI in London; the Ecologic Institute in Washington, DC and Berlin; the European Roundtable on Climate Change and Sustainable Transition (ERCST) in Brussels; and the Konrad-von-Moltke Fund. He is also an associated researcher with the Energy Policy Research Group (EPRG) at the University of Cambridge and a member of Climate Strategies, an international research network focussed on climate and energy policy. In the past, he has co-chaired the Scientific Committee of the Carbon Pricing Leadership Coalition (CPLC), served on the board of directors of the International Union for Conservation of Nature and Natural Resources US (IUCN-US) and contributed to the Fifth Assessment Report (AR5) of the Intergovernmental Panel on Climate Change (IPCC) and the Lazarowicz Report on Global Carbon Trading commissioned by the UK prime minister. He is the founder and editor-in-chief of the *Carbon & Climate Law Review*, the first academic journal in its field. Michael holds a law degree from the University of Constance, LLM and PhD degrees from the University of Helsinki, and is admitted to the Bar in the European Union.

EDITOR

Fabiano de Andrade Correa
Dr Fabiano de Andrade Correa is the Director of Legal Research at the BCI Secretariat. He is a lawyer and international consultant with more than fifteen years of experience across the private, public and international sectors. Over the past twelve years, he has been consulting in the area of international law, in particular sustainable development, climate change and related issues, with different intergovernmental organisations. He also serves as lead counsel for the Peace, Justice and Governance Programmes of the Centre for International Sustainable Development Law (CISDL); is a co-ordinator of the Climate Change and Agriculture Working Group with LACLIMA (a network of climate lawyers in Brazil); is Deputy Chair of the Climate Change Law Specialist Group of the IUCN World Commission of Environmental Law (WCEL); and is a guest lecturer in different universities in Brazil and Italy. Fabiano holds a PhD in law and LLM degrees from the European University Institute (EUI, Florence, Italy), a Master's in diplomacy and international relations (Diplomatic School of Madrid/ Complutense University Madrid, Spain) and an LLB (Federal University of Rio Grande do Sul, Porto Alegre, Brazil).

CO-AUTHORS

Dessanin Ewèdew Thierry Awesso
Dessanin Ewèdew Thierry Awesso is a PhD law student with a thesis being jointly supervised between Côte d'Azur University (France) and the University of Lomé (Togo). Currently a legal research officer at Research Division III of the BCI Secretariat, and working on artificial intelligence and environmental risks insurance in Africa, he is interested in the application of blockchain and distributed ledger technologies (DLTs) in regulatory enforcement.

Max Inglis
Max Inglis has extensive legal and commercial experience. His career began in legal private practice at the pre-eminent law firms of Linklaters and then Clifford Chance where he worked on multi-billion-pound transactions for private equity firms, financial institutions and FTSE 100 companies. Secondments to Europe and the Middle East provided opportunities to further develop his knowledge as well as business and transaction skills. In 2011, Max

founded his own professional services firm acting as an adviser to investment firms and banks on a variety of deals. Max has practised in a wide variety of disciplines and thus has been exposed to a broad spectrum of commercial situations, obtaining expertise in corporate finance, banking, securitisations and derivatives. Max holds an MBA with distinction from the University of Oxford, a BSc from the University of Southampton and a diploma from the University of Grenoble. He attended the College of Law, London where he gained a postgraduate diploma in law with commendation and a distinction on the legal practice course. He is also a legal adviser to the BCI Secretariat.

Justin Macinante
Dr Justin Macinante is a lawyer with thirty-five years of experience in banking and finance, environmental regulation and policy, and commercial practice in Europe, Australia and the Pacific. He was a legal counsel for the First Climate Group, a carbon trading firm based in Germany and Switzerland, for eight years and more recently has been consulting for the World Bank's Networked Carbon Markets initiative. Justin is part of the DLT4NCM project team at the University of Edinburgh, UK. He holds BSc and LLB degrees from the University of New South Wales, Australia; a Master's in environmental law (first-class honours) from the University of Sydney, Australia; and a PhD from Edinburgh Law School at the University of Edinburgh.

Constantine Markides
Constantine Markides is a qualified solicitor in England and Wales with experience working in the transport finance department at Norton Rose Fulbright LLP. He is currently a legal research officer at Research Division III of the BCI Secretariat and is also employed in the UK Export Finance team as a legal adviser.

Nicola Massella
Nicola Massella works as Legal Manager at STORM Partners providing advice on tokenisation projects and token offerings (i.e. initial coin offerings (ICOs), initial exchange offerings (IEOs) and security token offerings (STOs)). He also works with the BCI Secretariat as a legal research officer. A Doctor of Jurisprudence from Alma Mater Studiorum – the University of Bologna, his field of interest is fintech with a focus on crypto-assets and DLTs.

Sai Kishore Nellore
Sai K. Nellore is Principal Assistant Director-General overseeing the Fellowship Scheme Bureau of the BCI Secretariat, with more than twenty-four years of progressive international experience working with multilateral, government and corporate sectors. Experienced in low-carbon, climate change mitigation and sustainable development, with more than six years in senior leadership positions, he has a successful track record of conceptualising, developing and implementing innovative forestry and natural ecosystem projects and programmes. Along with programme delivery and inspiring and motivating teams in complex and multicultural environments, Sai's skill set includes large-scale project management, strong multi-stakeholder engagement and network management.

Clare Reynolds

Clare Reynolds is an English qualified lawyer, advising on financial services and fintech matters (including crypto-assets and cloud computing) as a senior associate at international law firm Taylor Wessing. She is also a principal legal research officer at the BCI Secretariat. She worked previously for other international law firms and non-governmental organisations, including ClientEarth. She has a first-class MA in geography from Oxford University and postgraduate qualifications in law.

Nicholas Scott

Nicholas Scott is a knowledge broker at the Hughes Hall Centre for Climate Change Engagement and a legal research officer at Research Division III of the BCI Secretariat. He holds an LLM from the University of California, Berkeley, with a specialisation in environmental law and a BA (honours) in law from the University of Cambridge.

Marco Zolla

Marco Zolla is a business lawyer, digital entrepreneur, technology enthusiast and climate champion with wide international experience and a Master's in corporate governance from the University of Milan, Italy. Marco has advised multinational corporations driving huge investments mainly in the renewable energy business and is now supporting tech-start-up projects, addressing the regulatory and legal challenges coming from the digital revolution. Currently, he is a senior legal research officer at Research Division III of the BCI Secretariat.

Foreword

In 2015, countries adopted the Paris Agreement and the 2030 Agenda for Sustainable Development, establishing a global framework for a low-carbon, climate-resilient and sustainable future for all. Historically, to reduce greenhouse gas (GHG) emissions and allow countries to meet their emission targets under the Kyoto Protocol, the parties under the climate convention allowed trading of emission credits (CO_2 equivalent) through 'market mechanisms', namely the Clean Development Mechanism (CDM) and joint implementation (JI). Similar regional or national schemes have also been developed in the past, for example, the EU Emissions Trading System (EU ETS) and national schemes in New Zealand, China and so on. Parties negotiating the Paris Climate Change Agreement wanted to maintain the benefits of countries co-operating to reduce emissions and agreed to create a new market mechanism building on the lessons learnt from previous schemes. The rules that apply to this new 'market mechanism' are defined in Article 6.2 of the Paris Agreement.

Contrary to present carbon market mechanisms, Article 6.2 moves away from centralised accounting, comprehensive rules and standardisation for issuing and transferring international units by offering decentralised co-operative approaches. This bottom-up approach requires parties unilaterally to 'ensure environmental integrity and transparency' and to 'apply robust accounting to ensure, inter alia, the avoidance of double counting' (Articles 6.2 and 6.3).

The Technology Mechanism was created under the United Nations Framework Convention on Climate Change (UNFCCC) to meet the developing countries' demands on technology transfer–related issues. Specifically, under the Paris Agreement and to facilitate its implementation, the technology framework was established to provide overarching guidance on issues related to technology. The theme of innovation features as a key component of the technology framework, underpinning actions and activities that accelerate and scale up innovation at different stages of the technology cycle; the aim is to develop environmentally and socially sound, cost-effective and better-performing climate technologies on a larger and more widespread scale to help countries build resilience and reduce their emissions.

Technologies including DLTs can offer new platforms to unlock innovation for climate change, which simultaneously contributes to the achievement of the Paris Agreement and the Sustainable Development Goals (SDGs) by enabling reductions in carbon emissions or supporting the monitoring and tracking of human impacts on the environment, for example.

Over the past decades, we have witnessed the increasing role of digitalisation in all aspects of global economies and systems, driven by technologies such as the Internet of Things (IoT), big data, artificial intelligence (AI) and blockchain. The Covid-19 pandemic accelerated this digital transformation and brought to the fore the potential of linking digitalisation and green agendas to solve environmental and climate change problems. Covid-19 recovery efforts bring opportunities for countries to embed digital technologies into their recovery plans as key enablers to enhance recovery, speed up the transition to a low-carbon economy and build back better.

However, as we consider these new technologies, we must be mindful of the inequality that stems from the digital divide, which has only been intensified by the coronavirus pandemic and risks worsening vulnerabilities to climate change. Unless, that is, we can bridge the digital divide by creating enabling environments for innovative solutions.

We also know that digital technologies can enhance transparency, accuracy, completeness and comparability in support of environmental integrity and market integrity for the climate. For example, carbon markets require implementing a reliable measurement, reporting and verification process to ensure their integrity and traceability and facilitate reporting and monitoring. However, current challenges to this implementation include lack of transparency and credibility, inconsistent standards and low digitalisation levels.

Recent research has analysed the suitability of using blockchain technology to implement the carbon market mechanism under the Paris Agreement and demonstrated that there is a strong case for implementing a blockchain-based system that offers enhanced tamper-resilience and more robust transparency and auditability features.

The evidence and case studies presented in this book demonstrate how a DLT-based system can deliver a digital infrastructure to existing and emerging carbon markets, which creates integrity and traceability. It builds on the needs of countries that are ready to embrace new and innovative technologies and adhere to transparency, accountability and verifiability in the actions they undertake to achieve the Paris Agreement and the SDGs.

As the UNFCCC Technology Mechanism's implementation arm, the Climate Technology Centre and Network (CTCN) is committed to working with developing countries, including the least developed countries and the small island developing states that are most vulnerable to climate change, to harness the potential of digital technologies in the pursuit of climate goals.

Rose Mwebaza, PhD
Director, CTCN, Economy Division, UN Environment

Preface

Technology is anything that wasn't around when you were born.

Alan Kay (1940–), American computer scientist

In July 2018, the BCI released the world's first book to combine the debates on blockchain technology and climate action. *Transforming Climate Finance and Green Investment with Blockchains* (ed. A. Marke, Academic Press 2018) collates a myriad use cases about blockchain applications in renewable energy, climate finance disbursement, emissions trading and the enforcement of green regulations. Following its success, the BCI is proud to present its second book, *Governing Carbon Markets with Distributed Ledger Technology*, as another pioneering effort that combines thought leadership on blockchain technology and regulation of the steadily expanding carbon market in an era of technological innovation and disruption.

Carbon markets involve complex governance challenges, which range from ensuring transparency of emissions and facilitating as well as recording transactions to overseeing market activity and preventing abuse. Conventionally, these have been addressed with a combination of regulatory, procedural and technical structures that impose significant burdens on market participants and administrators while remaining vulnerable to system shocks and illicit practices.

The carbon markets spearheaded by the Kyoto Protocol (notably the CDM) were aimed at assisting developed countries to reach their emissions targets. From 1997 onwards, several regional, national and subnational carbon markets have been established in the developed world, including the EU ETS in 2005.

Despite their proliferation, many carbon markets have struggled to meaningfully curb global emissions. Early carbon markets were handicapped by limited geographic and sectoral scope; international emissions trading under the Kyoto Protocol, for instance, was open for participation only to developed countries with emissions targets, and excluded both developing country parties – some of which were major emitters – and the private sector. Other challenges encountered in many carbon markets include an excessive supply of carbon credits, double counting of emissions reductions, carbon reduction projects having significant adverse local impacts owing to insufficient safeguards and creation of perverse incentives such as countries adopting lower emissions reduction standards to allow for selling of emissions reductions.

Under the Paris Agreement, all signatory countries have adopted climate targets, representing a shift from the Kyoto Protocol and signalling the potential to dramatically expand carbon markets. Despite omitting mention of the term 'carbon market', Article 6 of the Paris Agreement is the main provision for deployment of carbon trading. Among other things, Article 6.2 provides for co-operation through 'internationally transferred mitigation outcomes towards nationally determined contributions', thereby allowing for linking of different emissions trading systems (ETSs) and the transfer of carbon credits between such systems and countries. Article 6.4 mandates the establishment of a new mechanism similar to the CDM 'to contribute to the mitigation of greenhouse gas emissions and support sustainable development'. Notably, at the 26th United Nations Climate Change Conference in 2021 (COP26), parties adopted decisions concerning, among other topics, the operationalisation of Article 6, paving the way for the implementation of such mechanisms.

Given the Covid-19 pandemic, which has slowed progress on international climate co-operation and national climate action for more than eighteen months as GHGs continue to accumulate in the atmosphere, there is an unmistakable urgency to break the present deadlock in Article 6 negotiations by bringing in new perspectives and solutions.

To paraphrase the words of veteran American computer scientist Alan Kay, quoted at the beginning of this preface, DLT was not around when the concept of emissions trading was born in the 1970s to reduce various forms of air pollution in the United States. In the 2020s, the world has to race against time in order to reduce CO_2 emissions to avoid a global climate catastrophe. The key to accelerating the global efforts lies in emerging digital technologies such as DLT.

Transitioning the governance of carbon markets to a secure, decentralised architecture based on consensus algorithms promises to address problems of system cost and integrity, but the viability, conditions and implications of doing so have not yet been explored comprehensively, and nor have the complex governance requirements that will be faced in different carbon markets. In any event, DLT itself also needs to be adequately regulated in order to prevent deployment of DLT-supported ETSs from introducing new governance challenges.

This volume offers the first book-length exploration of how carbon markets can be governed using DLT, offering conceptual and theoretical analysis, practical case studies, as well as a roadmap for implementation of a DLT-based architecture in major existing and emerging carbon markets. This book builds on the academic debate that deals with the legal-institutional design of the carbon market regime. It identifies gaps in the conventional legal and administrative architecture that could be bridged through implementation of blockchain technology. However, this implies legal-institutional reform that would have disruptive implications for the regulatory environment. Using comparative legal analysis, the chapters in this book discuss an alternative crypto-legal structure that would be conducive to not only a secure but also an integrated and efficient carbon market.

In this volume, we do not intend to provide definite answers to any legal or policy questions; rather, we offer new resources that will enable climate negotiators and relevant stakeholders to take international negotiations and domestic policy debates on carbon trading in a fresh direction.

I am very grateful to the Legal Research Division of the BCI Secretariat for their assiduous efforts to complete this book project over the past year. I am also thankful to several senior climate negotiators and policy officials from a number of countries who have contributed to this project by sharing their insights with us through interviews and informal conversations.

Acknowledgements

This book has been developed as a collaborative effort by the Blockchain & Climate Institute's Legal Research Division. Over the past year, we have been grateful to Kamil Akdag (a former legal research officer in Research Division III), James Duchene (a legal adviser in the Director-General's Office), Jason Hsu (a legislative advocacy adviser in the Development Division) and Luke McMichael (a senior research officer in the Director-General's Office) for contributions to its preparation or finalisation.

We are also grateful to a number of external experts for their contributions to this book in various formats: Francisco Benedito (Chief Executive Officer at ClimateTrade), Eduardo Antonio Silva Besa (First Secretary, Chilean Embassy in Poland, Chilean Ministry of Foreign Affairs), Paolo Borchia (Member of the European Parliament for Italy), Aldyen Donnelly (co-founder and Director of Carbon Economics, Nori), Carlos Fuller (Lead Negotiator at AOSIS), Hussein Alfa (Seyni) Nafo (a former Chair of the African Climate Negotiators' Group), Dr Satyendra Prasad (Fiji's Permanent Representative to the United Nations), Michael Schneider (Assistant Director, Aviation Environment, IATA) and Professor Majid Shafie-Pour (former Chair of the Asia-Pacific Group of Climate Negotiators).

About BCI

The Blockchain & Climate Institute (BCI) is a progressive think tank providing leading expertise in the deployment of emerging digital technologies for climate and sustainability actions. As an international network of scientific and technological experts, BCI is at the forefront of innovative efforts to enable technology transfers in order to create a sustainable and clean global future. Headquartered in London, BCI achieves its missions by enabling global technology transfers and supporting governments in providing favourable policy and regulatory environments for innovations. By means of aggregation and distribution of new knowledge, BCI's international network for scientific and technological experts is able to enhance state and non-state climate actions through targeted technological interventions.

BCI'S LEGAL RESEARCH DIVISION (RESEARCH DIVISION III)

The Legal Research Division supports the creation of enabling legal and regulatory frameworks for the deployment of blockchain and emerging digital technologies in climate action and sustainable development efforts. The division's membership includes qualified (environmental) lawyers and jurists from a broad range of jurisdictions, which enables it to build on expertise across common and civil law jurisdictions and to provide top-notch legal research and legal advice on the governance of blockchain and wider DLT in the specific legal contexts of climate innovation programmes.

For more information about BCI's work and structure, please visit www.blockchainclimate.org.

Glossary

The following terms, when used in this book, have the meaning as ascribed by the International Organization for Standardization (ISO), as set out below. Unless otherwise indicated, these definitions are adopted from ISO/TC307.

artificial intelligence:	capability of an engineered system to acquire, process and apply knowledge and skills
block:	structured data comprising block data and a block header
blockchain:	a distributed ledger with confirmed blocks organised in an append-only, sequential chain using cryptographic links
blockchain system:	system that implements a blockchain; note that a blockchain system is a type of DLT system
block data:	structured data comprising zero or more transaction records or references to transaction records
block header:	structured data that include a cryptographic link to the previous block unless there is no previous block
block reward:	reward given to miners or validators after a block is confirmed in a blockchain system; it can be in the form of a token or cryptocurrency
confirmed:	accepted by consensus for inclusion in a distributed ledger
confirmed block:	block that has been confirmed
consensus:	agreement among DLT nodes that a transaction is validated and that the distributed ledger contains a consistent set and ordering of validated transactions; note that consensus does not necessarily mean that all DLT nodes agree – the details regarding consensus differ among DLT designs,

	and this is a distinguishing characteristic between one design and another
consensus mechanism:	rules and procedures by which consensus is reached
crypto-asset:	digital asset implemented using cryptographic techniques
cryptocurrency:	crypto-asset designed to work as a medium of value exchange
cryptographic hash function:	function mapping binary strings of arbitrary length to binary strings of fixed length, such that it is computationally costly to find for a given output an input that maps to the output, it is computationally infeasible to find for a given input a second input that maps to the same output, and it is computationally infeasible to find any two distinct inputs that map to the same output
cryptographic link:	reference, constructed using a cryptographic hash function technique, that points to data
cryptography:	discipline that embodies the principles, means and methods for the transformation of data in order to hide their semantic content, prevent their unauthorised use or prevent their undetected modification
decentralised application (DApp):	application that runs on a decentralised system
decentralised system:	distributed system wherein control is distributed among the persons or organisations participating in the operation of the system; note that in a decentralised system, the distribution of control among persons or organisations participating in the system is determined by the system's design
digital asset:	asset that exists only in digital form or which is the digital representation of another asset
distributed ledger:	ledger that is shared across a set of DLT nodes and synchronised among the DLT nodes using a consensus mechanism
distributed ledger technology (DLT):	technology that enables the operation and use of distributed ledgers
distributed system:	system in which components located on networked computers communicate and co-ordinate their actions by interacting with each other

DLT account:	distributed ledger technology account representation of an entity participating in a transaction
DLT address:	distributed ledger technology address value that identifies a DLT account participating in a transaction
DLT network:	distributed ledger technology network of DLT nodes which make up a DLT system
DLT node:	distributed ledger technology node
DLT platform:	distributed ledger technology platform set of processing, storage and communication entities which together provide the capabilities of the DLT system on each DLT node
DLT system:	distributed ledger technology system that implements a distributed ledger
DLT user:	distributed ledger technology user entity that uses services provided by a DLT system
double spending:	failure of a DLT platform where the control of a token or crypto-asset is incorrectly transferred more than once
entity:	item inside or outside an information and communication technology system, such as a person, an organisation, a device, a subsystem or a group of such items that has recognisably distinct existence
hash value:	string of bits which is the output of a cryptographic hash function
immutability:	property wherein ledger records cannot be modified or removed once added
Internet of Things (IoT):	infrastructure of interconnected entities, people, systems and information resources together with services which process and react to information from the physical world and from the virtual world
interoperability:	ability of two or more systems or applications to exchange information and to mutually use the information that has been exchanged
ledger:	information store that keeps records of transactions that are intended to be final, definitive and immutable to a distributed ledger
ledger record:	record containing transaction records, hash values of transaction records or references to transaction records recorded on a distributed ledger
miner:	DLT node which engages in mining

mining: activity, in some consensus mechanisms, that creates and validates blocks or validates ledger records

node: device or process, in DLT, that participates in a network and stores a complete or partial replica of the ledger records

off-chain: related to a blockchain system, but located, performed or run outside that blockchain system

off-ledger: related to a DLT system, but located, performed or run outside that DLT system

on-chain: located, performed or run inside a blockchain system

on-ledger: located, performed or run inside a DLT system

oracle: service that updates a distributed ledger using data from outside a DLT system

permissioned: requiring authorisation to perform a particular activity or activities

permissioned DLT system: permissioned distributed ledger system

permissionless: not requiring authorisation to perform any particular activity

permissionless DLT system: DLT system that is permissionless

private DLT system: private DLT system that is accessible for use only to a limited group of DLT users; note that public and private categories apply to DLT users and that permissioned and permissionless categories apply to DLT users and those entities that administer or operate the DLT system

public DLT system: public distributed ledger technology system which is accessible to the public for use

record: information created, received and maintained as evidence and as an asset by an organisation or person, in pursuit of legal obligations or in the transaction of business

token: digital asset that represents a collection of entitlements

transaction: smallest unit of a work process, which is one or more sequences of actions required to produce an outcome that complies with governing rules

transaction record: record documenting a transaction of any type

validated: status of an entity when its required integrity conditions have been checked validation: function by which a transaction, ledger record or block is validated

validator: entity in a DLT system that participates in validation; note that in some DLT systems, the DLT node that has the role of validator can digitally sign a ledger record or block

Abbreviations

ACE	Aviation Carbon Exchange
AFOLU	Agriculture, Forestry and Land Use
AI	artificial intelligence
AML	anti-money laundering
AR5	Fifth Assessment Report
AV	accreditation and verification
BCI	Blockchain & Climate Institute
CAEP	Committee on Aviation Environmental Protection
CCR	CORSIA Central Registry
CDM	Clean Development Mechanism
CEEPR	Center for Energy and Environmental Policy Research
CER	certified emission reduction (temporary tCER and long-term lCER)
CERT	ICAO CORSIA CO_2 Estimation and Reporting Tool
CISDL	Centre for International Sustainable Development Law
CLOB	central limit order book
CORSIA	Carbon Offset and Reduction Scheme for International Aviation
CPLC	Carbon Pricing Leadership Coalition
CTCN	Climate Technology Centre and Network
DAO	decentralised autonomous organisation
DApp	decentralised application
DeFi	decentralised finance
DL	deep learning
DLT	distributed ledger technology
DOE	designated operational entity
EC	European Commission
EPRG	Energy Policy Research Group
ERCST	European Roundtable on Climate Change and Sustainable Transition
ETS	emissions trading system

EU	European Union
EUA	European Union Allowance
EU ETS	European Union Emissions Trading System
EUTL	European Union Transaction Log
FRED+	Fuel Reporting and Emissions Database
GDPR	General Data Protection Regulation
GHG	greenhouse gas
IATA	International Air Transport Association
ICAO	International Civil Aviation Organization
ICO	initial coin offering
ICT	information communication technology
IoT	Internet of Things
IPCC	Intergovernmental Panel on Climate Change
IPCI	Integral Platform for Climate Initiatives
ITMO	internationally transferred mitigation outcome
IUCN-US	International Union for Conservation of Nature and Natural Resources US
JI	joint implementation
KYC	Know Your Customer
MBM	market-based measure
ML	machine learning
MRV	monitoring, reporting and verification
MSR	Market Stability Reserve
NDC	nationally determined contribution
NLP	natural language processing
ODR	online dispute resolution
OTC	over-the-counter
PA	predictive analytics
PII	personally identifiable information
QELRO	quantified emission limitation and reduction objective
SDGs	Sustainable Development Goals
UNCTAD	United Nations Conference on Trade and Development
UNEP	United Nations Environment Programme
UNFCCC	United Nations Framework Convention on Climate Change
VAT	value-added tax
VCS	Verified Carbon Standard
VCU	verified carbon unit
WCEL	World Commission of Environmental Law

1

Understanding 'Distributed Ledger Technology' and Its Potential as a Disruptive Technology for Climate Action

Alastair Marke[1]

1.1 INTRODUCTION: OVERVIEW OF THE ISSUES EXPLORED IN THIS BOOK

The global climate crisis is one of the most significant issues of our times. Although climate change itself is not a novel phenomenon, the rate at which the Earth's temperature is changing is unprecedented. This is in large part owing to anthropogenic causes – most notably elevated carbon dioxide (CO_2) emissions, among other greenhouse gases (GHGs).[2] To limit and ultimately reverse the impacts of anthropogenic climate change, immediate action is essential. At the international level, the most recent step forward is the Paris Agreement (PA),[3] an international and legally binding treaty that has been ratified by 189 signatories[4] and was adopted under the umbrella of the United Nations Framework Convention on Climate Change (UNFCCC).[5] The PA commits its signatories to '[h]olding the increase in the global average temperature to well below 2°C above pre-industrial levels and pursuing efforts to limit the temperature increase to 1.5°C above pre-industrial levels, recognising that this would significantly reduce the risks and impacts of climate change' (Article 2),[6] with a view to achieving a 'balance between anthropogenic emissions by sources and removals by sinks' of GHG emissions in the second half of the century (Article 4.1).

Putting a price on carbon emissions and creating a market for tradable emission allowances and credits – so-called carbon markets – is one of the most promising

1 Credit is given to Mr Luke McMichael, Senior Research Officer at the Director-General's Office, Blockchain & Climate Institute Secretariat for his editorial assistance in this chapter.

2 TJ Crowley, 'Causes of Climate Change Over the Past 1000 Years' (2000) 289(5477) *Science* 270–77. doi: 10.1126/science.289.5477.270.

3 Paris Agreement to the United Nations Framework Convention on Climate Change (adopted 12 December 2015, entered into force 4 November 2016) TIAS No 16–1104 (PA).

4 UNFCCC, Paris Agreement: Status of Ratification, https://unfccc.int/process/the-paris-agreement/status-of-ratification accessed 16 January 2021.

5 United Nations Framework Convention on Climate Change (adopted 9 May 1992, entered into force 21 March 1994) 1771 UNTS 107 (UNFCCC).

6 *Paris Agreement* [online](2015) https://unfccc.int/files/essential_background/convention/application/pdf/english_paris_agreement.pdf accessed 10 April 2018.

policy options for decarbonising the economy.[7] Indeed, a cost-effective means of achieving the foregoing goals of the PA may be through the 'tokenisation'[8] of carbon units. Article 6 of the PA, for instance, outlines co-operative approaches that parties can voluntarily pursue to allow 'for higher ambition in their mitigation and adaptation actions and to promote sustainable development and environmental integrity'. In particular, Article 6.2 provides for the use of 'internationally transferred mitigation outcomes (ITMOs) towards nationally determined contributions (NDCs)', allowing for, inter alia, linkage of different national and supranational emissions trading schemes (ETSs) and the transfer of carbon allowances and credits between countries. Going forward, the tokenisation of carbon units is likely to become an increasingly attractive option to incentivise emitters to transition towards cleaner technologies.[9]

One of the foci of this book is to consider the overlap between legal practices in the traditional legal and regulatory governance of carbon trading and the emergence of a 'crypto-legal' structure that is underpinned by the application of distributed ledger technology (DLT).[10] At present, there is no single approach to carbon trading, and various carbon markets have been shown to suffer from shortfalls related to their design and governance.[11] In some instances, existing infrastructures that proved vulnerable to abuse and fraud even necessitated drastic measures to secure the integrity of the carbon market.

One of the most notable features of current carbon markets is the centralisation of their governance.[12] The allocation of emission allowances or issuance of carbon credits is determined by a central entity, frequently a governmental authority, which then also oversees the trading process. This centralisation of governance functions has been a response to observed risks, but it leaves the market open to human error in governance operations. Also, it has contributed to the heterogeneity of design and implementation standards across markets and jurisdictions. This has engendered a complex and fragmented system that cannot fully harness the promised efficiency of carbon trading, inhibiting cross-market exchange of value and suffering from a lack of consensus about the methodology for determining the net environmental benefits of mitigation efforts.[13]

7 For details on the theory, rationale and evolution of carbon markets, see Chapter 2.

8 The tokenisation of assets involves the digital representation of real assets on distributed ledgers or the issuance of traditional asset classes in tokenised form. See OECD, 'The Tokenisation of Assets and Potential Implications for Financial Markets' *OECD Blockchain Policy Series* (2020) www.oecd.org/finance/The-Tokenisation-of-Assets-and-Potential-Implications-for-Financial-Markets.htm accessed 12 April 2022.

9 Center for Climate and Energy Solutions, 'Climate Change 101 – Cap and Trade' Climate Change 101: Understanding and Responding to Global Climate Change (2011).

10 This is further explored later in this chapter.

11 For details, see the case studies in the second part of this book.

12 See A Galenovich and others, 'Blockchain Ecosystem for Carbon Markets, Environmental Assets, Rights, and Liabilities: Concept Design and Implementation' in A Marke (ed), *Transforming Climate Finance and Green Investment with Blockchains* (Academic Press 2018).

13 ibid.

What has resulted from these shortcomings is an imbalance between demand and supply.[14] The complexity of the system also works against the incentivisation aspect inherent to a successful carbon trading ecosystem, with its inefficiencies acting as barriers to access, compounding the failure to incentivise the desired ethical trading behaviour and placing too great an emphasis on trust in a market that has not succeeded in propagating trustworthiness in the first instance and is disposed to corruption. Further, the centralised nature of the carbon market within each jurisdiction engenders a system that is highly susceptible to data privacy breaches. These issues are neither acceptable nor sustainable within a growing market model that seeks to make good on the aims of the PA.

1.2 UNDERSTANDING DLT AND BLOCKCHAIN

Since the cryptocurrency 'Bitcoin' emerged in 2009, a fresh way of recording, trading and enforcing items of value (including rights and entitlements) has increasingly interested businesses and governments around the world. The technology on which Bitcoin is based is called 'blockchain'. As the best-known example of DLT, blockchain refers to 'a distributed ledger', or a list of all transactions across a peer-to-peer network. It has been defined as 'an incorruptible digital ledger of economic transactions that can be programmed to record not just financial transactions but virtually everything of value'.[15] In fact, DLT uses 'nodes' (i.e. independent computers) to record, share and synchronise transactions in their individual electronic ledgers (i.e. databases) as opposed to storing data in a traditional, centralised ledger.[16]

Branded a 'trust machine',[17] blockchain introduces a new platform on which to build peer-to-peer transactions or interactions without a third party, central operator or authority. The algorithm adopted in blockchain reduces the dependence on humans to verify transactions. Users can co-own and co-operate blockchain platforms. On a blockchain, 'smart contracts' (see more on this term later) can automate and hence accelerate transaction flows. Thus, blockchain has recently become a juggernaut to disrupt business models in the finance sector.[18]

The first-ever blockchain application is the cryptocurrency Bitcoin, which, while dependent on the functioning of blockchain, should not be labelled a blockchain equivalent. Extensively discussed by governments and corporations lately,

14 Carbon Market Watch, 'Carbon Markets 101 – the Ultimate Guide to Global Offsetting Mechanisms' (Brief, 2020) https://carbonmarketwatch.org/publications/carbon-markets-101-the-ultimate-guide-to-global-offsetting-mechanisms/ accessed 12 April 2022.

15 D Tapscott and A Tapscott, *Blockchain Revolution: How the Technology Behind Bitcoin Is Changing Money, Business, and the World* (Penguin 2016).

16 World Bank, 'Blockchain & Distributed Ledger Technology' (*Brief*, 2018) www.worldbank.org/en/topic/financialsector/brief/blockchain-dlt accessed 20 December 2018.

17 Economist, 'The Promise of the Blockchain: The Trust Machine' [2015] *The Economist*.

18 S Meunier, 'Blockchain 101: What Is Blockchain and How Does This Revolutionary Technology Work?' in A Marke (ed), *Transforming Climate Finance and Green Investment with Blockchains* (Academic Press 2018).

'blockchain' has become a buzzword, overshadowing even the umbrella term DLT in many sectors. For simplicity, the terms DLT and blockchain are used interchangeably throughout this book.

With trust as, allegedly, the central issue hindering the development of the electronic marketplace, the use of DLT, which holds decentralisation as its fundamental tenet, would be a simple means of answering a number of these concerns. In short, DLT is a type of 'distributed database shared over a peer-to-peer network, where transaction data is synchronised between nodes of the network and the data is immutably stored and secured through cryptographic techniques. Decisions in the network are managed through consensus algorithms.'[19] A subclass of this is blockchain, which is defined as 'a transaction-based, chronologic, immutable and synchronised distributed ledger shared over a peer-to-peer network. In a blockchain, transactions are stored in interlinked transaction sets, referred to as blocks. They execute and record single transactions using consensus algorithms and bundle them into transaction sets using cryptographic techniques.'[20]

Utilising a distributed network enables autonomous individuals or groups to transfer or transact without the need for a trusted intermediary to moderate these trading interactions. Instead, the node system architecture ensures the creation of identical, immutable and verifiable registers, allowing for independent auditing and, crucially, public accountability in the supply chain. Fundamentally, the decentralisation of data via the implementation of blockchain can be expected to drive integration within the carbon market by means of instilling trust in the existing systems through removing the need for that trust directly. Another expected benefit of blockchain implementation would be increased efficiency, as the use of smart contracts streamlines application processes by reducing bureaucracy and minimising the chance of human error. This serves to bolster the integrity of a transaction, particularly as the process of identification and verification of transacting parties is simplified, enabling faster transactions from a commercial perspective. Decentralisation of information would also reduce government costs for access to census data, and, furthermore, individuals would have greater powers for accessing and controlling their personal information. Applying DLT will therefore allow for an ecosystem that cannot be controlled by single entities, providing a tool against the recorded abuses of existing systems.[21] In short, market functionality is preserved while efficiency is vastly improved. The expected knock-on effect is that individuals are then empowered to better use these systems with the goal of improving the global

[19] Maik Lange, Steven Chris Leiter and Rainer Alt, 'Defining and Delimitating Distributed Ledger Technology: Results of a Structured Literature Analysis' in Claudio Di Ciccio and others (eds), *Business Process Management: Blockchain and Central and Eastern Europe Forum*, Vol 361 (Springer International 2019) 6.

[20] ibid 7.

[21] M Rauch and others, 'Distributed Ledger Technology Systems – A Conceptual Framework' (Cambridge Centre for Alternative Finance Report, 2018) www.jbs.cam.ac.uk/wp-content/uploads/2020/08/2018-10-26-conceptualising-dlt-systems.pdf accessed 12 April 2022.

outlook on climate change, with greater assuredness that they are not vulnerable to fraudulent activity.

There are several attributes of DLT that make it appealing as a platform to facilitate emissions trading, namely (1) uniqueness, (2) validity, (3) consensus, (4) immutability and (5) authentication in the desired combination.[22]

(1) **Uniqueness**: In a blockchain environment, transactions are taken as an input to be run through a hashing algorithm[23] – taking an input string of any length and producing an output string of a fixed length of alphanumeric characters – to produce a unique identifier (e.g. Bitcoin uses secure hash algorithms of 256 bits as the signature for a text). This unique identifier functions as a serial number for tracking every piece of information in a transaction, which is critical for managing a huge amount of market data.

(2) **Validity**: All transactions on the blockchain network must be verified by a validator for their legality (which ensures that the network does not contain malicious information, double spends, etc.). Each transaction made is broadcast to the entire network where 'miners'[24] validate the legitimacy of a bunch of transactions in order to build a 'block'. The most notable mechanism is proof-of-work, which entails computers on the networks solving a cryptographic puzzle and the right/reward of adding a block is granted to the first computer or 'miner' able to solve the challenge. Therefore, DLT is capable of knowing whether a given proposed update to the system is valid.

(3) **Consensus**: Blockchain approves and records transactions through a process called a 'consensus algorithm'. Blocks of transactions are congregated and distributed for approval along to all network nodes that confirm them. Consensus entails agreeing on the ordering of validated transactions. When there is a conflict of copies, the version of the truth supported by the majority in the network prevails. Together with hashing, it results in a system that is immutable, resilient to cyber-attack (tamper-proof) and more powerful as the network grows. Any hacker attack is made much more difficult as it would have to compromise the majority of nodes instead of only a single point of

[22] Carla L Reyes, 'Conceptualizing Cryptolaw' (2017) 96 *Nebraska L Rev* 384; P Brody, 'How Blockchains Will Industrialise a Renewable Grid' in A Marke (ed), *Transforming Climate Finance and Green Investment with Blockchains* (Academic Press 2018).

[23] A hash is a one-way mathematical function that summarises a piece of data as a piece of unique, fixed-size, short data. A hash algorithm turns data into a key of random characters called a hash. A Jackson and others, 'Networked Carbon Markets: Permissionless Innovation with Distributed Ledgers?' in A Marke (ed), *Transforming Climate Finance and Green Investment with Blockchains* (Academic Press 2018).

[24] In blockchains, actors that maintain and audit transactions (typically called miners) receive rewards in exchange for their work or stake in sustaining a healthy network. J Duchenne, 'Blockchain and Smart Contracts: Complementing Climate Finance, Legislative Frameworks, and Renewable Energy Projects' in A Marke (ed), *Transforming Climate Finance and Green Investment with Blockchains* (Academic Press 2018).

failure in the middle, as would be the case when hacking, for instance, a server of a single online registry. In the face of conflicting updates to the system (by hackers), DLT is capable of knowing which, if any, of those updates parties should select as the one on which they all agree. Thus, mutually untrusted parties to a shared fact know that the fact they see is the same as the fact that other stakeholders see across the Internet or distributed ledgers.

(4) **Immutability**: Whereas most systems maintain a single, centralised copy of transactions and accounts, blockchain spreads them across all the key points in the network through a database consensually distributed and synchronised at multiple sites. It results in every location in the network having all the information it needs to function autonomously; and tampering with transactional data or committing fraud are almost impossible because of the huge redundancy of good copies. Nobody in the DLT system will accept a transaction from anyone who attempts to build that transaction on any modified version of the data that has already been accepted by other stakeholders. The immutability of a distributed ledger is thus crucial for building trusted registries.

(5) **Authentication**: Whereas traditional systems record only data in ledgers, blockchains let users exchange digital agreements alongside financial and/or non-financial value with smart contracts – also known as 'programmable ledgers'. For example, a buyer and a seller of carbon credit (futures) can agree upon a transaction (including prices and numbers) which cannot proceed until the receipt of due diligence information as the condition verified with an 'oracle'. An oracle is a trusted party (or a technical source, such as a database or a person assigned this role) functioning as the 'source of truth' for a smart contract. In addition, DLT associates every action in the system with a private key such that there is no 'master key' or 'administrator password' that overrides the smart contract settings agreed upon by parties. This smart contract is then distributed across all the network nodes and enforced automatically. It results in an impeccable integration of real-world actions with the exchange of value and payments online.

There are two other concepts related to smart contracts: (a) a decentralised autonomous organisation (DAO), which is an organisation run purely by rules written into smart contracts on a blockchain; and (b) a decentralised application (DApp), which contains a front-end user interface with a decentralised back-end that typically leverages DLT and smart contracts.[25]

An important part of blockchain is the choice between 'permissionless' (public and open to all participants) and 'permissioned' (private, where only authorised entities can hold a copy of the ledger or participate in transactions) blockchains.

[25] Meunier (n 18); Anand Audia, Busstra Gort and Sigrid Kaag, *The Legal Aspects of Blockchain* (UNOPS 2018).

That said, the current taxonomy of blockchain systems is much more structured than permissionless versus permissioned, and it may also be possible for a range of permissions to be applied to the system. In other words, a plethora of options exists between the two ends of the scale. For example, permission may be required to become a ledger node, but individuals may interact with ledger nodes without permissions; or anyone may be able to become a ledger node but may require permissions to add entries to the ledger; or there may be different permissions for adding entries compared to viewing entries; and so on.[26] Ultimately, the importance of the distinction is that permissionless and permissioned blockchains differ in the participation and rights of users – rules regarding privacy and governance. A permissionless blockchain such as Bitcoin allows everyone to freely participate as a standard user (anonymously) with no need of identification or authentication but only a pseudonym. There is not a single party 'in control'. In the interest of security, most permissionless blockchains adopt as the consensus mechanism a proof-of-work ('mining') system, which regularly appoints a 'random' computer to propose a block of transactions to the other computers in the network. Other computers can determine via mathematical proof (cryptography) that:

(i) this computer has indeed earned the right to make the proposal (proof: proof-of-work);
(ii) the proposed transactions come from a party permitted to execute these transactions and the contents have been untampered with (proof: digital signature); and
(iii) the proposed transactions can indeed be executed following the applicable rules (e.g. sufficient balance; proof: hash trees).

There are various consensus algorithms in DLT. Without going into too much detail, they can be categorised into two main groups. The first group is proof-based consensus (mentioned above). The second group is voting-based consensus, which requires nodes in the network to exchange their results of verifying a new block or transaction, before making the final decision.[27]

All transactions and information in a permissionless blockchain are public. In contrast, a permissioned blockchain is protected by an access control layer. Participation in permissioned blockchains is restricted to users who are approved by a 'super-user' for different read/write rights. This design can help safeguard privacy, improve control and proof of authority, and allow for a smaller pool of trusted actors when dealing with sensitive transactions.[28]

The applicability of blockchain for the governance of carbon markets, for example, in implementing an ETS and addressing the legal questions surrounding

[26] Jackson and others (n 23).

[27] G Nguyen and K Kim 'A Survey about Consensus Algorithms Used in Blockchain' (2018) 14 *J Info Process Systems* 101; Meunier (n 18); Audia, Gort and Kaag (n 25).

[28] Audia, Gort and Kaag (n 25).

these topics, is explored in the second half of this book, focussing on different mechanisms such as the European Union Emissions Trading System (EU ETS), voluntary carbon markets and others.

1.3 SHIFTING TO A CRYPTO-LEGAL STRUCTURE FOR REGULATED ENVIRONMENTS

The five attributes of blockchain, or DLT, outlined in Section 1.2 result in blockchain that may not be compatible with current regulatory frameworks. For one thing, DLT was invented with the rationale of creating self-governing and state-remote networks through infrangible internal rules balancing all the relevant interests with no judicial or regulatory intervention necessary, in theory.[29] Nevertheless, the blockchain (financial) networks, and the financial values transferred with distributed validation, should be regulated differently.

Regulatory instruments should be developed to address this friction by harmonising the outcomes under the internal rules of blockchain networks with the requirements of the law, particularly the assurance that the prerequisites for a valid transaction/contract still apply as a consequence. The most viable approach is to connect/transpose these internal rules into the law itself by recognising the generated outcomes, including dispositions and acquisitions, as enforceable against third parties,[30] in a 'crypto-legal structure' comprising 'crypto-laws' – a concept that Carla Reyes first suggested in 2018.[31]

1.3.1 *Defining Crypto-law and Crypto-legal Structure*

Lawrence Lessig famously advocated that 'code is law . . . we must understand . . . the software and hardware that make cyberspace what it is and regulate cyberspace as it is'.[32] 'Code' is the internet architecture that maintains the order of the cyberspace by binding users to a set of internal rules. Crypto-law is an emerging jurisprudence 'as a result of implementing and delivering the law of any subject matter through smart-contracting, semi-autonomous, intelligently developing cryptographic computer code', including the use of DLT in legal processes.[33]

Philipp Paech proposes a cross-cutting issue about the 'material scope' of regulation customised to the structure of blockchain financial networks.[34] The structure of blockchain financial networks is characterised by disintermediation, where accounts and intermediary–client (two-party) relationships are substituted by a distributed

[29] Philipp Paech, 'The Governance of Blockchain Financial Networks' (2017) 80 *Mod L Rev* 1073.
[30] ibid.
[31] Carla L Reyes, 'Cryptolaw for Distributed Ledger Technologies: A Jurisprudential Framework' (2018) 58 *Jurimetrics* 283.
[32] Lawrence Lessig, *Code: And Other Laws of Cyberspace* (Basic Books 1999).
[33] Reyes (n 31).
[34] Paech (n 29).

network built on 'multi-directional relationships' among its nodes connected through a software platform. Therefore, the suitable actors or entities against which to enforce the network-wide law and regulations, covering such basic requirements as continuity of service, systemic stability, availability and integrity, should be the platform providers and/or nodes, which can be well-established financial institutions and/or state-regulated legal persons. That is, platform providers have to guarantee the continuity and systemic stability of the platform on which its internal rules governing the acquisition of rights and execution of contracts must be aligned with relevant law.

Reyes also suggests that the 'crypto-law' should recognise the immutability of transaction records on a blockchain network with statutory legal provisions that transactions, once initiated, are irreversible by the blockchain network; and parties should file a claim for damages as the only remedy in a context similar to the outcomes of automated clearing processes for cash or securities, known as 'finality'. Nevertheless, there should be exceptional circumstances under which a transaction can be undone such as a software loophole identified to have caused unexpected outcomes discordant with the network rules. Otherwise speaking, the law should guide the handling of financial assets administered in blockchain financial networks.[35] Building these laws into computer-coded legal structures, or 'crypto-legal structures', will enable lawmakers to grasp the specific DLT features that can complement or substitute existing legal processes.[36] An example is the US State of Delaware, which has introduced amendments to its General Corporation Law allowing corporations to issue shares through blockchain technologies.[37]

Based on 'code is law', DLT codes, forming a set of crypto-law and then a crypto-legal structure, can be conceptualised as a foreign legal system for creating research space to study if – and under which circumstances – a crypto-legal structure is necessary.[38]

1.3.2 *Disruptive Effects of Crypto-legal Structure*

Below are the three scholar-recognised short-term disruptive effects that a crypto-legal structure can yield in regulated environments:

(A) **Simplification of existing substantive law**: Crypto-legal structures could simplify existing law by allowing a mixture of DLT services to resolve legal questions that the current legal rule, institutions or structures are struggling to address sufficiently.[39] An example is the security of data access. All

35 ibid.
36 Reyes (n 22).
37 Pete Rizzo, 'Delaware Governor Signs Blockchain Bill into Law' (*Coindesk*, 2017) www.coindesk.com/delaware-governor-signs-blockchain-legislation-law accessed 5 January 2019.
38 Reyes (n 31).
39 Reyes (n 22).

transactions, especially those proceeded digitally, contain sensitive data that raise concerns about infringement of privacy should cyber-attacks happen. Currently, much transactional data is stored on 'cloud' services offered by tech companies, meaning that the ultimate control of this storage infrastructure is in the hands of these contractors. On a blockchain, an encryption key is required for personal access to the data stored in a distributed ledger, guaranteeing data security for both regulators and the regulated. The use of smart contracts is 'a financial security held in escrow by a network that is routed to recipients based on future events, and a computer code'.[40] These security features will remove the distrust among contracting parties that empowers the application of the contract law. Regulators would no longer need to handle data theft and courts contract disputes, which in turn simplifies enforcement of the existing law.

(B) **Emergence of new legal elements and actors**: Effective regulation requires a right addressee against which to enforce the rules. There may be major variance between a legal rule implemented by humans and one implemented through computer code. The self-executing elements of blockchain applications – as new legal elements – designed by coders – as new legal actors – may exert more regulatory power on users than necessary, which may result in new regulatory drawbacks such as unintended biases and questions of access to redress for faulty decisions.[41] For example, if a blockchain financial network produced unintended outcomes owing to a software bug or loophole (in a smart contract), all financial institution users would immediately face the same operational difficulties because the decentralisation of ledgers on a blockchain means that all nodes are interconnected. There are no technical or legal options that can circumvent these difficulties. Therefore, Paech alludes to the material scope of regulation being extended to cover more/new legal elements and actors such as coders for blockchain-based transactions.[42]

(C) **New patterns of enforcement and regulation**: Crypto-legal structures imply the possibility that DLT leads to near-automatic compliance with regulatory requirements. This possibility offers both pros and cons: regulations to closely mirror socio-economic realities versus the risk of automatic restraint considerably eroding individual autonomy.[43] For instance, blockchain is known for its security and prevention of fraud such as payment scams. Smart contracts can protect buyers and sellers by ensuring that payment is not sent until agreed goods/services are delivered. Blockchain thwarts scams by recording all transactions so that a coin/credit cannot be counterfeited or double spent.

40 C DeRose, 'Smart Contracts Are the Future of Blockchain' [2016] *Am Banker*.

41 Reyes (n 22).

42 Paech (n 29).

43 Reyes (n 22).

Identity theft to conduct transactions is not possible because unique digital signatures (key pairs) are required to authorise transactions.[44] The roles of law enforcement agencies may have to evolve.

1.4 BLOCKCHAIN AND CLIMATE ACTION

Recently, the international climate change policy community has extended its focus to exploring how blockchain and emerging digital technologies (e.g. artificial intelligence (AI) and remote sensing) can facilitate implementation of the Paris Agreement. This increasing interest has focussed, in particular, on Article 6.2, which provides:

> Parties shall, where engaging on a voluntary basis in cooperative approaches that involve the use of internationally transferred mitigation outcomes (ITMOs) towards nationally determined contributions, promote *sustainable development* and ensure *environmental integrity* and transparency, including in governance, and shall apply *robust accounting* to ensure, inter alia, the avoidance of double counting, consistent with guidance adopted by the Conference of the Parties serving as the meeting of the Parties to this Agreement.[45]

Article 6.2 commits signatories to promoting 'sustainable development', 'environmental integrity' and 'transparency' of the international carbon markets. Can DLTs such as blockchain, recognised for improving efficiency and trust,[46] ensure the sustainability, environmental integrity and transparency of ITMOs or other typologies of carbon markets (e.g. domestic, regional or even voluntary ones)? Currently, the most established systems that could effectuate ITMOs are the transfers of allowances between the EU ETS (including Norway, Iceland and Liechtenstein) and the Swiss ETS. The applicable legal frameworks would epitomise that of global carbon markets to remain on the 2°C trajectory.

Deploying blockchain for the governance of carbon markets would necessarily encompass a series of institutional and regulatory reforms. Convery suggests that 'economists tend to pay relatively little attention to institutional design – and associated legal and administrative frameworks – but they are central considerations if emissions trading is to be successfully mobilised'.[47] These legal and administrative frameworks should ensure simplicity, strict accountability and

44 Paech (n 29).

45 *Paris Agreement* (n 6). Emphasis added.

46 Alastair Marke (ed), *Transforming Climate Finance and Green Investment with Blockchains* (Academic Press 2018).

47 F Convery, 'Emissions Trading and Environmental Policy in Europe' (Paper presented at the pre-summit conference – Knowledge and Learning for a Sustainable Society (Climate and Global Justice Session), Göteborg University, Sweden 12–14 June 2001) 1 www.emissionstradingnetwork.com accessed 12 April 2022.

flexibility concurrently.[48] Take the US SO_2 programme as an example, where 'simplicity' involves small units being exempted automatically. 'Strict accountability' involves legal systems dealing with non-compliance (e.g. automatic sanctions), and technical capability to detect violations almost automatically. 'Flexibility' involves bilateral trades not required to obtain prior government approval, which favours trading and reduces transaction costs.[49] Among others, 'strict accountability' has to be accomplished with some key components, including allocation of allowances; the monitoring, reporting and verification (MRV) process and related compliance cycle; transfers of carbon allowances; registry infrastructure; and trading of offset credits.

Despite the operator-level compliance rate within the EU ETS, arguably the most advanced example of a functioning carbon market nowadays, remaining high,[50] assessing the legal frameworks of the EU ETS that govern relevant ETS components can reveal numerous pending legal questions. For one thing, given the electronic nature of EU ETS allowances and Clean Development Mechanism (CDM) carbon credits, the cybersecurity of the electronic infrastructure tends to be a weak link of this carbon market. Cyber-attacks against the EU ETS trading accounts can lead to an overwhelming impact on the market order such as financial losses incurred by buyers or sellers. Cyber-attacks against the CDM registry can disturb the issuance and movement of carbon credits, resulting in double counting of emissions reductions in carbon markets such as the EU ETS to which its credits are transferred. The liabilities of all stakeholders in this context need to be clarified and unambiguous legal solutions to these legal questions are required to uphold the environmental integrity of the EU ETS and the CDM.

Thus, DLT, which boasts sophisticated security features, may be able to revolutionise the carbon markets and make them more secure and efficient. This book provides a comprehensive overview of these issues, demonstrating how emerging technologies such as DLT, AI and the Internet of Things (IoT), on their own merit but also combined, can significantly contribute to improving the governance of existing and future carbon markets. Notably, the book fills a gap in the literature focussing on these innovative and burning issues, providing cutting-edge analysis of (1) how these legal questions are being addressed in the current regulatory

48 AD Ellerman, 'Tradable Permits for Greenhouse Gas Emissions: A Primer with Particular Reference to Europe (Report No 69)' (2000) http://web.mit.edu/globalchange/www/MITJPSPGC_Rpt69.pdf accessed 12 April 2022.

49 J Goffman, 'Testimony at US House of Representatives: Accomplishments of the Clean Air Act, as Amended by the Clean Air Act Amendments of 1990', Hearing before the Subcommittee on Energy and Air Quality of the Committee on Energy and Commerce, House of Representative, 107th Congress, 2nd Session, Serial No 107-106 (1 May 2002). Scan available at https://bit.ly/38g55RB accessed 24 April 2022.

50 J Verschuuren and FM Fleurke, 'Report on the Legal Implementation of the EU ETS at Member State Level: Deliverable D2.4 ENTRACTE – Economic iNsTRuments to Achieve Climate Targets in Europe (EU/FP7)' (TSC 2014) http://entracte-project.eu/research/report-legal-studies/ accessed 12 April 2022.

frameworks and what the shortcomings or challenges are; and (2) how solutions could be implemented to alleviate these challenges and make the trading systems more secure and efficient, and at what cost.

1.5 AIMS OF THE BOOK

This book builds on two separate research strands: on the one hand, it explores the academic debate that deals with the legal-institutional design of carbon market mechanisms, its challenges and gaps; on the other hand, it looks at the field of emerging technologies, their roles and applications to different climate change challenges and solutions, as well as their underlying regulatory and institutional implications. In this regard, it offers an innovative and groundbreaking line of analysis uniting these different topics into practical conclusions and recommendations. Ultimately, this volume is to provide food for thought with regard to the design of a 'crypto-legal structure' that can support the decentralisation of carbon market governance in the new era.

The fresh analysis on the intersection of technology and carbon market regulations contained in this unique book seeks to inform climate negotiators and all related stakeholders of new perspectives to shape and progress the currently stagnant negotiations on the implementation of Article 6 of the Paris Agreement.

It identifies gaps in the conventional legal and administrative architecture that could be bridged through the implementation of blockchain technology. However, this implies a legal-institutional reform with disruptive implications to the regulatory environment. Using comparative legal analysis, this book discusses an alternative crypto-legal structure conducive to not only a secure but also an integrated and efficient carbon market.

As shown in an informal note by the co-chair of the Subsidiary Body for Scientific and Technological Advice (SBSTA) of the UNFCCC, blockchain technology has been extensively discussed during SBSTA meetings,[51] although it was finally omitted in the draft Article 6.2 guidance texts later released. At the 26th Conference of the Parties to the UNFCCC (COP26) in Glasgow, climate negotiators reached an agreement on the rulebook for Article 6, providing the rules necessary for a robust, transparent and accountable carbon market by eliminating double counting for compliance markets and establishing a strong carbon accounting framework. However, the negotiations on the specific technology types to support such international carbon market infrastructure have been postponed to upcoming COPs. These discussions may indicate the necessity of reviewing the current legal and regulatory frameworks governing the carbon markets to prepare them for a new organising principle in the 'blockchain era'. This book addresses these questions and

[51] SBSTA, 'Draft Elements for SBSTA Agenda Item 11(a) – Guidance on Cooperative Approaches Referred to in Article 6, Paragraph 2 of the Paris Agreement: Informal Note by the Co-chairs (12 November)' (2017).

studies some key elements of such plausible yet far-reaching regulatory reforms; it will thus fill the gap of academic legal research that could inform the development of new emissions trading regulations.

1.6 STRUCTURE OF THE BOOK

The book really falls into two halves. The first half covers the more general aspects of blockchain and carbon trading, beginning with Chapter 2, which explores concrete case studies of carbon markets and how transition to a DLT-based governance could be operationalised. The chapter establishes some basic concepts behind DLT and crypto-legal structure as well as the theoretical and historical aspects of carbon trading, exploring key governance aspects and challenges of carbon markets. Following this introductory chapter, Chapter 3 sets out the main functions of AI, IoT and DLT within the environmental sphere and how these technologies can be combined to create more effective climate solutions through weather-pattern prediction, increasing transparency and accounting, technical feasibility and carbon market resilience. Then Chapter 4 looks at the attributes that DLT has and how they can make it unique in solving climate issues. The chapter considers the overlap between the traditional legal structures in a system and the modern crypto-legal proposals and provides solutions to the security issues arising under the EU ETS.

The second half of the book has a more specific focus on key aspects of a transition to a blockchain-based governance model for carbon markets. It begins with Chapter 5, which considers the practical and legislative requirements for introducing an effective crypto-legal structure for DLT in the carbon trading economy. It also explores the roles of each stakeholder in this transitioning process towards achieving an efficient carbon economy. Chapter 6 explores the EU ETS and explains how the transition to a blockchain-based trading system could be operationalised. It also provides a legislative roadmap for aligning the EU ETS with the European Union Digital Strategy. Next, Chapter 7 focusses on the voluntary carbon markets by providing an overview of the CDM and the Verified Carbon Standard. It uses examples from the private sector to showcase the use of DLT in the voluntary carbon markets. Chapter 8 then considers the Carbon Offsetting Scheme for International Aviation and how a DLT-based system could achieve some of the aims of the Paris Agreement such as avoidance of double counting, shorter transaction times and lower transaction costs. Then Chapter 9 introduces the concept of networking of carbon markets and analyses the political, legal and practical reasons for using networking as opposed to linking. It also considers how the application of DLT can help to operationalise a networked carbon markets framework.

Finally, Chapter 10 summarises the conclusions and lessons from all the preceding chapters and provides recommendations and a potential roadmap for the transition into DLT-based governance for the carbon markets.

1.7 TARGET AUDIENCE

This book is intended for climate negotiators, policymakers and legislators, lawyers and the academic community at large who are interested in these issues. It particularly serves as a basis to inform the relevant negotiations at upcoming COPs in recognition of the added value it provides to MRV processes, cybersecurity and market efficiency.

2

Governing the Carbon Market

Michael A. Mehling

2.1 INTRODUCTION

'Carbon markets' is a collective term for a variety of approaches to carbon trading, that is, trade in intangible units that allow emission of a specified amount – usually a metric tonne – of greenhouse gases (GHGs). A carbon market can be implemented either as an emissions trading system (ETS), which imposes an absolute or relative ceiling ('cap') on aggregate emissions from covered entities and enables these and other market participants to trade in allowances, or as a baseline-and-credit system, which defines an emissions baseline and rewards emissions reductions beyond that baseline with tradable credits that can serve to offset emissions elsewhere.

Despite a turbulent history with several setbacks,[1] carbon markets have seen continued growth at the domestic level and in regional and international markets. As of 2022, 17 per cent of global GHG emissions are covered by some form of carbon trading, a figure that is set to rise as further markets are rolled out.[2] Expanding levels of market activity and an upward trend in carbon prices have seen the total value of global carbon trading break consecutive records in recent years.[3] In Europe, a regional trading system comprising thirty countries and more than 10,000 installations[4] – the European Union Emissions Trading System (EU ETS) – remains the largest carbon trading system with a market size of 682 billion euros in 2021,[5] but a national ETS currently under development in China will likely eclipse it in terms of emissions coverage and participation. Growth has also been

[1] See, for an assessment, Michael Arthur Mehling, 'Between Twilight and Renaissance: Changing Prospects for the Carbon Market' (2012) 6 CCLR 277.

[2] International Carbon Action Partnership (ICAP), 'Emissions Trading Worldwide: Status Report 2022' (ICAP 2022) 26 https://icapcarbonaction.com/system/files/document/220408_icap_report_rz_web.pdf accessed 16 May 2022.

[3] Refinitiv, 'Carbon Market Year in Review 2ß21' (Refinitiv 2022) https://www.refinitiv.com/content/dam/marketing/en_us/documents/gated/reports/carbon-market-year-in-review-2022.pdf accessed 16 May 2022.

[4] The EU ETS comprises all twenty-seven EU member states, as well as Iceland, Liechtenstein and Norway; for a detailed description, see Chapter 6 in this book.

[5] Refinitiv (n 3) 3.

seen in the market for carbon credits, where the historically largest crediting system, the Clean Development Mechanism (CDM) under the Kyoto Protocol, has mitigated more than 2 billion tonnes of GHG emissions and attracted USD 300 billion in carbon finance to developing countries.[6] Other crediting systems, including independent mechanisms governed by private standards, are, however, gaining ground and account for a majority of recently issued credits.[7]

While carbon markets offer a powerful tool to address climate change, they also place high demands on the institutional and regulatory architecture created for their implementation. Properly defined and enforced institutions – including property rights – are necessary for any market to achieve efficient outcomes,[8] especially where they affect public goods and common-pool resources.[9] Like other markets,[10] carbon markets are therefore embedded in and facilitated by government regulation.[11] Because they are premised on an artificially constrained supply of emission units, they are particularly dependent on a robust governance framework and credible policy mandates.

What this chapter describes, therefore, are the specific governance needs and challenges encountered in carbon trading. It begins with an overview of carbon trading, its theoretical underpinnings and historical evolution, and then proceeds to describe the central governance functions in carbon markets, focussing on environmental integrity, compliance and enforcement, transparency and market oversight. It concludes with some considerations about the potential role of technological innovations in carbon market governance as a transition to the subsequent sections of this book.

2.2 AN INTRODUCTION TO CARBON TRADING

2.2.1 *Theory and Rationale of Carbon Trading*

Policymakers seeking to address the causes and effects of climate change[12] – once described as 'the greatest market failure the world has ever seen'[13] – can have

6 United Nations Framework Convention on Climate Change (UNFCCC), 'Achievements of the Clean Development Mechanism 2001–2018: Harnessing Incentive for Climate Action' (UNFCCC 2018) 3 https://unfccc.int/sites/default/files/resource/UNFCCC_CDM_report_2018.pdf accessed 16 January 2021.

7 World Bank, *State and Trends of Carbon Pricing 2020* (World Bank 2020) 46.

8 Ronald H Coase, 'The Problem of Social Cost' (1960) 3 JL Econ 1.

9 Elinor Ostrom, *Governing the Commons: The Evolution of Institutions for Collective Action* (CUP 1990) 15.

10 Max Weber, *Wirtschaft Und Gesellschaft* (3rd edn, Mohr 1947) 364.

11 Markus Lederer, 'Market Making via Regulation: The Role of the State in Carbon Markets' (2012) 6 Regul Gov 524.

12 This section draws on Michael A Mehling, 'Governing Cooperative Approaches under the Paris Agreement' (2020) 46 Ecol LQ 765.

13 Nicholas Stern, *The Economics of Climate Change: The Stern Review* (CUP 2007) viii.

recourse to a portfolio of policy instruments, including corrective pricing and quantity rationing, performance standards, subsidies, agreements and informational instruments.[14] A subset of policy instruments influence behaviour through price signals[15] and are therefore commonly referred to as market-based or economic instruments.[16] Such instruments are credited with achieving climate policy objectives at the lowest cost because they incentivise abatement where it is cheapest.[17] Abatement decisions are decentralised, moreover, helping to overcome the information asymmetry between policymakers and polluters. By granting polluters flexibility to determine the allocation of resources, these instruments are thus better at avoiding path dependencies and sunk investments in dead-end technologies.[18]

One way of harnessing the benefits of economic instruments relies on quantity controls coupled with the creation of a market for tradable units.[19] While guaranteeing a defined policy outcome, such markets also generate an explicit price, thereby internalising some or all of the social cost of pollution in the private cost of underlying economic activity.[20] As prices for units rise in response to growing scarcity, the demand for them will gradually decrease, along with the associated emissions. Under conditions of perfect competition, this should result in an equilibrium where marginal abatement costs are equalised across all regulated entities, and abatement occurs where it yields the largest net benefit to society.[21]

Applied to climate change, this quantity rationing approach involves the issuance of tradable units conferring the right to discharge a specified quantity of GHG emissions for a specified duration. Variations of this approach range from ETSs based on a technological baseline or emissions ceiling ('cap') to crediting systems

14 Intergovernmental Panel on Climate Change (IPCC), *Climate Change 2014: Mitigation of Climate Change. Working Group III Contribution to the IPCC Fifth Assessment Report* (CUP 2015) 1155; Organisation for Economic Co-operation and Development (OECD), *Climate Change Mitigation: What Do We Do?* (OECD Publishing 2008) 18–22.

15 OECD, *Environmental Policy: How to Apply Economic Instruments* (OECD Publishing 1991) 117.

16 Johannes B Opschoor and Hans Vos, *Economic Instruments for Environmental Protection* (OECD Publishing 1989); Robert N Stavins, 'Market-Based Environmental Policies' in Paul R Portney and Robert N Stavins (eds), *Public Policies for Environmental Protection* (2nd edn, Routledge 2000).

17 Carolyn Fischer and Richard G Newell, 'Environmental and Technology Policies for Climate Mitigation' (2008) 55 J Env Econ Manag 142; Robert N Stavins (ed), *Project 88: Harnessing Market Forces to Protect Our Environment* (Project 88 1988) 15, 19.

18 Dieter Helm, 'Economic Instruments and Environmental Policy' (2005) 36 Econ Soc Rev 205, 215.

19 Thomas D Crocker, 'The Structuring of Atmospheric Pollution Control Systems' in Harold Wolozin (ed), *The Economics of Air Pollution: A Symposium* (WW Norton 1966); John H Dales, *Pollution, Property and Prices: An Essay in Policymaking and Economics* (University of Toronto Press 1968); W David Montgomery, 'Markets in Licenses and Efficient Pollution Control Programs' (1972) 5 J Econ Theory 395.

20 While quantity controls with trading are fundamentally distinct from Pigovian pricing set at the level of the social cost of externalities (see Arthur C Pigou, *The Economics of Welfare* (Macmillan & Co 1920)), the variable market price of transacted units does send a price signal to market participants, thereby internalising the externality at least in part.

21 William J Baumol and Wallace E Oates, *The Theory of Environmental Policy* (2nd edn, CUP 1988) 177; Thomas H Tietenberg, *Emissions Trading: Principles and Practice* (2nd edn, Resources for the Future 2006) 27.

based on mitigation efforts at project, sectoral or economy-wide level.[22] Collectively referred to as 'carbon markets',[23] they have in common a quantity limitation which generates demand for units, and an ability of market participants to purchase or sell units at the respective market price, signalling the opportunity costs of pollution as determined by the forces of demand and supply.

A market-based approach is particularly suited to address climate change because GHGs are not in themselves toxic and the damage function of their accumulation in the atmosphere is shallow in the short run,[24] which allows for spatial and temporal flexibility in the policy response.[25] Climate change is unique, moreover, in that the underlying causes are diffuse, widely heterogeneous and virtually ubiquitous activities, necessitating policy solutions that are scalable and cost-effective. As abatement costs rise over time – with cheap abatement options being, by design, exhausted first – the cost-effectiveness of market-based instruments will become increasingly important to sustain policy ambition over the long term, explaining the continued expansion of carbon markets around the world.

2.2.2 *Evolution of Carbon Trading*

Not long after first being described in the theoretical literature,[26] carbon markets were already being implemented as an instrument of climate policy.[27] At the domestic level, experimentation with market mechanisms began as early as 1974,[28] and its perceived success in addressing air pollution prompted a surge in the public interest and scholarly

22 OECD, *Domestic Transferable Permits for Environmental Management: Design and Implementation* (OECD Publishing 2001) 19.

23 Although other GHGs may be included, the term 'carbon market' is widely used because carbon dioxide (CO_2) is the main GHG in terms of its overall contribution to climate change and because tradable units are mostly denominated in terms of carbon dioxide equivalent (CO_2e); see Richard G Newell, William A Pizer and Daniel Raimi, 'Carbon Markets 15 Years after Kyoto: Lessons Learned, New Challenges' (2013) 27 J Econ Perspect 123, 124.

24 This is the case because climate change is a stock externality: its consequences depend not on emissions in a single year but on the accumulated stock of emissions over time; see Richard G Newell and William A Pizer, 'Regulating Stock Externalities under Uncertainty' (2003) 45 J Env Econ Manag 416, 417.

25 Helm (n 18) 223; Alan J Krupnick and Ian WH Parry, 'What Is the Best Policy Instrument for Reducing CO_2 Emissions?' in Ruud de Mooij, Michael Keen and Ian WH Parry (eds), *Fiscal Policy to Mitigate Climate Change: A Guide for Policymakers* (International Monetary Fund (IMF) 2012) 1.

26 This section draws on Michael A Mehling, 'Market Mechanisms' in Lavanya Rajamani and Jacqueline Peel (eds), *The Oxford Handbook of International Environmental Law* (2nd edn, OUP 2021) 920.

27 Daniel H Cole, 'Origins of Emissions Trading in Theory and Early Practice' in Stefan E Weishaar (ed), *Research Handbook on Emissions Trading* (Edward Elgar 2016) 25.

28 Early markets for transferable pollution allowances in the United States included a 1977 amendment of the Clean Air Act to include an offset system which gave new installations the right to commence operations in certain areas only after the resulting emissions had been offset against a reduction in emissions by other, existing sources, as well as a major amendment of the same act in 1990 that created a market for allowances to emit sulphur dioxide (SO_2); see, generally, Hugh S Gorman and Barry D Solomon, 'The Origins and Practice of Emissions Trading' (2002) 14 J Policy Hist 293.

engagement. The central benefit ascribed to market mechanisms arises from differences in abatement cost and greater efficiency gains in a larger market, from which to derive an economic theory that endorsed the broadest possible deployment. Unsurprisingly, therefore, market approaches were also soon considered for global environmental challenges. With its global scale, high economic stakes and unique physical features, climate change attracted the most active discussion of markets as part of intergovernmental co-operation.[29]

Perhaps the most pivotal moment for the integration of market-based approaches into the fabric of international environmental governance occurred during the negotiations resulting in the adoption of the Kyoto Protocol,[30] when the United States insisted on the inclusion of carbon trading as a condition for agreement.[31] Under the Kyoto Protocol, those developed country parties that entered quantified emission limitation and reduction obligations (QELROs) were able to meet these through a set of flexibility mechanisms: international emissions trading and two project mechanisms, Joint Implementation (JI) and the CDM.[32] Additional modalities, procedures and guidelines were eventually adopted by the parties through a series of decisions that govern the implementation of the Kyoto Protocol.[33] Under these rules, the use of the flexibility mechanisms is voluntary but subject to several eligibility requirements.[34]

As countries proceeded to render this framework operational, they were able to draw on prior work by legal scholars that 'borrowed'[35] insights from domestic experiences to recommend how market instruments should be implemented under international law.[36] This trend accompanied a broader shift in international relations from the enforcement of binary rules in 'regulatory' treaties to a more 'managerial' style relying on transparency and facilitation through flexible co-operative arrangements.[37] In this

29 Published in 1997, the 'Economists' Statement on Climate Change' was by then the largest public statement in the history of the profession and endorsed an 'international emissions trading agreement' to address the climate challenge; see Stephen J Decanio, *The Economics of Climate Change: A Background Paper* (Redefining Progress 1997) 2.

30 Kyoto Protocol to the United Nations Framework Convention on Climate Change (adopted 10 December 1997, entered into force 16 February 2005), 2303 UNTS 162 (Kyoto Protocol).

31 Sebastian Oberthür and Hermann E Ott, *The Kyoto Protocol: International Climate Policy for the 21st Century* (Springer 1999) 189.

32 See Articles 6, 12 and 17 of the Kyoto Protocol; for further details on the CDM, see Chapter 7 in this book.

33 Suraje Dessai and Emma Lisa Schipper, 'The Marrakech Accords to the Kyoto Protocol: Analysis and Future Prospects' (2003) 13 Global Env Chang 149.

34 To participate in international emissions trading, for instance, countries had to, inter alia, calculate their assigned emissions budgets pursuant to specified accounting modalities, establish a national system for the estimation of GHG emissions by sources and removals by sinks, and create the necessary infrastructure to account for the issuance, holding, transfer, cancellation and retirement of tradable units.

35 Jonathan B Wiener, 'Something Borrowed for Something Blue: Legal Transplants and the Evolution of Global Environmental Law' (2001) 27 Ecol LQ 1295.

36 Richard B Stewart and Jonathan B Wiener, 'The Comprehensive Approach to Global Climate Policy: Issues of Design and Practicality' (1992) 9 Arizona J Intl Comp L 83.

37 Abram J Chayes and Antonia H Chayes, *The New Sovereignty: Compliance with International Regulatory Agreements* (Harvard University Press 1998).

process, traditional intergovernmental co-operation has ceded terrain to a fragmented topography of informal networks and partnerships, in which varying constellations of state and non-state actors resort to the public as well as private norms when addressing transboundary challenges.[38] International carbon trading under the Kyoto Protocol is emblematic of this trend, with its reliance on private actors such as project developers and verifiers.

Following the inclusion of the flexibility mechanisms in the Kyoto Protocol in 1997, carbon markets saw a gradual diffusion to the domestic level, starting with national ETSs in a number of European countries and, in 2005, the launch of the EU ETS as the largest carbon market at the time.[39] Over the following decade, additional carbon markets began to emerge in North America and the Asia-Pacific region, and more recently momentum has shifted to the developing world, with several countries in Latin America and Asia at various stages of introducing domestic carbon markets.[40] Continued expansion of these compliance markets into new geographies and sectors, coupled with gradually rising carbon prices as climate policies align with decarbonisation targets in a growing number of jurisdictions, will likely sustain this trend into the future.

In parallel, the voluntary carbon market – driven by a number of private carbon crediting standards – has seen dramatic growth, extending participation in carbon trading to new constituencies.[41] Evolving consumer preferences, investor pressure and shareholder expectations have accelerated growth in this segment of the carbon market, a trend that is likewise expected to continue. Overall, as of 2022, 25 ETSs for GHG emissions were in place at the supranational, national and subnational levels,[42] and 14,550 carbon crediting projects had been registered under 23 national, international and independent carbon crediting mechanisms.[43] While predictions about the future trajectory of carbon markets are highly speculative, current policy commitments and market fundamentals suggest further growth.

Even as some market segments are likely to decline in the longer term because the underlying sectors phase out GHG emissions, other sectors that are particularly difficult to decarbonise will rely partly or entirely on offset crediting to achieve carbon neutrality. By the end of the century, this could result in an overall market that exceeds 1 trillion US dollars per year.[44] Offset crediting alone, driven by new markets and market segments such as the Carbon Offset and Reduction Scheme for

38 Kati Kulovesi, Michael A Mehling and Elisa Morgera, 'Global Environmental Law: Context and Theory, Challenge and Promise' (2019) 8 Transnatl Env L 405.

39 For a more detailed description of the EU ETS, see Chapter 6 of this book.

40 For a recent overview, see ICAP (n 2).

41 Stephen Donofrio and others, 'State of the Voluntary Carbon Markets 2020: Voluntary Carbon and the Post-Pandemic Recovery' (Ecosystem Marketplace 2020) www.forest-trends.org/publications/state-of-the-voluntary-carbon-markets-2020-2 accessed 16 January 2021.

42 ICAP (n 2) 35.

43 World Bank (n 7) 51.

44 Jae Edmonds and others, 'The Economic Potential of Article 6 of the Paris Agreement and Implementation Challenges' (International Emissions Trading Association 2019) 7 www.ieta.org/resources/International_WG/Article6/CLPC_A6%20report_no%20crops.pdf accessed 13 October 2019.

International Aviation (CORSIA),[45] is forecast to grow from 0.6 billion US dollars in 2019 to as much as 200 billion US dollars in 2050.[46]

2.3 GOVERNANCE CHALLENGES IN THE CARBON MARKET

2.3.1 *What Is Governance and Why Does It Matter in Carbon Trading?*

As stated in the introduction to this chapter (Section 2.1), carbon markets – which are based on an artificially constrained supply of emission units and thus rely on credible policy mandates – place high demands on the institutional and regulatory framework governing their establishment and operation.[47] This chapter therefore defines the notion of governance and establishes its relevance in carbon trading. 'Governance' is, of course, an ambiguous concept. For the Commission on Global Governance, it represented 'the sum of the many ways individuals and institutions, public and private, manage their common affairs. It is the continuing process through which conflicting or diverse interests may be accommodated and co-operative action may be taken.'[48] Importantly, governance is widely seen as extending beyond traditional state authority to include, for instance, authority at multiple levels – international, national, regional and local – as well as private forms of governance.[49]

Applied to the context of climate change, governance thus broadly understood can be defined as 'all purposeful mechanisms and measures aimed at steering social systems towards preventing, mitigating, or adapting to the risks posed by climate change, established and implemented by states or other authorities'.[50] For climate policy design and implementation, more specifically, the Intergovernmental Panel on Climate Change (IPCC) has acknowledged that 'institutions[51] and processes of governance shape and constrain policy-making and policy implementation in multiple ways relevant for a shift to a low carbon economy' by setting the incentive

45 For further details, see Chapter 8 of this book.

46 Frank Watson, 'Global Carbon Offsets Market Could Be Worth $200 Billion by 2050: Berenberg' S&P Global (13 May 2020) www.spglobal.com/platts/en/market-insights/latest-news/natural-gas/051320-global-carbon-offsets-market-could-be-worth-200-bil-by-2050-berenberg accessed 16 January 2021.

47 Ruth Greenspan Bell, 'The Kyoto Placebo' (2006) 22 Issues Sci Technol 28, 29.

48 Commission on Global Governance, *Our Global Neighborhood: The Report of the Commission on Global Governance* (OUP 1995) 2.

49 'Governance, in other words, encompasses the activities of governments, but it also includes the many other channels through which "commands" flow in the form of goals framed, directives issued, and policies pursued.' See James N Rosenau, 'Governance in the Twenty-First Century' (1995) 1 Global Gov 13, 14.

50 Sverker C Jagers and Johannes Stripple, 'Climate Governance Beyond the State' (2003) 9 Global Gov 385, 385.

51 'Institutions', a term closely related to governance, denotes 'rules and norms held in common by social actors that guide, constrain, and shape human interaction. Institutions can be formal, such as laws and policies, or informal, such as norms and conventions.' See IPCC (n 14) 1768.

structure and political context of decision-making and by affecting patterns of thinking and understanding of policy choices.[52]

When it comes to carbon trading, governance can hence manifest itself in a variety of ways, from the treaty provisions and implementing decisions adopted at the international level to operationalise the flexibility mechanisms of the Kyoto Protocol, to the rules and procedures enacted by legislative or executive bodies to implement a domestic ETS, all the way to the private standards determining the eligibility of mitigation projects for offset crediting or guiding the activities of accredited verifying entities. Governance frameworks will differ for each carbon market, but some common elements can be identified across geographic and normative contexts. At a minimum, carbon markets require a process to ensure transparency of emissions, including a regulatory framework for measurement, reporting and verification (MRV), as well as the required infrastructure to track distribution and ownership of carbon units and their transfer.[53] But, depending on the context, governance of carbon trading extends well beyond these minimum elements to encompass further aspects of transparency, compliance and enforcement, and market oversight. These and the associated governance challenges are described in further detail in Section 2.3.2.

As with any market,[54] the economic benefits of carbon trading are thus predicated on an adequate governance framework to secure the conditions needed for an efficient allocation of resources. At the same time, however, excessive regulation can prove detrimental, counteracting the allocative efficiency achieved through corrective measures. Policymakers face considerable difficulties in identifying the optimal balance between too much or too little governance, and any balance they might strike will in turn be subject to political pressures and stakeholder influences. If they opt for a restrictive governance framework, the resulting transaction costs may affect the operation of carbon markets,[55] diminishing liquidity and the efficiency of price discovery. Overly stringent restrictions can deter market actors from participating in the market altogether.[56] Taken as a whole, the governance of carbon markets calls for reconciling contending visions of the appropriate balance between

52 ibid 1149.

53 Suzi Kerr and others, 'Emissions Trading in Practice: A Handbook on Design and Implementation' (World Bank and ICAP 2016) 108879 http://documents.worldbank.org/curated/en/353821475849138788/Emissions-trading-in-practice-a-handbook-on-design-and-implementation accessed 16 January 2021; Erik F Haites and Geoffrey Bird, *An Emerging Market for the Environment: A Guide to Emissions Trading* (United Nations Environment Programme (UNEP) and United Nations Conference on Trade and Development (UNCTAD) 2002).

54 Joseph E Stiglitz, 'Government Failure vs. Market Failure: Principles of Regulation' in Edward J Balleisen and David A Moss (eds), *Government and Markets: Toward a New Theory of Regulation* (CUP 2012) 15.

55 Robert N Stavins, 'Transaction Costs and Tradeable Permits' (1995) 29 J Env Econ Manag 133.

56 William Nordhaus, 'Life After Kyoto: Alternative Approaches to Global Warming' (Working Paper 11889, National Bureau of Economic Research 2005) 18 www.nber.org/papers/w11889 accessed 16 January 2021.

prescriptiveness and flexibility, or between securing ambition and reducing cost, encompassing inevitable trade-offs.

2.3.2 *Governance Risks and Vulnerabilities in the Carbon Market*

That carbon markets raise particular governance challenges was already observed early on.[57] As the conceptual notion of carbon trading moves from theory to implementation, its elegant simplicity gives way to complex governance risks and vulnerabilities. These are all the more relevant because incentive structures in carbon markets differ fundamentally from those in more established markets: buyers and sellers can afford indifference about whether transacted units reflect actual emissions reductions, making evasion a positive-sum game for both parties. Absent adequate safeguards, the intangible nature and limited, inelastic supply of emissions units renders carbon markets relatively more susceptible to price volatility and strategic or fraudulent behaviour.[58] Another challenge arising from the unique incentive structure of carbon markets is the intertemporal – or dynamic – inefficiencies discussed in the theoretical literature,[59] including in the context of emissions trading[60] and offset crediting.[61]

Like other climate policies, carbon markets are exposed to rent seeking and regulatory capture at various stages of their implementation, but their technical complexity arguably expands the number of entry points for influencing behaviour.[62] Stakeholder pressures can weaken the stringency of mitigation targets or influence the design of carbon markets in ways that favour certain market participants.[63] More generally, governments tend to suffer from information asymmetries and capacity constraints that limit their ability to identify and implement the

[57] Assessing governance needs of the CDM, for instance, Peter Newell, Nicky Jenner and Lucy Baker, 'Governing Clean Development: A Framework for Analysis' (2009) 27 Dev Policy Rev 717.

[58] Beat Hintermann, 'Market Power, Permit Allocation and Efficiency in Emission Permit Markets' (2011) 49 Env Resour Econ 327, 327; generally, Robert W Hahn, 'Market Power and Transferable Property Rights' (1984) 99 QJ Econ 753.

[59] Baumol and Oates (n 21) 212.

[60] Jared C Carbone, Carsten Helm and Thomas F Rutherford, 'The Case for International Emission Trade in the Absence of Cooperative Climate Policy' (2009) 58 J Env Econ Manag 266; Carsten Helm, 'International Emissions Trading with Endogenous Allowance Choices' (2003) 87 J Pub Econ 2737; Bjart Holtsmark and Dag Einar Sommervoll, 'International Emissions Trading: Good or Bad?' (2012) 117 Econ Lett 362.

[61] Jon Strand, 'Carbon Offsets with Endogenous Environmental Policy' (2011) 33 Energ Econ 371.

[62] Jonas Meckling, *Carbon Coalitions: Business, Climate Politics, and the Rise of Emissions Trading* (MIT Press 2011); on the underlying concepts, see James Buchanan and Gordon Tullock, 'Polluters' Profits and Political Response: Direct Controls versus Taxes' (1975) 65 Am Econ Rev 139; Anne O Krueger, 'The Political Economy of the Rent-Seeking Society' (1974) 64 Am Econ Rev 291; George J Stigler, 'The Theory of Economic Regulation' (1971) 2 Bell J Econ Manag Sci 3.

[63] Peter Markussen and Gert Tinggaard Svendsen, 'Industry Lobbying and the Political Economy of GHG Trade in the European Union' (2005) 33 Energ Policy 245; Irja Vormedal, 'The Influence of Business and Industry NGOs in the Negotiation of the Kyoto Mechanisms: The Case of Carbon Capture and Storage in the CDM' (2008) 8 Global Env Polit 36.

most appropriate intervention.[64] It has even been argued that climate change stretches the capability of governments to process and react to the attendant information.[65] Establishing adequate governance structures is frequently constrained by insufficient technical and administrative capacities, including resources and suitable personnel.[66]

For one prominent commentator, the intractable governance challenges encountered in the context of carbon trading suggested that 'cheating will probably be pandemic in an emissions trading system that involves large sums of money'.[67] And indeed, several of the foregoing vulnerabilities have already been observed in practice, with harmful effects for the functioning of carbon markets and their support among market participants and the broader public. Trading on regulated exchanges has at times been exceeded by less transparent over-the-counter (OTC) transactions, and actual compliance trading is often rivalled by speculative trading through financial intermediaries. Individual market participants and speculators have been periodically reported to influence the price of carbon units in the market and exaggerate price moves to their advantage. Risks to market functioning became particularly visible in a string of criminal activities encountered early on in the EU ETS, including value-added tax (VAT) fraud,[68] phishing attempts on the German national registry, and a series of subsequent cyber-thefts affecting several million European Union Allowances.[69]

As carbon markets expand to include new states and regions, these governance risks are likely to intensify. Different jurisdictions show great variation in their legal and administrative systems, their regulatory cultures and their traditions of transparency, accountability and access to information, affecting the operation of carbon trading; in some geographies, weak enforcement capacities, less robust adherence to the rule of law, and an absence of effective civil society and public interest monitoring groups increase the risk of non-compliance with, or abuse of, trading rules.[70] In

64 Friedrich A von Hayek, *Law, Legislation, and Liberty: Rule and Order* (University of Chicago Press 1973) 14; Brian E Dollery and Joe L Wallis, *Market Failure, Government Failure, Leadership and Public Policy* (Macmillan & Co 1999) 37.

65 Max H Bazerman, 'Climate Change as a Predictable Surprise' (2006) 77 Climatic Change 179.

66 Thomas L Brewer and Michael A Mehling, 'Transparency of Climate Change Policies, Markets, and Corporate Practices' in Jens Forssbæck and Lars Oxelheim (eds), *The Oxford Handbook of Economic and Institutional Transparency* (OUP 2015) 179, 188.

67 Nordhaus (n 56) 19.

68 Patrick Keyzer and others, 'Carbon Market Integrity: Integrity and Oversight of the European Emissions Trading System' (Carbon Market Institute (CMI) 2012) 13 www.carbonmarketinstitute.org accessed 16 January 2021; Dominique Guegan, Antonin Lassoudiere and Marius-Cristian Frunza, 'Missing Trader Fraud on the Emissions Market' (2011) 18 J Fin Crime 183.

69 Point Carbon, 'Carbon Market Monitor: A Review of 2012' (Point Carbon 2012) 3.

70 Ruth Greenspan Bell, 'Choosing Environmental Policy Instruments in the Real World' (OECD 2003) CCNM/GF/SD/ENV(2003)10/FINAL 11 www.oecd.org/environment/cc/2957706.pdf accessed 16 January 2021; with specific examples for China: Coraline Goron and Cyril Cassisa, 'Regulatory Institutions and Market-Based Climate Policy in China' (2016) 17 Global Env Polit 99.

the literature, such challenges have been discussed under the broader label of non-market or government failures, including cognitive, organisational and political barriers.[71] Governance functions that are amenable to technological innovation acquire relevance, in particular, for three aspects of carbon trading: emissions transparency through MRV and enforcement (often referred to as the 'compliance cycle'), broader system transparency, and market oversight and activity tracking, which are described in greater detail in Sections 2.3.2.1–2.3.2.3, respectively.

2.3.2.1 Emissions Transparency and the Compliance Cycle

Carbon trading is not an end in itself; its very *raison d'être* is the achievement of emissions reductions. In order to safeguard this purpose, carbon trading must be governed by a rigorous system of emissions transparency as well as provisions to secure compliance.[72] Emissions transparency is ensured by way of monitoring, reporting and verification (MRV), which provide an important means of tracking the progress of individual market participants towards the achievement of their defined mitigation objectives, establishing baselines for offset projects and allowing for recognition of certain actions, such as emissions reductions through such projects.[73] Importantly, a credible MRV framework can also strengthen confidence in the carbon market, fostering stronger market participation; MRV obligations are generally tolerated by market participants because they impose only a relatively modest burden.[74]

In the context of carbon trading, 'monitoring' refers to the observation and measurement of GHG emissions and compliance with emission mitigation obligations, be it through on-site and remote monitoring, or through use of inferences and indirect indicators. Inventories of GHG emissions, for instance, are calculated on the basis of direct and indirect activity data, such as the amount of fuel and electricity used, industrial output and distances covered in transportation. 'Reporting', by contrast, requires communication of information obtained through monitoring, with a view to facilitating the assessment of public policies and measures or individual performance.[75]

71 Michael C O'Dowd, 'The Problem of "Government Failure" In Mixed Economies' (1978) 46 S African J Econ 242; Gordon Tullock, Gordon L Brady and Arthur Seldon, *Government Failure: A Primer in Public Choice* (Cato Institute 2002); Burton Allen Weisbrod, 'Problems of Enhancing the Public Interest: Toward a Model of Governmental Failures' in Burton Allen Weisbrod, Joel F Handler and Neil K Komesar (eds), *Public Interest Law: An Economic and Institutional Analysis* (University of California Press 1978); Charles Wolf Jr., *Markets or Governments: Choosing between Imperfect Alternatives* (2nd edn, MIT Press 1993).

72 Kerr and others (n 53) 120.

73 Additionally, verification of individual progress can also enhance action through expert advice on opportunities for improvement.

74 Clare Breidenich and Daniel M Bodansky, 'Measurement, Reporting and Verification in a Post-2012 Climate Agreement' (Pew Center on Global Climate Change 2009) 1–4 www.c2es.org/site/assets/uploads/2009/04/mrv-post-2012-climate-agreement.pdf accessed 16 January 2021.

75 In the context of financial accounting, however, reporting can also acquire a different meaning. Under accounting rules, entities may be required to report allowance or credit holdings in line with

Information to be reported depends on the context and nature of commitments, but may include emissions data, activity levels and technology investments. Its usefulness generally depends on the precision and reliability of reported information, and on the degree to which information is presented in a transparent and standardised way so as to allow for comparisons between reports and verification by others. Finally, 'verification' refers to a process through which the accuracy and reliability of reported information or the procedures used to generate information are independently assessed. Verification can play a preliminary role in compliance procedures by providing a factual basis for later legal determinations. Unlike reporting, verification cannot be performed by the regulated entity itself; it is typically carried out by independent, accredited verification entities.[76]

In most carbon trading systems, an enforcement system with appropriate penalties – which can involve a combination of measures – provides assurance that the emissions transparency requirements, as well as other compliance obligations related to the carbon market, are observed. Penalties can consist of a reputational deterrent – 'naming and shaming' – under which the names of non-compliant entities are published, a financial penalty or fine, requirements to 'make good' any compliance shortfalls, and further measures, including criminal charges.[77]

2.3.2.2 System Transparency

As part of their transparency framework, carbon markets set out a number of disclosure requirements for information related to the trading system, variously requiring communication and publication of such information to the public or specific stakeholders, such as other market participants or compliance entities. These disclosure requirements are distinct from the monitoring and reporting obligations that compliance entities are subject to with regard to GHG emissions, and instead serve to improve the smooth functioning of the market as well as to promote public trust, goodwill and credibility in the ETS.[78] They thus contribute to transparency in a broader sense, which can be defined as 'the extent to which information is made publicly available within a given social system',[79] covering the flow of information itself as well as its quality and the method of dissemination.[80]

accounting standards adopted by national governments or private institutions, such as the Financial Accounting Standards Board and the International Accounting Standards Board.

76 Breidenich and Bodansky (n 74) 3–9.

77 Kerr and others (n 53) 131.

78 Felicity Deane, Evan Hamman and Yilin Pei, 'Principles of Transparency in Emissions Trading Schemes: The Chinese Experience' (2017) 6 Transnl Env L 87.

79 M Jae Moon, Eric W Welch and Wilson Wong, 'What Drives Global E-Governance? An Exploratory Study at a Macro Level', *Proceedings of the 38th Annual Hawaii International Conference on System Sciences* (2005).

80 James R Hollyer, B Peter Rosendorff and James Raymond Vreeland, 'Measuring Transparency' (2017) 22 Polit Analysis 413.

Generally speaking, these transparency requirements are an expression of the broader trend towards increased public access to information, public participation and access to justice in environmental matters, all of which are accepted as central pillars of robust environmental governance and even emerging norms in environmental law.[81] Transparency therefore occupies a prominent position in the international climate regime, with relevant obligations – primarily related to the communication and measurement of emissions – for both developed and developing country parties. It acquires similar importance in the context of carbon trading, where a sophisticated policy instrument addressing a highly complex threat will quickly challenge the capacity of stakeholders and the broader public to comprehend technical nuances and the implications and impacts of alternative policy choices.

Robust transparency requirements encompass three different dimensions of transparency: (1) consideration of who possesses the information; (2) consideration of which data or documents need to be disclosed; and (3) consideration of who is entitled to those documents.[82] Importantly, to be meaningful, transparency should not only be internal to a policy regime, meaning that only those managing and participating in that regime are privy to relevant information; it should also extend beyond the regime to include wider dissemination of information, including its availability to the public.

Accordingly, in the context of carbon trading, information disclosure requirements can relate to various aspects of system design and operation. Aside from the duties to collect, report and verify installation- or company-level emissions data described in Section 2.3.2.1, transparency obligations can extend to information on aggregate emissions and emission trends under the trading system, information about allowance distribution, including auction results and use of proceeds, information on offset credit issuance, market and transaction data, as well as information related to compliance and enforcement. Likewise, the subjects of these requirements – that is, the entities under an obligation to disclose information – can range from public authorities, such as the government body administering the ETS, to market facilitators and intermediaries, such as exchanges, to the compliance entities themselves.

With a view to increased transparency about market and transaction data, exchanges and other facilitating entities may be required to publicise daily information on settlement prices, volume, open interest, and opening and closing ranges for all allowances, credits and carbon derivatives traded on the trading facility.[83] By

81 David B Hunter, 'The Emerging Norm of Transparency in International Environmental Governance', *Research Handbook on Transparency* (Edward Elgar 2014).

82 Frederick Schauer, 'Transparency in Three Dimensions' (2011) 2011 Uni Ill L Rev 1339.

83 An effective means of increasing market transparency, moreover, can be to require the use of an automated quotation system or a central limit order book (CLOB). Operated by either a public agency or a private exchange, such a CLOB provides a central location to consolidate unexecuted market orders, either automatically ('hard' CLOB) or by providing market participants with

contrast, OTC trading is typically not standardised, and transaction data are consequently more difficult to obtain and aggregate; to improve access to OTC transaction data, all market participants – not just exchanges and professional intermediaries – could be asked to register with an oversight institution and provide pricing information for transactions exceeding certain volume thresholds, for instance, where such transactions are determined to have a significant effect on carbon price discovery owing to their size and relevance. Additionally, they might be required to maintain trading protocols and detailed records of all transactions for the purposes of identifying and providing evidence of manipulation.

2.3.2.3 Market Oversight and Activity Tracking

Provided the overall environmental integrity of the carbon market is maintained, subsequent operation of the carbon market may seem of secondary importance. Yet efficient and secure market operation is important to ensure that emission reductions are met at the lowest available cost. Abatement cost, in turn, has a direct influence on the definition of economically viable levels of mitigation. Accordingly, maintaining market functionality is a priority in its own right, yet once again is subject to a number of challenges. As outlined earlier, some particularities of carbon trading may render it more susceptible to speculation and manipulation than conventional markets, potentially compromising its ability to incentivise investment and reveal low-cost abatement opportunities. Unlike traditional commodities, carbon is subject to an artificially constrained supply of allowances and credits, which can make it easier for one or more market participants to influence trading activity. When trading systems allow banking, moreover, the absence of any storage cost for allowances or credits makes it viable to accumulate large positions for sale at a later date.[84]

Regarding market operation, therefore, attention has focussed on, inter alia, the need to avoid strategic market behaviour by dominant players, for instance, when large volumes of carbon units become concentrated in the hands of a small group of market participants, vesting them with considerable market power. Deceptive and fraudulent behaviour to influence prices can involve 'wash trades', in which a firm, acting through agents, is itself both the beneficial buyer and the seller of the instrument, pushing prices higher to eventually conduct a large genuine sale; or price manipulation through aggressive purchasing on a market with low liquidity, geared towards increasing profits on maturing derivative positions; or achievement

information to facilitate trading ('soft' CLOB). At a minimum, it shows orders to buy and sell as well as the name of the intermediary (market maker) posting each order.

84 Jonas Monast, Jon Anda and Timothy H Profeta, 'U.S. Carbon Market Design: Regulating Emission Allowances as Financial Instruments' (Nicholas Institute for Environmental Policy Solutions 2009) Working Paper CCPP 09–01 15 https://nicholasinstitute.duke.edu/climate/carbon-market-oversight/u.s.-carbon-market-design-regulating-emission-allowances-as-financial-instruments accessed 12 February 2019.

of the defined threshold, or 'trigger', prices to activate certain regulatory consequences, such as relaxed constraints on borrowing and offset use, or execution of strategic reserve auctions.[85] Even manipulation across different markets is conceivable, given that, for instance, developments in the carbon market will affect prices in energy markets.[86]

Concern has been voiced about the ability of OTC transactions to discover a uniform price for carbon, given that these transactions occur on the basis of bilateral bargaining and usually without public disclosure of the price.[87] Another tradable asset giving rise to the controversy are carbon-based derivatives. In compliance markets such as the EU ETS, a large share of transactions are conducted through forward and futures contracts, which are financial products embodying promises to deliver emission allowances or credits in a certain quantity, at a certain price, by a specified date. Derivative trading is seen by some as a highly leveraged and risky speculative activity driven more by the desire for capital gains than to reduce GHG emissions.[88] While theoretically increasing liquidity and thereby helping allocate risks and set appropriate carbon prices, derivatives transactions are commonly effected not by regulated entities seeking to minimise compliance costs and risk exposure but by financial intermediaries seeking to profit from developments in the carbon price.[89] Yet speculation with carbon-based derivatives can artificially inflate prices and create detrimental cycles in the market, while incentivising risky projects or outright fraud. Securitisation of derivatives – a process by which often sophisticated contractual arrangements are sold in tranches on capital markets after origination – further reduces transparency and accountability.

From these challenges arise a number of governance requirements in carbon trading that relate to day-to-day market operation. Here, governance ensures oversight of who may participate in the market, and under what conditions; what transaction data and other information can be collected and disseminated to ensure market transparency; what regulatory restrictions can be imposed to address excessive speculation and other undesirable trading behaviour; and what measures should

85 William C Whitesell and Stacey L Davis, 'Preventing Market Disruptions in Cap-and-Trade Programs' (Center for Clean Air Policy (CCAP) 2008) 8 http://ccap.org/assets/Preventing-Market-Disruptions-in-Cap-and-Trade-Programs_CCAP-Oct-2008.pdf accessed 16 January 2021.

86 Michelle Chan, 'Lessons Learned from the Financial Crisis: Designing Carbon Markets for Environmental Effectiveness and Financial Stability' (2009) 3 CCLR 152.

87 Without effective price-revealing mechanisms in place, there is a high likelihood that information asymmetries between governments and participating entities will prevent adequate price discovery and thus equalisation of prices at the margin of abatement costs; that, in turn, will reduce the overall efficiency of the carbon market as a mitigation policy, see Christian Flachsland, Robert Marschinski and Ottmar Edenhofer, 'Global Trading versus Linking: Architectures for International Emissions Trading' (2009) 37 Energy Policy 1637, 1639.

88 Larry Lohmann, 'Regulatory Challenges for Financial and Carbon Markets' (2009) 3 CCLR 161.

89 Jillian Button, 'Carbon: Commodity or Currency? The Case for an International Carbon Market Based on the Currency Model' (2008) 32 Harv Env L Rev 571, 572.

be implemented to avoid large price swings and excessive volatility.[90] Accountability of market participants and especially intermediaries[91] can, for instance, be improved by requiring them to register with the market oversight institution, and by introducing training, licensing and registration duties for traders before these are allowed to solicit, act as a dealer or make markets. Specific reporting requirements may apply, as well as a duty to retain records and allow access for inspection through the oversight authority. For activities considered particularly prone to abuse or risk, such as derivatives transactions, trading might be limited to registered exchanges, with facilitation by intermediaries who are 'members in good standing' with the exchange. Sanctions for violations can include temporary or permanent injunctions, such as a suspension from trading, civil monetary penalties, rescission of all related transactions, disgorgement and restitution.

Finally, robust data management plays an important role in carbon market oversight. In conventional carbon trading systems, a registry or some other form of electronic database will typically assign a unique serial number to each unit and track those serial numbers from their issuance onward, capturing information on who has been issued allowances, who holds those allowances as well as other units, and when and from where units are surrendered or cancelled.[92] Prior to engaging in unit transfers, market participants have to sign up to the registry and create an account to obtain and hold allowances. Many of the criminal activities observed in the EU ETS during its second trading period were possible only owing to vulnerabilities of the registry infrastructure, and improvements that have since been carried out include enhanced control for account opening with harmonised Know-Your-Customer checks, enhanced transactions security with a waiting period prior to transfers, a trusted account list and improved authentication methods for transactions, strengthened registry oversight with expanded administrator powers to suspend registry access and block transfers, and enhanced protection of good faith acquirers through irrevocability of transfers.[93]

2.4 CONCLUSION

As this chapter has shown, carbon markets are technically and administratively complex. Carbon units are intangible, and the dynamics in the market entirely dependent on policy decisions. That makes carbon trading particularly vulnerable

90 Such measures can include, for instance, limits on the number of tradable units that may be purchased or held by a market participant, for instance, through bidding limits in allowance auctions or aggregate position limits in the secondary market, as well as minimum margin requirements to limit the risk from leverage, for instance, through a minimum level of collateral, usually in percentage terms of the new position, that the purchaser must hold to proceed with a transaction.

91 Such market intermediaries include brokers, dealers, exchanges and clearing houses. These are facilities that execute or settle trades or other transactions and are typically required to register or seek a licence prior to assuming operations.

92 Kerr and others (n 53) 129.

93 ibid 130.

to governance shortfalls. Sound governance of carbon markets is critical to ensure their operation, and existing carbon markets have revealed past weaknesses in emissions transparency, system transparency, as well as market integrity and oversight. Currently, these governance functions are provided by a range of public and private actors, including system administrators, accredited verifiers and various market intermediaries such as trading exchanges. Going forward, however, some of these governance functions may be carried out more securely and efficiently through innovative technologies, drawing on the potential of distributed ledger technology, artificial intelligence and Internet of Things technologies. How these may contribute to improved governance of carbon trading is discussed in Chapter 3.

3

Potential Interaction among Artificial Intelligence, Internet of Things and Distributed Ledger Technology

Dessanin Ewèdew Thierry Awesso, Marco Zolla and Alastair Marke

3.1 INTRODUCTION

This chapter provides an initial explanation of two key emerging technologies: artificial intelligence and Internet of Things while exploring how they work and their potential interaction with distributed ledger technology (DLT). These considerations will be key for further exploring how the main features of these technologies can be employed to overcome challenges and build a better governance structure for carbon markets, as discussed in the second half of the book.

3.2 AN OVERVIEW OF AI

3.2.1 *Definition of AI*

The term artificial intelligence (AI) was coined in the 1960s when it emerged as a sub-domain of computer science,[1] following numerous technological advances such as Turing's paper on 'the possibility of programming an electronic computer to behave intelligently',[2] in which he outlined the revolutionary imitation game that we know as the Turing Test.

In the past decades, many definitions of AI have been created. Finlay refers to AI as 'the replication of human analytical and/or decision-making capabilities'.[3] Other definitions suggest that AI refers to 'manifold tools and technologies that can be combined in diverse ways to sense, cognise and perform with the ability to learn from experience and adapt over time'.[4]

1 Ipsita Pradhan, 'Driving Transformation through Engaged Teams, 13th Sep 2016' (2017) www.theirm.org/news/artificial-intelligence-the-new-normal/ accessed 5 December 2018.

2 Bruce G Buchanan, 'A (Very) Brief History of Artificial Intelligence' (2005) 26 *AI Magazine* 53 https://ojs.aaai.org/index.php/aimagazine/article/view/1848 accessed 8 April 2022.

3 Steven Finlay, *Artificial Intelligence and Machine Learning for Business: A No-Nonsense Guide to Data Driven Technologies* (3rd edn, Relativistic 2018) 11.

4 Rajendra Akerkar, 'Artificial Intelligence for Business' [2019] *Am J Roentgenology* 1 http://link.springer.com/10.1007/978-3-319-97436-1 accessed 8 April 2022.

What Akerkar refers to when mentioning 'manifold tools and technologies' is a combination of technologies such as machine learning (ML), predictive analytics (PA), deep learning (DL) and natural language processing (NLP), which altogether fall under the umbrella term of AI.[5] For instance, most of today's AI systems rely heavily on ML,[6] which is a field of AI capable of detecting patterns and learning 'how to make predictions and recommendations by processing data and experiences, rather than by receiving explicit programming instruction'.[7] The capability of ML to provide predictions is often regarded as predictive modelling or predictive analytics. It is 'a form of advanced analytics which examines data or attempts to answer the question – "What is going to happen?" – or more precisely – "What is likely to happen?"'.[8] Other types of advanced analytics enabled by AI/ML are descriptive and prescriptive analytics. The former commonly refers to 'the examination of data or content' to provide context for historical data,[9] while the latter 'addresses the questions [of] "What should be done?"' by relying on techniques such as recommendation engines and neural networks.[10]

As LeCun, Bengio and Hinton highlight,[11] ML is currently capable of efficiently performing tasks such as providing recommendations on e-commerce websites, identifying objects in images, transcribing speech into text and matching news items. Nevertheless, DL has the possibility of solving many more complicated AI tasks.[12] As a type of ML capable of processing a larger set of data resources, DL entails less data pre-processing by humans and produces more accurate results than traditional ML approaches.[13] Besides its current applications in image recognition and speech recognition, DL 'has produced auspicious results for various tasks in natural language understanding, particularly topic classification, sentiment analysis, question answering and language translation'.[14]

Similarly, NLP solutions leverage ML and DL so that computers can 'understand' spoken and written language. Thus, NLP can be defined as the '[a]bility of computers to process spoken or written human (natural) language'.[15] Current applications of NLP

5 ibid.

6 Finlay (n 3).

7 McKinsey, 'An Executive's Guide to AI' (2018, last updated 2020) www.mckinsey.com/business-functions/mckinsey-analytics/our-insights/an-executives-guide-to-ai accessed 8 April 2022.

8 Gartner, 'Definition of Descriptive Analytics – Gartner Information Technology Glossary' (2019) www.gartner.com/en/information-technology/glossary/descriptive-analytics accessed 8 April 2022.

9 ibid.

10 Thomas Oestreich and Mike Rollings, 'The Fundamentals of AI Success for Data and Analytics Leaders' (2017) www.gartner.com/en/documents/3792883/the-fundamentals-of-ai-success-for-data-and-analytics-le accessed 8 April 2022.

11 Yann LeCun, Yoshua Bengio and Geoffrey Hinton, 'Deep Learning' (2015) 521 *Nature* 436.

12 Yoshua Bengio, 'Learning Deep Architectures for AI' [2009] 2 *Foundations and Trends® in Machine Learning* 1–55.

13 McKinsey (n 7).

14 LeCun, Bengio and Hinton (n 10).

15 Neil Mehta and Murthy V Devarakonda, 'Machine Learning, Natural Language Programming, and Electronic Health Records: The Next Step in the Artificial Intelligence Journey?' (2018) 141 *J Allergy Clin Immunology* 2019.

include Google search, language translation, next-word suggestion in text-messaging apps, and IBM's Watson Jeopardy – a supercomputer capable of answering questions posed in a natural language. Other applications include meaning-extraction, such as sentiment analysis of user reviews of restaurants, movies and products. To emphasise the importance of the language processing part of NLP, Akerkar points out not only that a core aspect of human intelligence is using and understanding natural language 'but also [that] its successful automation would have an incredible impact on the usability and effectiveness of computers themselves'.[16]

Furthermore, since 'more than 90 per cent of data has been created in the last two years',[17] AI will be central to delivering new products and services in fintech and other industries. This is because AI can provide 'insights that human analysts do not see on their own' and is capable of making 'predictions with ever-higher degrees of accuracy'[18] so that, by analysing large volumes of data and identifying new patterns, it will be able to reshape how businesses respond to operational challenges and inefficiencies.[19] To demonstrate AI's future impact, a recent study by PricewaterhouseCoopers shows how, by 2030, the accelerating development and uptake of AI will have led to a 14 per cent growth in gross domestic product, adding USD 15.7 trillion to the global economy.[20]

3.2.2 *ML: The Backbone of AI-Supported (Security) Risk Management*

As that brief introduction showed, ML could form the backbone of AI-supported risk management. Broadly speaking, ML can be categorised as:

- **supervised learning** (including semi-supervised), which involves the use of labelled training data (e.g. annotated data that teaches the algorithm) and comprises two categories of tasks:
  - regression-supervised tasks in which the dependent variable (what needs to be predicted) is numerical, and
  - classification-supervised tasks in which the dependent variable (what needs to be predicted) is categorical (non-numerical);
- **unsupervised learning**, which does not use any labelled data. The most popular type is known as clustering, which involves identifying patterns emerging from clusters of data points; and

16 Akerkar (n 4).

17 Miklos Dietz and others, 'FinTechnicolor: The New Picture in Finance' (2016) www.mckinsey.com/~/media/mckinsey/industries/financialservices/ourinsights/bracing for seven critical changes as fin techmatures/fintechnicolor-the-new-picture-in-finance.ashx accessed 8 April 2022.

18 ibid.

19 Deloitte, 'Artificial Intelligence Innovation Report', vol 46 (2016) https://dokumen.tips/documents/artificial-intelligence-innovation-report-deloitte.html?page=1 accessed 8 April 2022.

20 Anand S Rao, Gerard Verweij and Euan Cameron, 'Sizing the Prize: What's the Real Value of AI for Your Business and How Can You Capitalise?' (PwC 2017) www.pwc.com/gx/en/issues/analytics/assets/pwc-ai-analysis-sizing-the-prize-report.pdf accessed 8 April 2022.

- **reinforcement learning**, which concerns how software agents ought to take actions in an environment to maximise some notion of cumulative reward to achieve a balance between exploration (of uncharted territory) and exploitation (of current knowledge). It differs from supervised learning as it does not use labelled input/output pairs.

There are many other subfields of ML that are derived from the above categorisation. Some examples include NLP, recommender systems, image analysis (computer vision), anomaly detection, to name but a few. Three specific reasons explain why AI/ML has reached the current level of real-life applications:

- improved algorithms demonstrated through the sophisticated results obtained by DL and reinforcement learning;
- the exponential growth of computing power as per Moore's Law; and
- the unprecedented amount of big data generated every day, which continues to increase without any sign of a slowdown.

Combining the three drivers' effects makes possible the development of new algorithms such as those by Yann LeCun and colleagues.[21] There are several examples of AI applications in the finance sector already disrupting the service models of banks and insurers. For example, AI is used to detect fraud and money laundering to enable financial institutions to meet regulatory requirements. Some authors describe how AI can be used to assist investigations by citing that 'neural networks and fuzzy logic have aided tasks such as link analysis, where associations between accounts or individuals are analysed for common features'.[22] Heterogeneous hybrid technology is applied to allow artificial agents to select the best analysis method for each case. The agents, known as sentinels, can identify and compare individuals' unusual transaction activities to those of peer groups to further verify their findings.

3.2.3 *AI and Climate Change*

With AI becoming increasingly popular, its capabilities and its ability to perform critical tasks are growing at a fast pace. However, the most crucial thing will be to take great care when specifying its goals. Could one of these goals be not only to enable new disrupting business models but also to allow organisations to take on new initiatives to address climate change issues? The World Economic Forum[23] proposes that AI could help the environment in eight ways:

- autonomous and connected electric vehicles
- distributed energy grids

[21] LeCun, Bengio and Hinton (n 10).
[22] Jason Kingdon, 'AI Fights Money Laundering' (2004) 19 *IEEE Intelligent Systems* 87.
[23] Celine Herweijer, '8 Ways AI Can Help Save the Planet' (24 January 2018) www.weforum.org/agenda/2018/01/8-ways-ai-can-help-save-the-planet/ accessed 10 January 2021.

- smart agriculture and food systems
- next-generation weather and climate prediction
- smart disaster response
- AI-designed intelligent, connected and liveable cities
- a transparent, digital Earth
- reinforcement learning for Earth sciences breakthroughs.

For example, AI could be used to predict changes in the weather patterns. A vast amount of climate data is available to enable producing weather forecasting models and global warming projections with greater accuracy. Climate data represent 'a rich and fertile playground for future data mining and ML research'.[24] Monteleoni and colleagues point out the large scale of the datasets, which are 'running into millions or billions of data points', as well as their high-dimensional nature.[25] Cho remarks that leveraging AI and its higher capability for making better predictions could helping researchers achieve '89 to 99 percent accuracy in identifying tropical cyclones, weather fronts and atmospheric rivers, the latter of which can cause heavy precipitation and are often hard for humans to identify on their own .... [T]hese types of programs can help keep people safe.'[26]

Thus, AI and DL techniques can include many more types of data, such as atmospheric data, atmospheric chemistry, ocean dynamics and ocean chemistry, into their analysis to increases the accuracy of climate modelling and simulations.[27] With more data to analyse and higher complexity incorporated into the calculations, AI could help decision-makers improve climate resilience.

3.3 AN OVERVIEW OF IOT

3.3.1 *The Breakthrough of IoT*

The Internet of Things (IoT) belongs to those technologies that are contributing to the phenomenon defined as the fourth industrial revolution or the digital revolution.[28] The convergence among the physical, biological and digital dimensions is considered one of the most radical innovations brought by this revolution. While the third industrial revolution saw the deployment of technological devices confined to boxes (PCs, mobile phones, etc.), nowadays, technological devices are

[24] Claire Monteleoni and others, 'Climate Informatics' [2013] *Computational Intelligent Data Analysis for Sustainable Dev* 81.

[25] ibid.

[26] Renee Cho, 'Artificial Intelligence – A Game Changer for Climate Change and the Environment' (5 June 2018) https://news.climate.columbia.edu/2018/06/05/artificial-intelligence-climate-environment/ accessed 8 April 2022.

[27] ibid.

[28] Klaus Schwab, 'The Fourth Industrial Revolution: What It Means, How to Respond' *World Economic Forum* (14 January 2016) www.weforum.org/agenda/2016/01/the-fourth-industrial-revolution-what-it-means-and-how-to-respond/ accessed 8 April 2022

increasingly embedded in all types of artefacts. Besides, they are also connected to the Internet, making homes, offices, factories, cars and cities smarter. Thus, IoT can be considered the bridge between the physical and the digital worlds, capable of creating a smarter world from interconnected devices.

That said, IoT technologies are not a particularly recent phenomenon. We can date their birth to a period between the end of the 1990s and the beginning of the 2000s.[29] However, in the last ten years we have been experiencing their spread to different market sectors. The number of connected devices is expected to continue to grow to 21.5 billion units worldwide by 2025.[30] Although IoT has existed for several years, it is not easy to find a well-recognised definition.[31] In fact, IoT is not a single technology but rather an aggregate of technologies at both the hardware and the software levels. More than just a particular technology for connecting objects via the Internet, IoT is foremost an ecosystem in which certain automated interactions among different systems are envisaged for a specific purpose. This ecosystem is beneficial in its making the human environment smarter; the IoT world opens to undiscovered opportunities from the traditional embedded systems to new professional and data-driven markets. Through this perspective, we can identify the IoT in smart devices and sensors interconnected with each other via the Internet and a cloud platform or server, capable of generating digital data on certain processes or performances. These devices can be qualified as smart not merely because they are connected to the Internet but because they can produce reliable data, even without any human action, and allow quicker and more efficient responses to change needs.

Going back to the fourth industrial revolution, this historical phenomenon apparently only arises from the progressive penetration of technology into daily-life processes. The fourth industrial revolution was born when technological innovations became able to generate a value that can be spent in our daily lives. It is widely recognised that generating digital data creates value; thus, access to digital data is a new form of power, as data allow stakeholders to make better decisions more quickly. In the specific case of IoT, its value consists mainly in creating and circulating new digital data through the digitisation of the physical world. The new data that IoT makes available create value that can be evaluated from an

[29] The expression 'Internet of Things' (IoT) was coined back in 1999 by Kevin Ashton.

[30] Statista Research Department, 3 March 2020.

[31] Various definitions of IoT have been adopted by different institutions; according to the EU Parliament briefing paper 'The Internet of Things: Opportunities and Challenges' (2015), IoT is defined as 'a distributed network connecting physical objects that are capable of sensing or acting on their environment and able to communicate with each other, other machines or computers'. According to the OECD, '[t]he Internet of Things includes all devices and objects whose state can be altered via the Internet, with or without the active involvement of individuals. While connected objects may require the involvement of devices considered part of the "traditional Internet", this definition excludes laptops, tablets and smartphones already accounted for in current OECD broadband metrics.' OECD, 'IoT Measurement and Applications', OECD Digital Economy Papers No 271 (OECD Publishing 2018) https://doi.org/10.1787/35209dbf-en accessed 22 April 2022.

economic point of view. For example, IoT may optimise industrial processes and increase production performance through a data-driven decision-making system; therefore, a physical sensor becomes a new type of product once it can capture and transmit digital data. Thanks to digital data, we are already witnessing change in various players' economic roles in multiple production chains; producers of smart devices are increasingly changing their role from manufacturers to data providers, from product makers to service providers. In IoT, the generated data's value is often an essential part of the business model, thus opening the possibility of easily monetising the device data.

3.3.2 *The Main Challenges in IoT*

Despite the benefits that IoT can bring in multiple processes, only a small part of the potential of this technology has been duly exploited. The broad categories of challenges are: (1) interaction and communication; (2) data management; (3) data reliability; (4) security; (5) governance and liabilities; and (6) intellectual property (IP) management.

The need for interaction among IoT devices in order to bring about efficient results leads to several difficulties. First, it is uncertain whether the devices can interact at both the hardware and the software levels owing to their differences in nature and manufacturing. Establishing communication protocols between tools produced by different manufacturers can often create insurmountable technical problems, as many devices are unable to communicate with devices from other manufacturers, which may be competitors. The communication obstacles between devices and the lack of protocol standardisation have undermined the possibility of implementing IoT solutions on a large scale.[32] As devices come in different shapes and forms, it is to be expected that other technical solutions will be enforced to address this challenge. Collaboration among device manufacturers' network providers, platform providers, app developers and end-users will be pivotal to ensure interaction among different devices.

Moreover, the fast circulation of data is only possible with a strong communication layer. The data generated by smart devices must be transmitted, through a robust communication network, into a platform that can analyse them and the related patterns. Connectivity issues and network overload problems undermine the spread of IoT. In this regard, the deployment of a new generation of technology standards for cellular networks, such as 5G, is expected to be the catalyst for increasing the reliability of an IoT infrastructure.[33]

32 Currently there are several international initiatives to promote the IoT protocol standardisation, interoperability and common architecture, especially for IIOT; one of these is the Industrial Internet Consortium (https://iiconsortium.org/index.htm accessed 8 April 2022), which aims to deliver a trustworthy IIoT in which the world's systems and devices are securely connected and controlled to deliver transformational outcomes.

33 By increasing download speeds, 5G can send data to and from as many as a million devices per square kilometre. TR Staff, 'The 5G Economy: How 5G Will Impact Global Industries, the Economy, and

Another challenge to the spread of IoT exists in the management of the IoT platform. As indicated in the previous paragraph, IoT uses physical devices, with built-in connectivity tools, interacting with each other via the Internet; this interaction creates digital data that must be deposited or archived in a certain way and then eventually used. Therefore, it is necessary to set technological solutions offering data management, where data can be monitored and where it is possible to control the devices connected. In this sense, the IoT platform will be the heart of the ecosystem. It includes software applications, data management and infrastructure that allows transmission between data centres and data providers. However, building and maintaining this kind of platform requires great effort and care. The platform needs to simultaneously monitor the data received, detect anomalies, eliminate these anomalies and maintain the collected data's integrity and security.

The data generated by IoT have value only if they are reliable. The circulation, storage and analysis of these data by an IoT platform presents a series of technical and legal issues that must be correctly addressed. In the absence of verification mechanisms and control tools, the data are unreliable and therefore worthless, not unsuitable for being used to make data-based decisions. Only technological solutions able to produce reliable data can lead to integrating different hardware and software solutions to ensure that these technologies can participate in an IoT ecosystem. This will enable the value of the data thus created to be unlocked, and new business models based on providing data will be able to generate profitability for the IoT ecosystem participants.

Data security in the IoT is a deeply analysed issue,[34] and one that plays a key role, especially for IoT applications in industrial processes where confidential data concerning trade secrets (i.e. industrial processes) can be transmitted. To enable a trusted end-to-end IoT service, all devices that get connected must be secured. Their data must be protected from external cyber-attacks; therefore, a set of protection measures must be implemented to preserve the confidentiality, integrity and availability of the data. A considerable volume of connected devices requires structured security automation and enhanced security analytics capabilities. Cyber risk concerns the server where the data are stored and the communication layer that needs sophisticated encryption and authentication mechanisms. In this context, the management of security issues poses additional costs for developing a well-functioning IoT ecosystem. Since it is not possible to build an interconnection protocol for many devices that has eliminated all security risk, an IoT solution will be effective if it can offer a reasonable, proportionate and cost-effective security level.

You' *MIT Technology Review* (1 March 2017) www.technologyreview.com/2017/03/01/153487/the-5g-economy-how-5g-will-impact-global-industries-the-economy-and-you/ accessed 8 April 2022.

34 Alasdair Gilchrist, *IoT Security Issues* (De|G Press 2017) www.degruyter.com/view/title/526420 accessed 8 April 2022. C Skouloudi and others, 'Guidelines for Securing the Internet of Things – Secure Supply Chain for IoT' European Union Agency for Cybersecurity (9 November 2020) www.enisa.europa.eu/publications/guidelines-for-securing-the-internet-of-things accessed 8 April 2022.

Collaboration needs trust, and trust can be granted only if the actors play in an environment where standard rules (including obligations and liabilities) are well-defined. For this reason, it is necessary to create an appropriate regulatory framework that provides answers to a series of open points including, for example, who owns the data, who is entitled to process the data and how the data are managed. For example, an IoT solution that captures individuals' data should be privacy compliant; in this regard, it is necessary to identify who manages personal data and set ad hoc procedures to protect the individual data collected by IoT devices.

The legal framework should also specify the liability regime (i.e. strict liability, limited liability) and the remedies available for each network actor. The liability regime should identify a certain threshold of duty of care, which might be differentiated among the participants and linked to their different ecosystem contributions. In particular, the allocation of responsibility among the network participants in the case of a data breach or data mismanagement must be set. Providing answers to these legal questions will inspire confidence so that, for example, the maker of a smart device can be confident that it will not incur any responsibility in case of a duty-of-care breach by the supplier of the software that manages the data generated by the device.

Finally, some issues regarding the IP protection of IoT have emerged with the spread of IoT inventions.[35] The legal requirements to obtain IP protection for an IoT business-related invention are not uniform across different jurisdictions. There is no consensus about the patentability of integrated inventions that combine data structures with software data processing and hardware equipment. In such an environment, it might be challenging to obtain judicial protection in case of cross-border infringement of IoT inventions. Besides, the necessity of adopting a widely standardised technology in order to make a working IoT system might affect the competition in the market and impede the IoT industry's growth. In this scenario, the patent of the most adopted technology may create a barrier to developing new solutions.

All of the above challenges lead to the conclusion that IoT solutions will likely find a greater spread if they can operate within a clear legal framework, are inclusive, offer effective governance combined with a transparent risk management model, are capable of communicating the different levels of risk to the actors and identify unknown threats.

3.3.3 *Current Developments and Potential Future Scenarios in the IoT World*

In recent years the evolution of IoT solutions has been surprisingly rapid. The convergence among technologies is directly affecting the broader technological

[35] In the United States the cumulative number of IoT-litigated patents witnessed an increase of more than 400 per cent from 2013 to 2018. Tim Pohlmann, 'Patent Litigation Trends in the Internet of Things' IAM (20 March 2019) www.iam-media.com/patent-litigation-trends-internet-things accessed 8 April 2022.

development seen in the fourth industrial revolution. As American scientist and futurist Roy Amara famously said, 'we tend to overestimate the effect of a technology in the short run and underestimate the effect in the long run'.[36] It is undoubtedly easier to praise the immediate and marvellous benefits of a recently launched technology. Simultaneously, it is more difficult to determine how a certain tech-solution may impact our lives in the future.

It is important to remember that, instead of being a single technology, IoT is an aggregator of technologies. Thus, IoT benefits from innovations from every technological domain that it can aggregate in its system. Owing to this aggregating nature, IoT solutions have seen significant acceleration of their development; we have seen the launch of ecosystems that integrate IoT with other recent technologies such as DLT, AI/ML and robotics. The convergence of IoT solutions with other technologies is leading to the creation of new business models, new services and solutions that are seeing unprecedented partnerships between actors operating in different sectors. These solutions are potentially able to change business relations, supply chains and the mechanisms for resource distribution. Technological development has led to structured IoT solutions that are increasingly capable of creating new markets.

At the IoT platform architecture level, while traditional IoT systems required collected data to be stored in centralised servers, various storage options are now possible thanks not only to cloud technologies but also to DLT. A decentralised and distributed ecosystem allows peer-to-peer co-operation among different actors within a network. Instead of a vertical and hierarchical approach, these actors may offer their services, such as data providing, data management and risk management, circularly. Creating an IoT platform that requires co-operation among different actors also allows disintermediation within the network so that different subjects with a common interest can directly interact with each other to achieve certain benefits. Interaction among participants requires trust, which is a prerequisite for every IoT system. As mentioned in Section 3.3.2, if the IoT ecosystem players do not trust the data generated or analysed, their interest in and willingness to be part of the network will necessarily disappear. Therefore, integrating IoT with other technologies capable of ensuring transparency in the collection and storage of data and their analysis is essential for facilitating the creation of a trustworthy system that puts the network players in a position to co-operate effectively.

The integration between DLT, for example, blockchain, and IoT is one of the clearest examples of the results achieved by the convergence between technologies. The intersection of IoT with blockchain has been deeply analysed, and several solutions have been already deployed.[37] For example, instead of transmitting data through a centralised server, an IoT device can

[36] Susan Ratcliffe (ed), *Roy Amara 1925–2007, American Futurologist, Oxford Essential Quotations, Vol. 1* (4th edn, OUP 2016).

[37] The IOTA Foundation (https://www.iota.org/ accessed 8 April 2022) is one of the most well-known business-case examples promoting integration between the IoT and blockchain. To date, IOTA has

package its data together with metadata and a timestamp, hash the data and electronically sign it with its private key, then the hash can be sent to the blockchain through a smart contract. In this way, the data is both sealed (by the hash) and made uniquely identifiable and findable. Thus, DLT guarantees transparency, traceability and immutability, while IoT allows reliable data to be registered automatically.

In conclusion, that large companies are pouring enormous economic resources into IoT[38] shows a strong desire to spread the IoT adoption. The use cases of converging IoT with other tech innovations are indeed expected to increase further. As described in this chapter, IoT's growth requires a complex awareness of its potential and its challenges from both a technological point of view and an economic, political and regulatory one. Nowadays, there are several favourable conditions to unlock the expected growth of IoT; thus, to adapt a well-known aphorism, we can say that the road to the future is paved with useful IoT inventions.

3.4 UNLOCKING THE POTENTIAL OF INTEGRATING AI, IOT AND DLT: ADVANTAGES, CHALLENGES AND TECHNICAL FEASIBILITY

This section provides an overview of the intersection between IoT and DLT by highlighting the benefits of the integration process. The growth of IoT is undeniable, and it can be advantageous to unlock the potential of DLTs in the carbon market (explored in Chapter 4), particularly by collecting data in real-time (as explained in Section 3.3).

3.4.1 *Integration of IoT with DLTs*

The number of IoT devices around the world was expected to reach 50 billion in 2020.[39] By 2025, forecasts suggest that there will be more than 75 billion IoT connected devices in use.[40] This would be a nearly threefold increase from the IoT installed base in 2019. Considering this prediction, constraints associated with

developed a technology to securely connect machines and people by using a decentralised and open-source protocol. The IOTA Tangle – the data structure behind IOTA – holds all the transactions in an immutable DLT and allows secure data transfers without transaction fees. Additionally, IOTA provides solutions for data encryption (IOTA streams), data access (IOTA access) and a decentralised marketplace where humans and machines exchange goods and services (IOTA Industry Marketplace).

38 The International Data Corporation has estimated that worldwide spending on the IoT was USD 745 billion in 2019. www.idc.com/getdoc.jsp?containerId=prUS44596319 accessed 8 April 2022.

39 Ericsson, 'CEO to Shareholders: 50 Billion Connections 2020' (13 April 2010) www.ericsson.com/en/press-releases/2010/4/ceo-to-shareholders-50-billion-connections-2020 accessed 22 April 2022.

40 Statista, 'Internet of Things (IoT) Connected Devices Installed Base Worldwide from 2015 to 2025' (27 November 2016) www.statista.com/statistics/471264/iot-number-of-connected-devices-worldwide/ accessed 22 April 2022.

the centralised architecture of the IoT system need to be addressed.[41] The primary limitations of IoT's centralised architecture are lack of scalability, cost, privacy, security, single 'point of failure', access and diversity, and inflexibility.

The major concern that stands as a barrier to the distribution of IoT devices is that all computing operations of the network are executed through a single server. This situation creates a single point of failure. Therefore, should this single server go down, the entire system would become unavailable. Also, IoT's centralised architecture is an easy target of cyber-attacks, since all IoT data collected are under the full control of a single server. An advisable solution is using DLT to secure it.[42] Indeed, DLT has gained popularity in recent years as an innovative approach that provides a transparent and verifiable transaction record.

Integrating IoT with DLT, particularly blockchain, which is the most popular type of DLT, has many advantages.[43] It provides an autonomous, distributed, decentralised and trustless environment. In contrast to the traditional centralised architecture, which presents several issues regarding a single point of failure and scalability, blockchain uses a decentralised and distributed ledger. Adopting a decentralised architecture for the IoT system can resolve security issues. The increasing number of IoT networks attacks is making it even more important to create an IoT with a very high-security level. Many experts see blockchain as a key technology in providing the much-needed security improvements to IoT.[44]

This technology utilises the processing capabilities of all the participating nodes in the blockchain network. That is what makes it more efficient. Also, there is no need for a third party, which improves business friendliness and guarantees a trusted workflow. Moreover, DLT delivers a high level of transparency by sharing transaction details among all participant nodes involved in those transactions.[45]

It seems clear, then, that DLT can provide increased security for IoT applications. It offers an immutable and tamper-proof ledger to protect data against attacks in which any data modification will not be added unless the majority of participating nodes verify it. Further, the peer-to-peer communication model can process a significant number of transactions between IoT devices. This model can significantly decrease the costs of installing and maintaining centralised data centres and distributing computation and storage among billions of IoT devices.[46] The

[41] Hany F Atlam and Gary B Wills, 'Chapter Three – Intersections between IoT and Distributed Ledger' in Shiho Kim, Ganesh Chandra Deka and Peng Zhang (eds), *Advances in Computers*, vol 115 (Elsevier 2019) 73–113 http://dx.doi.org/10.1016/bs.adcom.2018.12.001 accessed 8 April 2022.

[42] ibid.

[43] Malak Alamri and others, 'Blockchain for Internet of Things (IoT) Research Issues Challenges & Future Directions: A Review' (2019) 19 *IJCSNS* 244.

[44] Ana Reyna and others, 'On Blockchain and Its Integration with IoT. Challenges and Opportunities' (2018) 88 *Future Generation Computer Systems* 173.

[45] Atlam and Wills (n 42); Reyna and others (n 45).

[46] Atlam and Wills (n 42); Hanshu Hong, Bing Hu and Zhixin Sun, 'Toward Secure and Accountable Data Transmission in Narrow Band Internet of Things Based on Blockchain' (2019) 15 *Intl J Distributed Sensor Networks*.

decentralisation feature will also prevent the whole network from being unavailable if one node goes down. Figure 3.1 illustrates an IoT system with centralised architecture on the left and decentralised DLT integration on the right.

Integrating DLT with IoT therefore creates a system with more benefits and fewer issues. It is:

- responsive, working in different situations and adapting to changing conditions;
- resilient, without a single point of failure;
- robust, with an ability to contain billions of nodes and transactions without affecting the performance of the network;
- reductive, with optimised costs and increased efficiency;
- highly available in real-time and featuring smooth data flow;
- revenue-generating, providing opportunities to new business models;
- radically open, endlessly evolving and capable of updating the network with new inputs; and
- reliable, ensuring data integrity and trustworthiness of nodes.[47]

However, it is crucial to bear in mind that corrupt IoT data can arise from environmental issues, vandalism, device failure and/or malicious attacks.[48] For that reason, it is recommended that IoT devices are thoroughly tested before being integrated with DLT, and they should be located and encapsulated in the right place to avoid physical damage. They should also include systems that can detect device failures in real-time.[49]

Integrating IoT with DLT is not just theoretical; there are already many use cases in practice.[50] For instance, Chain of Things provides an integrated blockchain and IoT hardware solution to solve IoT challenges regarding identity, security and interoperability.[51] Waltonchain runs a trustworthy and traceable business network with complete data sharing and information transparency.[52] It is designed by integrating fadio-frequency identification (RFID) and blockchain technologies. Figure 3.2 illustrates the initial idea of blockchain and an IoT-based integrated application domain for users.

Despite all these elements favouring integration of blockchain with IoT, the advantages of such a choice should be analysed carefully and any decisions taken with caution.[53] Owing to the diversity of solutions available for integrating blockchain with IoT and the different types of IoT devices and applications, IoT designers

47 Atlam and Wills (n 42). D Tapscott and A Tapscott, *Blockchain Revolution: How the Technology Behind Bitcoin Is Changing Money, Business, and the World* (Penguin Random House 2016).

48 Rodrigo Roman, Jianying Zhou and Javier Lopez, 'On the Features and Challenges of Security and Privacy in Distributed Internet of Things' (2013) 57 *Computer Networks* 2266 http://dx.doi.org/10.1016/j.comnet.2012.12.018 accessed 21 March 2020.

49 Reyna and others (n 45).

50 Atlam and Wills (n 42); Reyna and others (n 45).

51 'Chain of Things' www.chainofthings.com/ accessed 21 March 2020.

52 'WALTONCHAIN – Building a New Business Ecosystem Integrating Blockchain with the IoT' www.waltonchain.org/en/ accessed 21 March 2020.

53 Reyna and others (n 45).

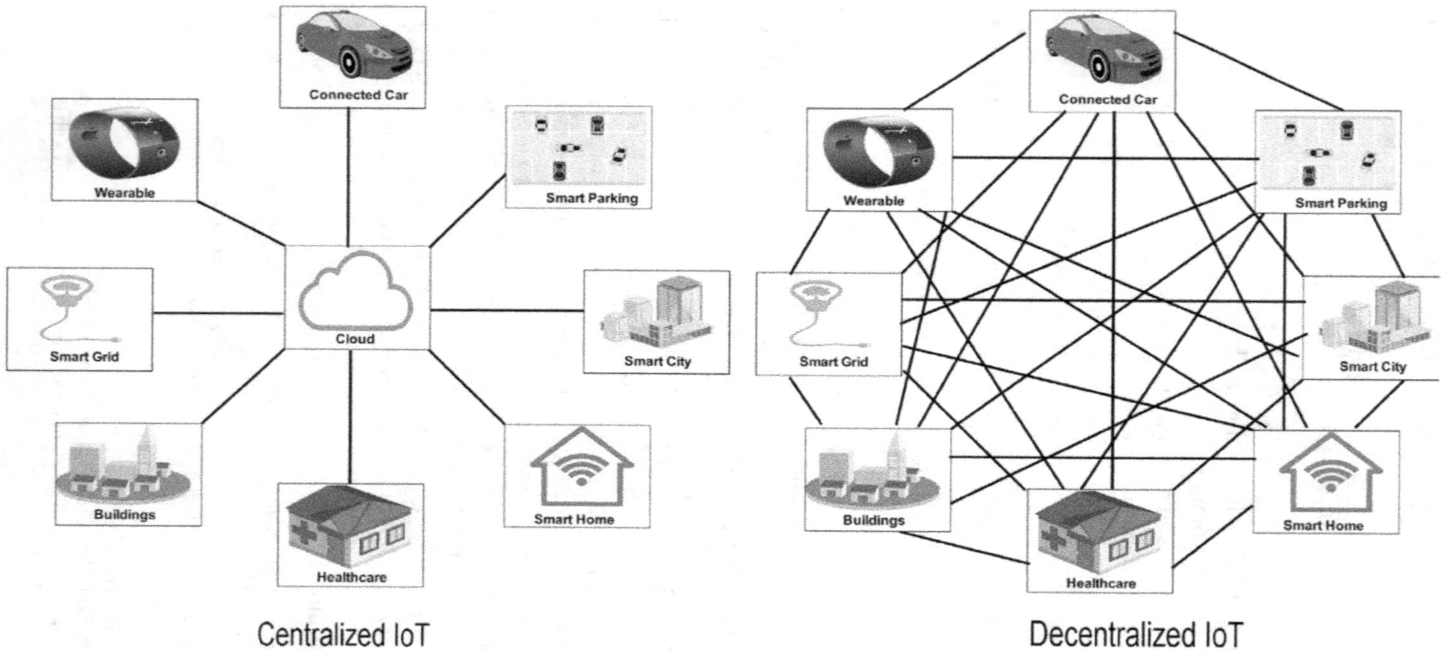

FIGURE 3.1 Left: centralised IoT where a central authority manages and controls all operations of the communicating nodes; right: integrated blockchain and IoT, creating a decentralised IoT with no central authority or single point of failure
Source: Hany F. Atlam and Gary B. Wills, 'Chapter Three – Intersections between IoT and Distributed Ledger' (2019).

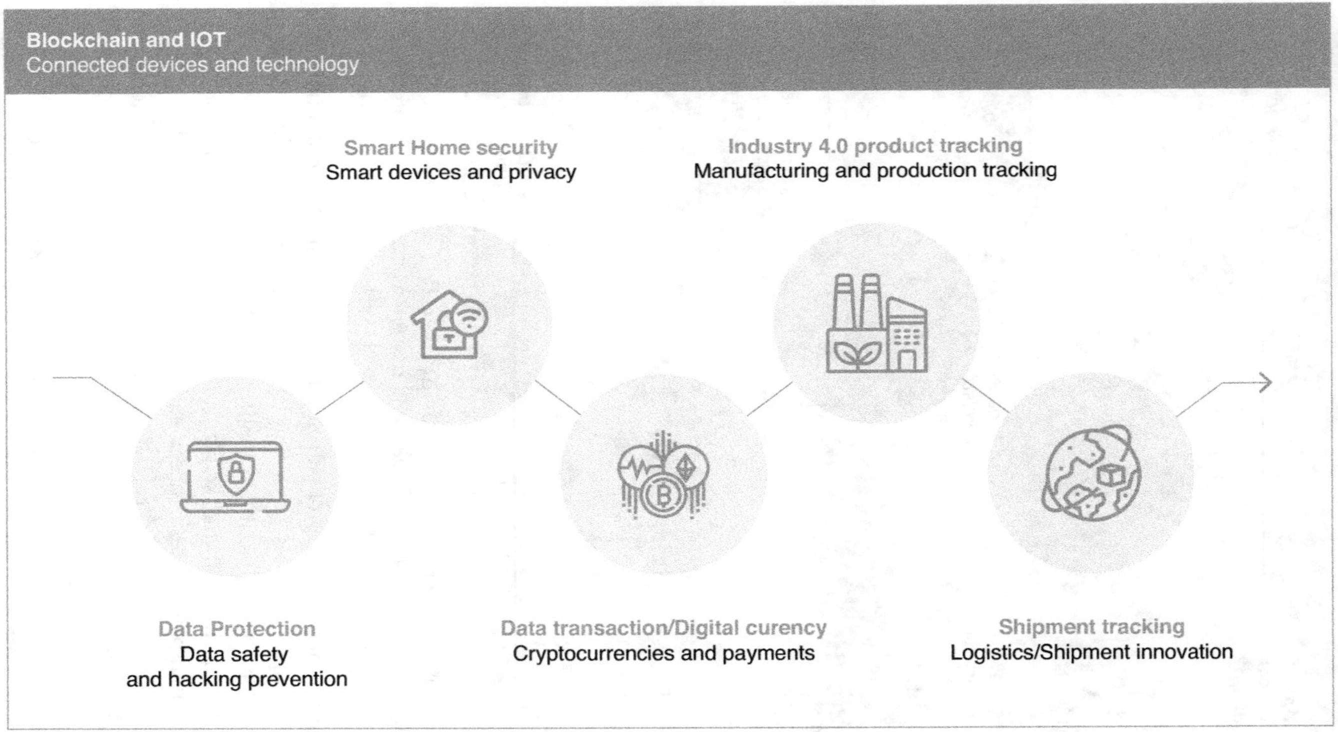

FIGURE 3.2 How integration of DLT with IoT works
Source: Adapted from Progresif, 'How Blockchain Will Revolutionise Our Lives', https://progresif.com/how-blockchain-will-revolutionise-our-lives/.

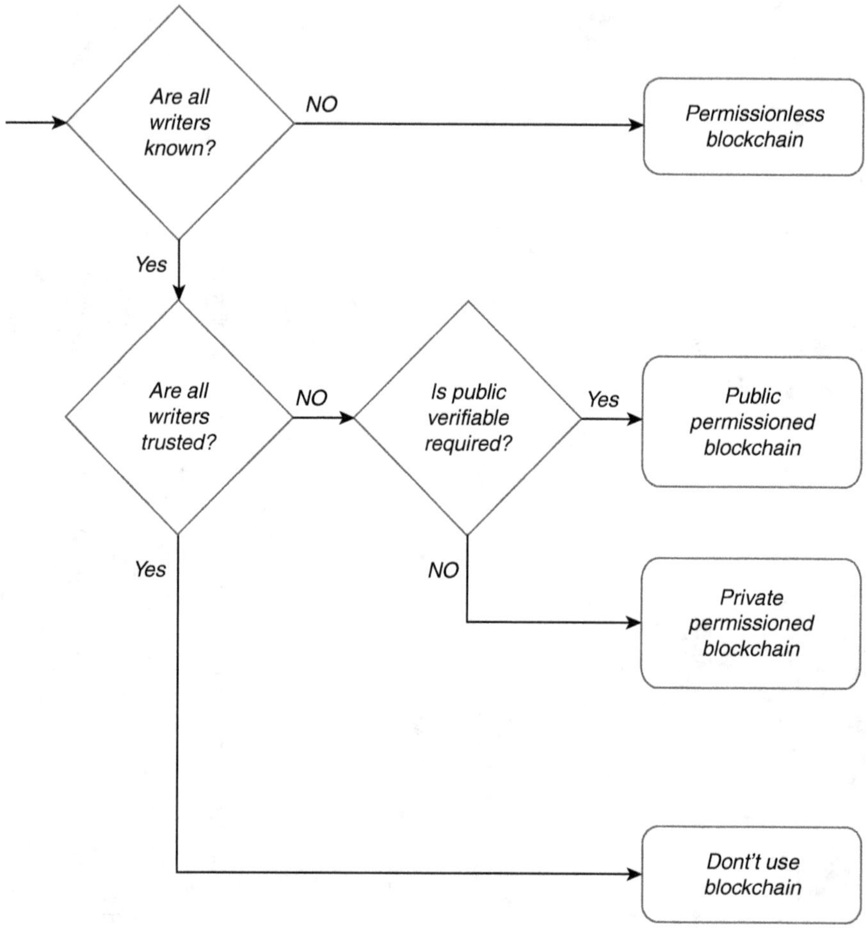

FIGURE 3.3 Facilitated flow chart of blockchain type selection
Source: Mohammad Maroufi, Reza Abdolee and Behzad Mozaffari Tazekand, 'On the Convergence of Blockchain and Internet of Things (IoT) Technologies' (2019).

must take care to choose an appropriate solution based on their restrictions and requirements.[54] Figure 3.3 presents a flow chart for determining which kind of blockchain is suitable for different IoT applications.

In sum, integrating IoT with blockchain can bring several benefits to both technologies, such as transparency, resilience, identity management, immutability, autonomy, security and decentralisation. Table 3.1 illustrates how, for example, blockchain can address IoT challenges with its integrated blockchain features and protocols.[55]

54 Mohammad Maroufi, Reza Abdolee and Behzad Mozaffari Tazekand, 'On the Convergence of Blockchain and Internet of Things (IoT) Technologies' (2019) 14 *Journal of Strategic Innovation and Sustainability* http://arxiv.org/abs/1904.01936 accessed 7 March 2020.

55 ibid.

TABLE 3.1 *How blockchain can address the challenges of IoT*

IoT challenges	Blockchain solutions
Security	Blockchain provides an immutable and secure environment for various types of IoT device. It also ensures data integrity since any change should be verified by the majority of the participating nodes in the blockchain network.
Point of failure	Blockchain uses decentralised and distributed communication between participating nodes in the network, which eliminates the issue of a single point of failure.
Third-party authority	Blockchain provides a decentralised and distributed environment for IoT devices, so there is no need for a centralised server or service provider to build the required trust between communicating nodes in the IoT system.
Address space	In contrast to IPv4 with 32-bit and IPV6 with 128-bit address space, blockchain has 160-bit address space, allowing it to generate and allocate addresses for about $1.46*10^{48}$ IoT devices offline.
Susceptibility to manipulation	Updates of IoT devices are approved only after obtaining the consent of most of the participating nodes in the blockchain network.
Ownership and identity	Blockchain can provide trustworthy authorised identity registration, ownership tracking and monitoring.
Data integrity	Blockchain provides an immutable and tamper-proof ledger that cannot be updated unless the majority of the participating nodes provide their consent and verify the update.
Authentication and access control	Smart contracts can provide decentralised authentication rules and logic that can enable efficient authentication for IoT devices.
Flexibility	With various commercial and open-source choices for blockchain, IoT organisations can use it to realise several targets without spending a considerable amount of money on research and development.
Costs and capacity constraints	Since there is no need for a centralised server, IoT devices can communicate securely, exchange data and carry out actions automatically through smart contracts.

Source: Adapted from Hany F. Atlam and Gary B. Wills, 'Chapter Three – Intersections between IoT and Distributed Ledger' (2019).

The combination of both technologies can be useful to avoid carbon market failure (see Chapter 4).

3.4.2 *Integration of DLT with AI*

Section 3.4.1 focussed on the potential of integrating DLT with IoT. This section will analyse how DLT, particularly blockchain, could match with AI and the challenges that lie ahead of such an integration. To begin with, AI expresses the theory and practice of building machines capable of performing tasks that require intelligence.[56] On the other hand, blockchain can provide security, privacy, decentralisation, anonymity and immutability. It seems that we could get significant advantage from combining AI and blockchain.[57] Integration of blockchain with AI has been called 'blockchain intelligence'.[58]

Even if, at this moment, applications of the combination of these technologies are still sparse, we can expect this situation to evolve very soon. The benefits of AI and DLT fusion are:

- **Encrypted data processing**: AI could unlock the encrypted DLT data's value, using techniques that securely process encrypted data. An emerging field of AI is building algorithms that can process or operate with encrypted data (Section 5.3.1.1).[59]
- **Decision-making recording**: DLT could record the decision-making process of AI. If decisions are recorded, they can simply be audited with certainty that the record has not been altered. Moreover, recording the decision-making process could help achieve the level of transparency necessary to gain public trust.
- **Management of consensus protocols**:[60] AI can be used to manage DLT protocols more efficiently. Basically, computers require a large amount of processing power to process encrypted data. For example, the hashing algorithms used to mine blocks on the Bitcoin blockchain take a brute force approach, trying every combination of characters until they find one that fits to validate a transaction. An AI-powered mining algorithm could enable using another method, meaning that tasks could be managed more intelligently and more efficiently.[61]

A recent systematic literature review on blockchain and AI cross-uses found that security is the most significant advantage of AI and blockchain convergence. Some studies focussed on detecting fraud behaviour and malware or reporting incidents and attacks. These studies prove that an AI-based blockchain can lead to automatic

56 Bernard Marr, 'Artificial Intelligence and Blockchain: 3 Major Benefits of Combining These Two Mega-Trends' *Forbes* (2 March 2018) www.forbes.com/sites/bernardmarr/2018/03/02/artificial-intelligence-and-blockchain-3-major-benefits-of-combining-these-two-mega-trends/ accessed 28 March 2020.

57 Ala Ekramifard and others, 'A Systematic Literature Review of Integration of Blockchain and Artificial Intelligence' in Kim-Kwang Raymond Choo, Ali Dehghantanha and Reza M Parizi (eds), *Blockchain Cybersecurity, Trust and Privacy: Advances in Information Security* (79th edn, Springer International 2020) 152 https://doi.org/10.1007/978-3-030-38181-3_8 accessed 8 April 2022.

58 Zibin Zheng, and Hong-Ning Dai, 'Blockchain Intelligence: When Blockchain Meets Artificial Intelligence' (December 2019) 2 www.researchgate.net/publication/337944266_Blockchain_Intelligence_When_Blockchain_Meets_Artificial_Intelligence accessed 8 April 2022.

59 ibid 4–6.

60 Marr (n 57).

61 ibid.

attack detection and defence approaches (see, for example, Chapter 6 on the use of AI for EU ETS security).[62]

Actually, a significant number of studies reveal issues and challenges in the blockchain, such as security and performance. These can be addressed by applying AI technologies. For instance, DL approaches can automatically classify the behavioural patterns of blockchain peers. They also help to identify strange behavioural patterns of malicious peers. Further, ML prediction has also been used to detect unknown root exploits to increase blockchain-based health-care applications' security.[63] Not only this, but an ML algorithm can detect and stop most attacks or anomaly behaviours in the blockchain network.[64] Additionally, AI can be used to manage blockchain and improve its performance. Examples are using the DL concept instead of consensus[65] or using neural networks in edge computing to optimise mobile blockchain's mining process.[66]

As described, integrating AI and blockchain could empower applications in different fields, including health, trading, security and IoT, help with management and decision-making, and provide security and privacy.[67] However, security remains the hottest topic in recent studies. Some studies demonstrate that ML algorithms' blockchain can detect and prevent attacks and improve safety and privacy. A review of these studies also shows that AI and blockchain's integrated features can play an essential role in the medical field, including at various stages of gathering, analytics and decision-making on health-care datasets. Nevertheless, many research challenges are to be addressed, such as scalability, lack of standards and issues around consensus protocols.[68]

To date, most of the research on integrating blockchain with AI concentrates on exploiting blockchain for AI to overcome its security challenges.[69] But our demonstration is principally focussed on solving blockchain issues by using AI technologies. Figure 3.4 summarises the opportunities brought by AI to enhance blockchain

62 Ekramifard and others (n 58) 155.

63 Ahmad Firdaus and others, 'Root Exploit Detection and Features Optimization: Mobile Device and Blockchain Based Medical Data Management' (2018) 42 *Journal of Medical Systems* 112 https://doi.org/10.1007/s10916-018-0966-x accessed 8 April 2022.

64 Somdip Dey, 'Securing Majority-Attack in Blockchain Using Machine Learning and Algorithmic Game Theory: A Proof of Work' 2018 10th Computer Science and Electronic Engineering Conference (CEEC) (IEEE 2019); Andreas Bogner, 'Seeing Is Understanding – Anomaly Detection in Blockchains with Visualized Features', *UbiComp/ISWC 2017 – Adjunct Proceedings of the 2017 ACM International Joint Conference on Pervasive and Ubiquitous Computing and Proceedings of the 2017 ACM International Symposium on Wearable Computers* (2017).

65 Rui-Yang Chen, 'A Traceability Chain Algorithm for Artificial Neural Networks Using T–S Fuzzy Cognitive Maps in Blockchain' (2017) 80 *Future Generation Computer Systems*.

66 Cong Nguyen and others, 'Optimal Auction for Edge Computing Resource Management in Mobile Blockchain Networks: A Deep Learning Approach' (November 2017) www.researchgate.net/publication/320944201_Optimal_Auction_For_Edge_Computing_Resource_Management_in_Mobile_Blockchain_Networks_A_Deep_Learning_Approach accessed 8 April 2022.

67 Ekramifard and others (n 57) 156.

68 ibid 157.

69 Khaled Salah and others, 'Blockchain for AI: Review and Open Research Challenges' (2019) 7 *IEEE Access* 10127 1044–46.

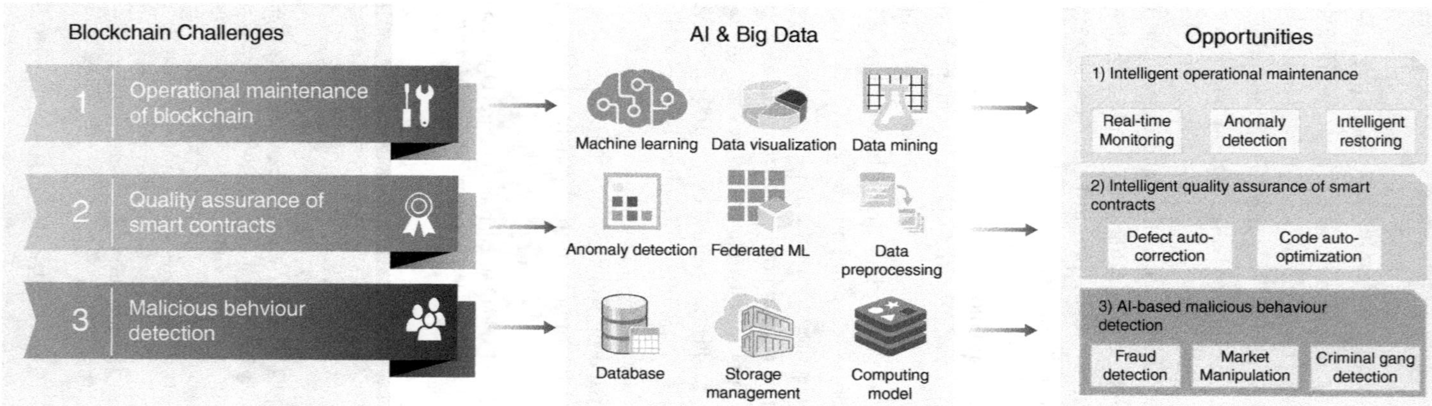

FIGURE 3.4 Opportunities brought by AI to address the challenges of blockchain
Source: Zibin Zheng and Hong-Ning Dai, 'Blockchain Intelligence: When Blockchain Meets Artificial Intelligence' (2019).

systems: intelligent operational maintenance of blockchain (real-time monitoring, anomaly detection, intelligent restoring); intelligent quality assurance of smart contracts (defect auto-correction, code auto-optimisation); and malicious behaviour detection (fraud detection, market manipulation, criminal gang detection).[70] Such technical feasibility offers the potential to prevent carbon market failure with DLTs.

It is clear that blockchain and AI are two technologies that have the potential to become even more ground breaking when they are combined. Both serve to enhance the capabilities of the other.[71]

3.4.3 *Integration of IoT with AI*

This section provides an overview of the integration of IoT with AI by highlighting its benefits. Our previous developments demonstrate that IoT would be useful for the evolution of the carbon market as they can, for example, be used to monitor the implementation of carbon offsetting projects all over the world. Also, IoT devices enable remote and real-time monitoring and there are many use cases for this in various sectors, such as health, agriculture, insurance and the environment.

In the environmental domain, IoT systems have been mainly developed for forest monitoring. Early detection is the safest way to protect forests against the threats posed by fires or deforestation. In this aspect, thermal infrared cameras, Lidar sensors and Synthetic Aperture Radar devices have been proposed and implemented globally. For example, 'Forest Guardian'[72] is a system that detects the sound produced by deforestation activities using acoustic signal evaluation and network node communication principles. This system offers improvements such as permanent monitoring of critical forest areas and rapid response to deforestation activities at a theoretical level.[73] However, in practice, IoT technology faces many challenges (see Table 3.1).

On the other hand, AI is applied in many domains to understand techniques that require intelligent action and solving of complex problems. Thus, integrating IoT with AI will create a powerful technology that can solve many IoT problems related to the massive amount of data generated by different IoT devices. With the substantial analytic capabilities of AI, IoT data can be analysed efficiently to extract meaningful information.[74]

The typical layered architecture of IoT comprises five layers, as shown in Figure 3.5: perception, network, middleware, application and business. The

70 Zheng and Dai (n 59) 2–3.

71 Marr (n 57).

72 J Papán, M Jurečka and J Púchyová, 'WSN for Forest Monitoring to Prevent Illegal Logging', Federated Conference on Computer Science and Information Systems (2012).

73 AE Marcu and others, 'IoT System for Forest Monitoring', 2019 42nd International Conference on Telecommunications and Signal Processing (TSP) (IEEE 2019).

74 Hany F Atlam, Robert J Walters and Gary B Wills, 'Intelligence of Things: Opportunities Challenges' 3rd Cloudification of the Internet of Things Conference (CIoT) (2018) 1.

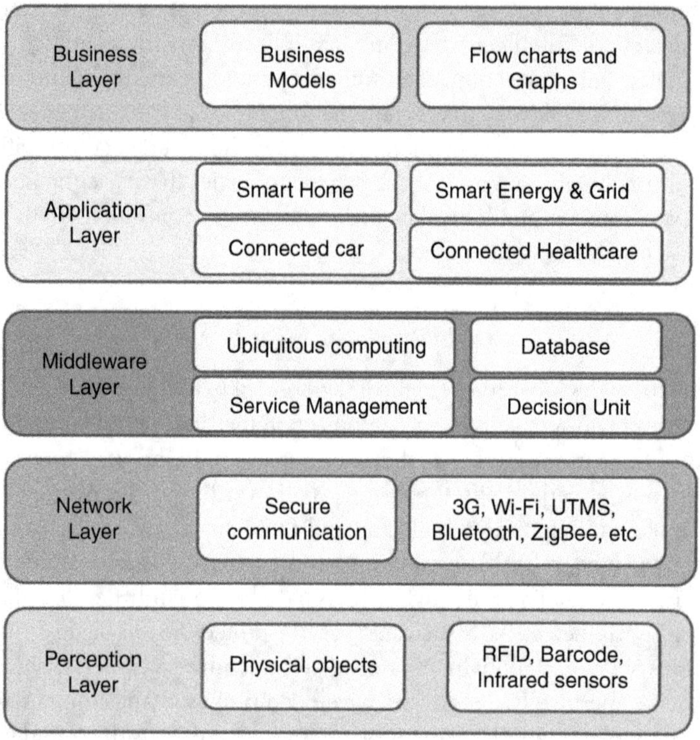

FIGURE 3.5 IoT referenced layer architecture
Source: Hany F. Atlam, Robert J. Walters and Gary B. Wills, 'Intelligence of Things: Opportunities Challenges', 3rd Cloudification of the Internet of Things Conference (CIoT) (2018).

perception layer involves physical objects and sensor devices. The purpose of this layer is to collect environment information such as location, humidity and temperature. Then the collected data is transferred to the network layer. This layer conveys collected data securely from sensors to the information processing system. The network layer transfers the collected data from the perception layer to the middleware layer. The middleware layer consists of a set of sub-layers used to manage data, software, models and platforms. It is located between the network layer and the application layer. The application layer provides global governance of the applications that use the processed information of the middleware layer. Finally, the business layer manages the whole IoT system, including the applications and services. It generates graphs and flow charts based on the data received from the application layer.[75]

[75] Manisha Gunturi, Harika Devi Kotha and M Srinivasa Reddy, 'An Overview of Internet of Things' (2018) 10 *J Adv Res Dynamical and Control Systems* 659; Atlam, Walters and Wills (n 75) 2–3.

Owing to the analytic capabilities of AI, IoT data can be analysed to make better-informed decisions. Collecting data is one thing, but sorting, analysing and making sense of that data is an entirely different thing.[76] Thus, AI is the driver that will allow analytics and decision-making from the data collected by IoT devices[77] when monitoring offsetting programmes remotely. However, even though integrating AI and IoT will release the full benefits of IoT data, many challenges stand in the way of successful convergence of IoT and AI. These challenges include heterogeneity, security and privacy, accuracy and speed, centralised architecture, legal aspects and artificial stupidity.[78]

3.4.4 *Combination of AI, IoT and DLT*

This section gives an overview of the potentialities resulting from the intersection of three major technologies: AI, IoT and DLT. The previous developments focussed on the technical advantages of integrating IoT with DLT (Section 3.4.1), DLT with AI (Section 3.4.2) and IoT with AI (Section 3.4.3). The purpose of this approach is to explain how emissions trading systems (ETSs) can benefit from the combination of these technologies.

The convergence of DLT, particularly blockchain, AI and IoT, maximises each of these technologies' benefits while minimising the risks and constraints associated with them. It will form an impactful combination of security, interconnectivity and autonomy.[79] Blockchain, as a decentralised architecture, enables many computers to perform their tasks together and to store information in a decentralised, unchanging and accessible way.

Since IoT networks cover many connected devices, there are many weaknesses in the system, exposing it to cyber-attacks, fraud and theft. To prevent security problems, AI can proactively defend itself against malware and cyber-attacks. Network and data security can be further improved through blockchain technology that can prevent unauthorised access to the network's data. Additionally, AI can enhance the functional capacity of the IoT network by making it autonomous and smarter.[80] Figure 3.6 illustrates the results of the intersection among these technologies.

A proven example of convergence among blockchain, AI and IoT is Fujitsu's algorithm, which continuously monitors workers' physiological data (temperature, activity levels, pulse, etc.) using portable in-vitro diagnostic devices (IVDs) and sensors

76 Ahmed Banafa, 'Why IoT Needs AI' BBVA OpenMind (18 July 2017) www.bbvaopenmind.com/en/technology/digital-world/why-iot-needs-ai/ accessed 8 April 2022.

77 Atlam, Walters and Wills (n 75) 5.

78 ibid 6.

79 Jan Veuger, 'Convergence Blockchain, AI En IoT' (2019) 12 *Res Dev Material Sci* 1245 https://crimsonpublishers.com/rdms/pdf/RDMS.000777.pdf accessed 8 April 2022.

80 ibid. Sushil Kumar Singh, Shailendra Rathore and Jong Hyuk Park, 'BlockIoTIntelligence: A Blockchain-Enabled Intelligent IoT Architecture with Artificial Intelligence' [2019] Future Generation Computer Systems https://doi.org/10.1016/j.future.2019.09.002 accessed 7 March 2020.

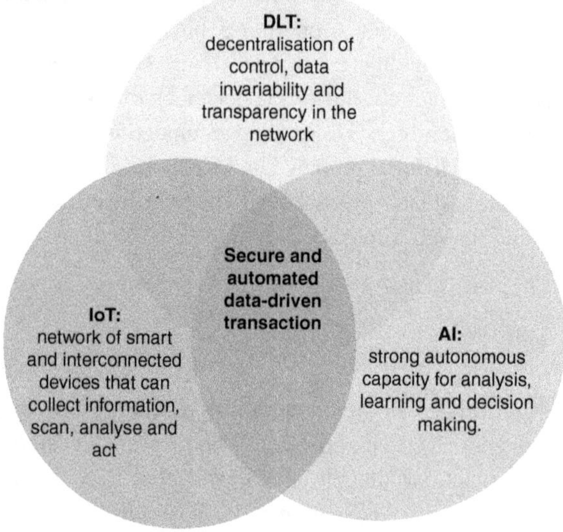

FIGURE 3.6 The intersection among DLT, AI and IoT

to track the links between different factors and workers' health. The analysis can help organisations improve working conditions and prevent workers' health problems. Applying blockchain to this system can help keep track of more personalised data by ensuring privacy or paying out health insurance amounts using smart contracts.[81]

For the moment, the expected impact of the convergence of blockchain, AI and IoT is incalculable, and its existing applications will certainly develop. However, findings from the applications are at an early stage and are not as advanced as is necessary to achieve real transformation and scalability. The same remark can be made concerning IoT and blockchain (see Section 3.4.1). With increased interest, investment and innovation, the convergence of blockchain, AI and IoT will become a reality.[82]

In this sense, Singh and colleagues propose an IoT architecture with blockchain and AI to support effective big data analysis – BlockIoTIntelligence – and give an overview of the potential result of the intersection.[83] Figure 3.7 explains the proposed architecture, divided into four 'bits of intelligence', namely cloud intelligence, fog intelligence, edge intelligence and device intelligence. It demonstrates how to converge blockchain and AI to achieve big data analysis, security and centralisation of IoT applications such as smart health care or smart city.[84]

81 Veuger (n 80) 1246. Fujitsu Limited, 'Fujitsu Estimates Workers' Heat Stress Levels with New AI-Based Algorithm – Fujitsu Global' (2017) www.fujitsu.com/global/about/resources/news/press-releases/2017/0712-02.html accessed 7 April 2020.

82 Veuger (n 80) 1246.

83 Singh, Rathore and Park (n 81).

84 ibid 5.

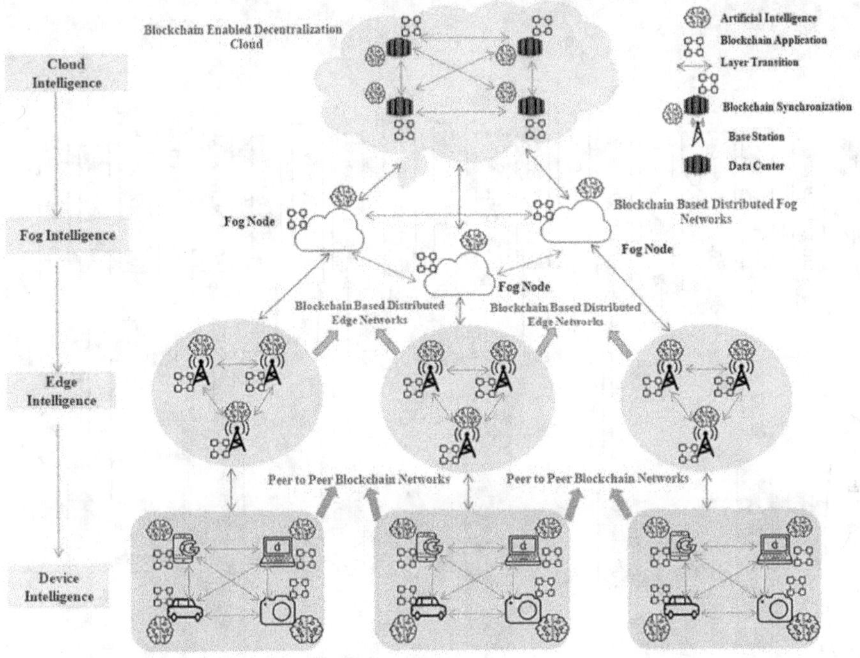

FIGURE 3.7 Design overview of the proposed BlockIoTIntelligence architecture
Source: Sushil Kumar Singh, Shailendra Rathore and Jong Hyuk Park, 'BlockIoTIntelligence: A Blockchain-Enabled Intelligent IoT Architecture with Artificial Intelligence' (2019).

Device intelligence consists of various IoT devices with AI and blockchain applications; it produces a massive amount of data, which is transferred to the edge intelligence. Subsequently, edge intelligence consists of AI-enabled base stations connected to the blockchain at the network's edge. Each AI-enabled base station is connected to several sensing devices, and it analyses and processes the traffic data from these devices. The process data from the edge intelligence are reported to the fog intelligence, which is a combination of several AI-enabled fog nodes with blockchain. Each AI-enabled fog node with blockchain is associated with composing AI-enabled base stations at the edge intelligence and responsible for processing data to the cloud intelligence. Finally, cloud intelligence consists of AI-enabled data centres connected to the blockchain to provide decentralised and secure big data of IoT.[85]

A methodological flow of the proposed BlockIoTIntelligence architecture is illustrated in Figure 3.8.[86] It describes the IoT platform as a combination of six layers: physical layer, communication layer, link control layer, service layer,

[85] ibid 6.
[86] ibid 8.

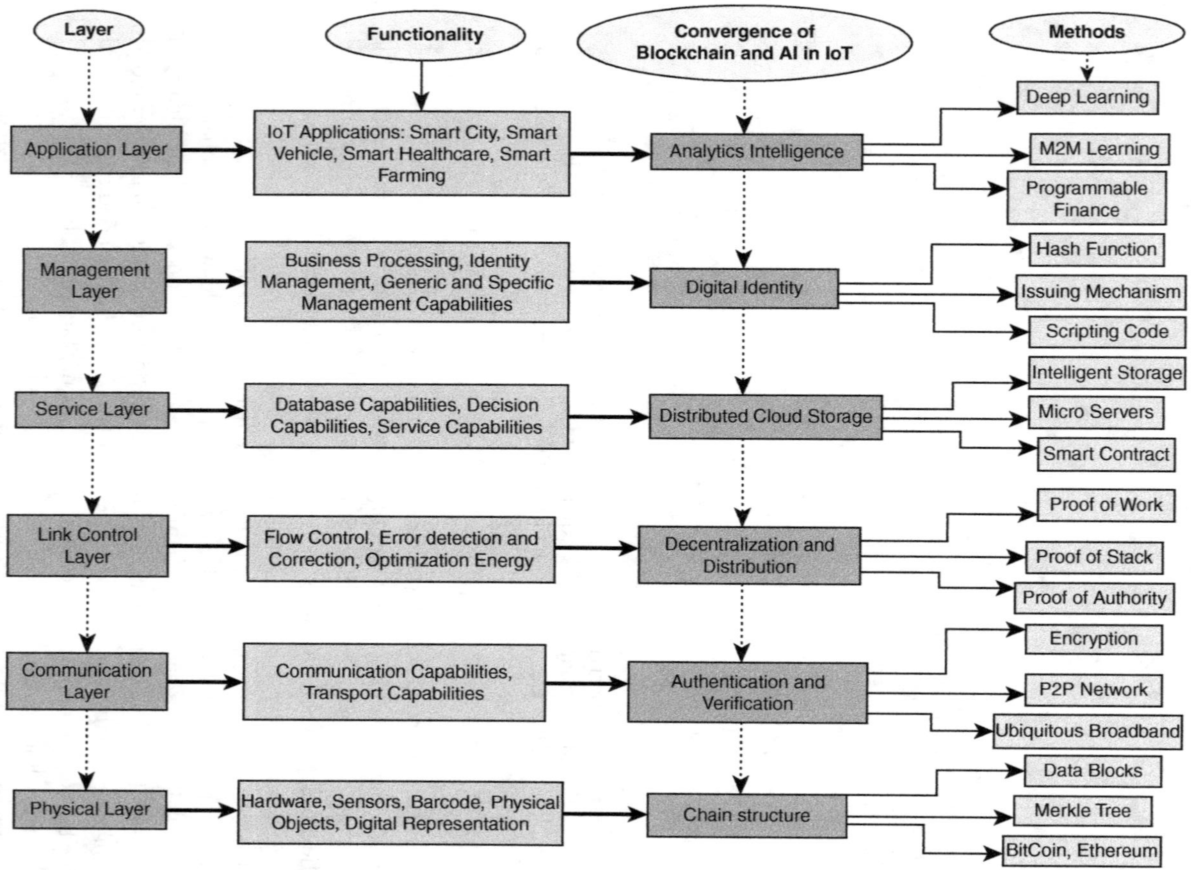

FIGURE 3.8 The methodological flow of the proposed BlockIoTIntelligence architecture
Source: Sushil Kumar Singh, Shailendra Rathore and Jong Hyuk Park, 'BlockIoTIntelligence: A Blockchain-Enabled Intelligent IoT Architecture with Artificial Intelligence' (2010).

management layer and application layer. The physical layer is correspondent to device intelligence and communication. The link control layer is related to edge intelligence and service. The management layer is connected to fog intelligence. Finally in the proposed architecture, the application layer is relevant to cloud intelligence.[87] The physical layer identifies data such as temperature, location and agriculture in cloud intelligence. This layer has different kinds of security threats and issues, such as transferring the information from one place to another, making it insecure from malicious persons. The concept of blockchain intelligence is used to mitigate these issues. The collected data are transferred to the communication layer, which is a medium for transmitting the information.[88]

The convergence of blockchain and AI for IoT uses consensus protocols for scalability and security. It provides a distribution and decentralisation mechanism. Information is stored in decentralised form using this layer. Stored data are transferred to the service layer, which provides essential services such as decision support, database support, service composition and organisation, virtual entity resolution and IoT service monitoring for IoT applications.[89] The system uses distributed cloud and intelligent storage, micro-servers and smart contracts for secure authentication and validation in this layer. The transfer of this information to the management layer provides data management, software, criteria and infrastructure between networks to the application layer. Finally, information shared with the application layer serves to ensure the global management of the applications used in IoT applications such as smart vehicles, smart health care, smart farming, intelligent transportation and others. The convergence of blockchain and AI for IoT also uses other techniques such as analytics intelligence, DL, machine-to-machine learning and programmable learning used in smart technology.[90]

3.5 CONCLUSION

Based on the analysis in this chapter, DLT features appear to answer current carbon market gaps and challenges. However, an efficient global carbon market, with fewer gaps, cannot rely on only one technology. All technologies have their weaknesses, and DLT presents numerous, such as the lack of data analytics and the need for real-time data collection.

Nowadays, it is almost impossible to talk about DLT without considering AI and IoT. These last two present interesting features that can help solve some of the challenges related to the use of DLT. Each technology presented in this triptych can tackle the challenges of the other two. This chapter aims to demonstrate that it is possible and beneficial to combine AI, IoT and DLT to develop the carbon market. Using AI, IoT and DLT to address carbon market issues such as transparency and

87 ibid 7.
88 ibid.
89 ibid.
90 ibid.

accounting is technically feasible even if it does present some challenges. It also creates advantages that could be useful in preventing the carbon market's failure and strengthening its resilience.

As explained in Chapter 1, DLT has many key attributes that make it well-suited to addressing regulatory challenges. It does, however, have certain weaknesses, including a lack of data analytics capabilities and the need for real-time data collection. Two promising emerging technologies that offer potential applications in climate solutions and being integrated with DLT are AI and IoT. Of these, AI can foster efficient and intelligent decision-making, whereas IoT allows DLT to interact more closely and intricately with the physical world. When combined, these technologies can address each other's flaws and create a complex system that can effectively, securely and comprehensively collect and handle data. Chapter 4 will, among other things, explain how the combination of these technologies may enhance carbon trading.

4

Emerging Technologies and Their Applicability to Solving Challenges in the Carbon Markets: An Overview

Alastair Marke, Max Inglis and Constantine Markides

4.1 INTRODUCTION

One of the foci of this book is to consider the overlap between the legal solutions available in the 'traditional' legal structure and the emerging 'crypto-legal' structure, underpinned by the application of distributed ledger technology (DLT) to the governance of carbon market initiatives, such as compulsory mechanisms like the European Union Emissions Trading System (EU ETS) and other voluntary carbon markets.

This chapter builds on the explanation of the main features and challenges of carbon markets presented in Chapter 2, as well as on the potential use of and interaction among artificial intelligence (AI), Internet of Things (IoT) and DLT as explored in Chapter 3, to analyse how the main features of these emerging technologies can be applied to improve the governance of carbon markets.

4.2 CURRENT CHALLENGES OF THE CARBON TRADING ECONOMY

There are multiple advantages of the increasing development of carbon markets as a climate action tool, chiefly that it enables environmental incentives to become tradable financial assets, allowing people anywhere in the world to earn tradable assets in exchange for participation in the reduction of greenhouse gas (GHG) emissions.

As touched on in Chapter 1, several of the main issues with the current carbon trading platforms are the lack of trust, cost-effectiveness, funding, transparency and efficiency resulting from these platforms. The centralised nature of the system places too much control in the hands of a single body, which has led to a fall in the cost-effectiveness of the system. For example, approximately USD 979 million is spent annually administering emissions trading systems (ETSs) supported by intermediaries.[1] This is a significant amount of money that could be allocated

[1] Future Thinkers, '7 Ways the #Blockchain Can Save the Environment and Stop Climate Change' (*Medium*, 2017) https://medium.com/futurethinkers/7-ways-the-blockchain-can-save-the-environment-and-stop-climate-change-724d48287dfc accessed 21 December 2018.

more effectively. The difficulty arises because a centralised system suffers from the issues referred to above and depends on individual countries interpreting and enforcing market regulations effectively and fairly. The cost of human error in the process is deeper than just the functional error, as it involves relationships between people.

The issues referred to above are cyclical in nature since a lack of an effective uniform trading system that can be applied across jurisdictions subsequently leads to a lower desire among potential new participants to join the system. This eats away at the efforts made for many years by the existing participants to establish a fair playing field for all trading actors. The centralised nature of the system and decision-making has been considered distant by some participants, which nurtures the distrust among non-participants. It is very possible that DLT-based solutions can settle these issues.

4.3 APPLICABILITY OF DLT TO CARBON TRADING

In support of the view that DLT can be a relevant tool to improve the governance of carbon trading, a policy paper by Moniz and colleagues reports that a DLT-supported verification platform could reduce the transaction costs of the carbon market by 30 per cent.[2] An appropriate example would be the EU ETS, the main market tool used by the EU to curb its carbon emissions. At present, it limits emissions from more than 11,000 heavy energy-using installations (power stations and industrial plants) and airlines operating between these countries and covers approximately 40 per cent of the EU's carbon emissions.[3] As the largest and oldest major carbon market, the EU ETS serves as a useful case study on how DLT supported by AI and IoT could enhance the monitoring, reporting and verification (MRV) for carbon markets generally.

4.3.1 *DLT-Supported MRV, Compliance and Allocation Processes*

The regulations of ETSs govern the MRV process and related compliance cycle, the registry infrastructure and the allocation, use and transfers (i.e. market transactions) of allowances. Carbon trading schemes, such as the EU ETS, which involve significant transfers of data and assets can benefit from a mix of the five DLT attributes mentioned in Chapter 1 to improve the MRV process.

In a DLT-supported EU ETS, firms in covered sectors such as power stations and oil refineries could trade 'emission allowances' (European Union Allowances

2 Ernest J Moniz and others, 'Promising Blockchain Applications for Energy: Separating the Signal from the Noise' (Policy Paper, Energy Futures Initiative, 2018) https://static1.squarespace.com/static/58ec123cb3db2bd94e057628/t/5b4e59751ae6cf086c4450a5/1531861368631/EFI_Blockchain_July2018_FINAL+.pdf accessed 12 April 2022.

3 EU Emissions Trading System (EU ETS) | Climate Action (europa.eu) https://ec.europa.eu/clima/eu-action/eu-emissions-trading-system-eu-ets_en accessed 24 April 2022.

(EUAs)) on a DLT. In the 'MRV module' of this DLT, 'independent accredited verifiers' would form a distributed network of 'gatekeepers' connecting the European Commission (EC) and the EU ETS. Verifications could be carried out by a legal person or legal entity accredited by a 'national accreditation body' under the EU Accreditation and Verification Regulation Commission Regulation (EU) No. 600/2012. They can be regulators, universities or environmental consultancies. These verifiers can provide a service package comprising 'on-chain' assessment and 'off-chain' reports.

Firstly, the verifiers retrieve the details of EUAs of all installations from the EU ETS-covered firms from the DLT, holding the Union Registry with transaction data already input by the EC, to establish the carbon emission standards of the installations against which to conduct an assessment. The verifiers assess whether the submitted annual emissions reports (AERs) are compliant with the Monitoring & Reporting Regulation (MRR) Commission Regulation (EU) No. 601/2012 and Commission Implementing Regulation (EU) 2018/2066 (in the case of aircraft operators), relevant GHG emissions permits, and approved monitoring plan; and ensure the data in AERs being free of material misstatements.[4] At the facility-level, the evaluation criteria are standardised, systematic and compatible with the technicalities of DLT that verifiers simply need to complete an 'e-form'. The inputs from verifiers will serve as (one of) the 'oracle(s)' to trigger a 'smart contract' that surrenders the relevant EUAs for the firms and update their 'holding and trading' accounts, the Union Registry and national inventories automatically.

Secondly, the verifiers provide 'off-chain' services that may include matching consultancy services. They also calibrate the assessment data input on the DLT into a standard, machine-readable format. Data from these summary reports will be fed into a 'big data' repository managed by the EC. Then, AI will be deployed off-chain to conduct data analytics to facilitate the allocation of allowances for the following year. It will also be able to determine the EUAs to be required by the firms, which could optimise the Market Stability Reserve mechanism, and even if and how the EU-level carbon emissions threshold or annual 'linear reduction factor' should be adjusted. Such AI-generated data can then be transferred back to the DLT to start another compliance year.

4.3.2 *Added Value to the MRV and Compliance Cycle*

Successful ETSs require an effective MRV process that relies on robust legal, accounting and regulatory structures. The accuracy and transparency of MRV are crucial for the sustainability of the EU ETS because inadequate MRV results in accountability issues.

[4] European Commission, 'EU ETS Handbook' (2015).

Generally, embedding the MRV and allocation processes 'on-chain' can significantly improve the transparency of facility/company-level compliance, enhancing the accountability of participants. If all emissions-related information is accessible for public scrutiny on a DLT (with a certain level of privacy), participants are forced to be responsible and accountable.

Another added value is the security of information on the EU ETS DLT. As all data on GHG emissions permits, monitoring plans and verifiers' assessment results are availed on the trusted, immutable DLT, it helps strengthen the monitoring and verification of the credit source and ownership when there are transactions/transfers of allowances between participants. This will protect the ETSs from fraud and double counting issues, among other important matters.[5]

By itself, DLT cannot streamline the allocation of allowances or guarantee the credibility of input data. Unless supplemented with IoT and AI, whether at facility, company, national or regional level, enhanced MRV capabilities owing to DLT-based ETSs' infrastructure could not ensure the accuracy and credibility of emissions data input, allow near-real-time tracking of environmental impacts of environmentally friendly measures or forecast the number of allowances needed in the allocation procedure for sufficiently offsetting a given process.

As the EU ETS will be expanded to cover more sectors post-2020, DLT could be conducive to creating a more liquid marketplace that allows more participants not meeting the current emissions threshold to join and automatically connect to it cost-effectively through 'application programming interfaces', for example. It represents that over-the-counter carbon credit transactions would be within reach for all stakeholders who wish to participate more easily in the EU ETS.

4.3.3 *Limited Disruptive Effects of DLT-Supported MRV on Regulatory Enforcement*

Even if the MRV process may be migrated entirely to a DLT, the process of issuing, distributing and surrendering allowances would remain unchanged.[6] The disruptive effects of such a DLT-supported MRV process on the EC's enforcement of the MRR and AV in the EU ETS is likely to be very limited.

Similar to a DLT financial network in nature, a DLT-supported EU ETS would also raise a series of new legal questions. Regulators and market participants need to work together to ensure the compliance of future standards and define new supervisory models through a new 'crypto-legal structure', as discussed in Chapter 1 surrounding some or all of the five regulatory services and the three short-term disruptive effects mentioned.

5 K Khaqqi, 'Incorporating Seller/Buyer Reputation-Based System in Blockchain-Enabled Emission Trading Application' (2018) 209 *Applied Energy* 8.

6 ibid.

4.4 FILLING CARBON MARKET GAPS WITH AI, IOT AND DLT

4.4.1 *Current Data Management*

Carbon pricing mechanisms, such as ETSs, are commonly data-driven, and there is a multitude of MRV practices and technologies encompassing data collection, data processing and data analysis that support these mechanisms.[7] For instance, ETSs are facilitated by the use of registries into which allowances are issued, and that enable tracking as they are traded between different participants.[8]

Since the 1990s, new technologies have brought more accurate and comprehensive accounting to MRV practices, organisational and subnational inventories and project-specific calculations. More recently, innovative MRV practices and technologies, such as mobile and remote monitoring, are being advanced for transportation, distribution of household appliances and land-use mitigation activities.[9] Despite significant advances in technological adoption and automation of MRV, most MRV practices still involve manual processes that rely on disconnected data trails, spreadsheets and static PDF files to achieve market and environmental integrity.[10] Figure 4.1 illustrates the key steps in the GHG data process.[11]

4.4.2 *New Data Management Design*

While DLT can provide a secured, shared, distributed and transparent registry system, the data stored in the registry cannot be useful if it is not accurate. That is, DLT can only guarantee that the datasets have not been altered; it cannot ensure

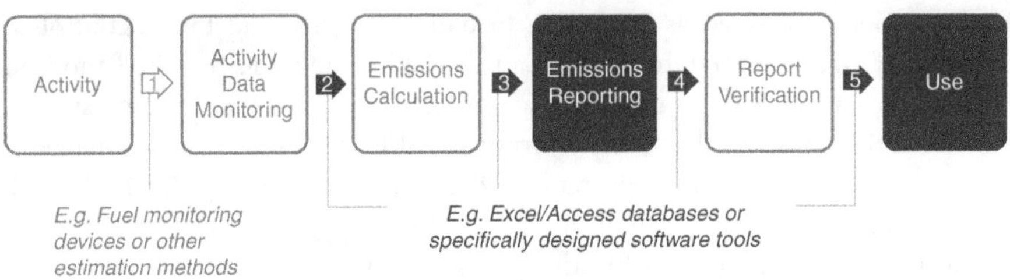

FIGURE 4.1 Key steps and links in the GHG data process with GHG data management systems highlighted
Source: PMR, 'Supporting GHG Mitigation Actions with Effective Data Management Systems' (2013).

7 World Bank, 'Blockchain and Emerging Digital Technologies for Enhancing Post-2020 Climate Markets' (2018) 8.
8 PMR, 'Emissions Trading in Practice: A Handbook on Design and Implementation' (2016) 6.
9 World Bank (n 7) 8.
10 ibid.
11 PMR, 'Supporting GHG Mitigation Actions with Effective Data Management Systems' (2013) 6.

that the data stored on the ledger are correct. Controlling access to the registry through DLT is just a part of the answer, however; IoT can help in providing real-time data to the registry. The data collected can relate to the specific projects that generate allowances that are traded on the market. For example, if the project relates to reforestation, monitoring can be realised with a satellite that can measure the evolution of the vegetation on the field.

Furthermore, AI can help to analyse the data provided directly by the different actors or collected by IoT. It can detect fraud and notice and prevent data manipulation. In the case of a reforestation project, AI can determine whether the data provided match with the satellite tracking. Moreover, for projects for which real-time monitoring is not available, AI can check whether the data provided are correct considering previous projects with similar conditions. Thus, if the algorithm detects an attempt of fraud, it can take action. For example, it could suspend the suspicious account, and mark the suspect data that has been registered before the intervention of the registry manager. The manager can decide further actions such as unlocking the blocked account, deleting the questionable data or asking corrections.

Another essential capacity of AI is to process the data collected and stored in the registry. It can help the market by avoiding unplanned downtime while increasing operating efficiency. Therefore, the data provided by the different actors can be analysed in real-time. This analytic capacity will be useful in comparing the achievements to the goals. Moreover, it can be a tool for making a double check of the data stored on the registry, to prevent double counting.

4.4.3 *Market Risk Management*

Carbon pricing emerged as a solution to climate change and the uncontrolled emission of GHGs around the world. Canada, China, South Korea, the European Union and some US states have imposed or scheduled a carbon pricing system. However, studies show that these instruments still face significant challenges.[12] There are at least three primary reasons that can explain this failure. The first concerns the link between carbon markets in the developed world and offsetting opportunities in developing countries. The second is linked to corruption and transparency issues in carbon markets. Finally, carbon markets have reportedly indirectly promoted unsustainable practices.[13]

Figure 4.2 shows a generic functional architecture of the different IT systems and databases that can share connections and exchange information with a registry. The upper middlebox 'GHG inventories' refers to the systems that record physical GHG data (e.g. emissions and removals) at the national, programme and project levels. The

[12] Jeffrey Ball, 'Why Carbon Pricing Isn't Working: Good Idea in Theory, Failing in Practice' (2018) 97 *Foreign Affairs* 134.

[13] Steffen Bohm, 'Why Are Carbon Markets Failing?' *The Guardian* (12 April 2013) www.theguardian.com/sustainable-business/blog/why-are-carbon-markets-failing accessed 12 April 2022.

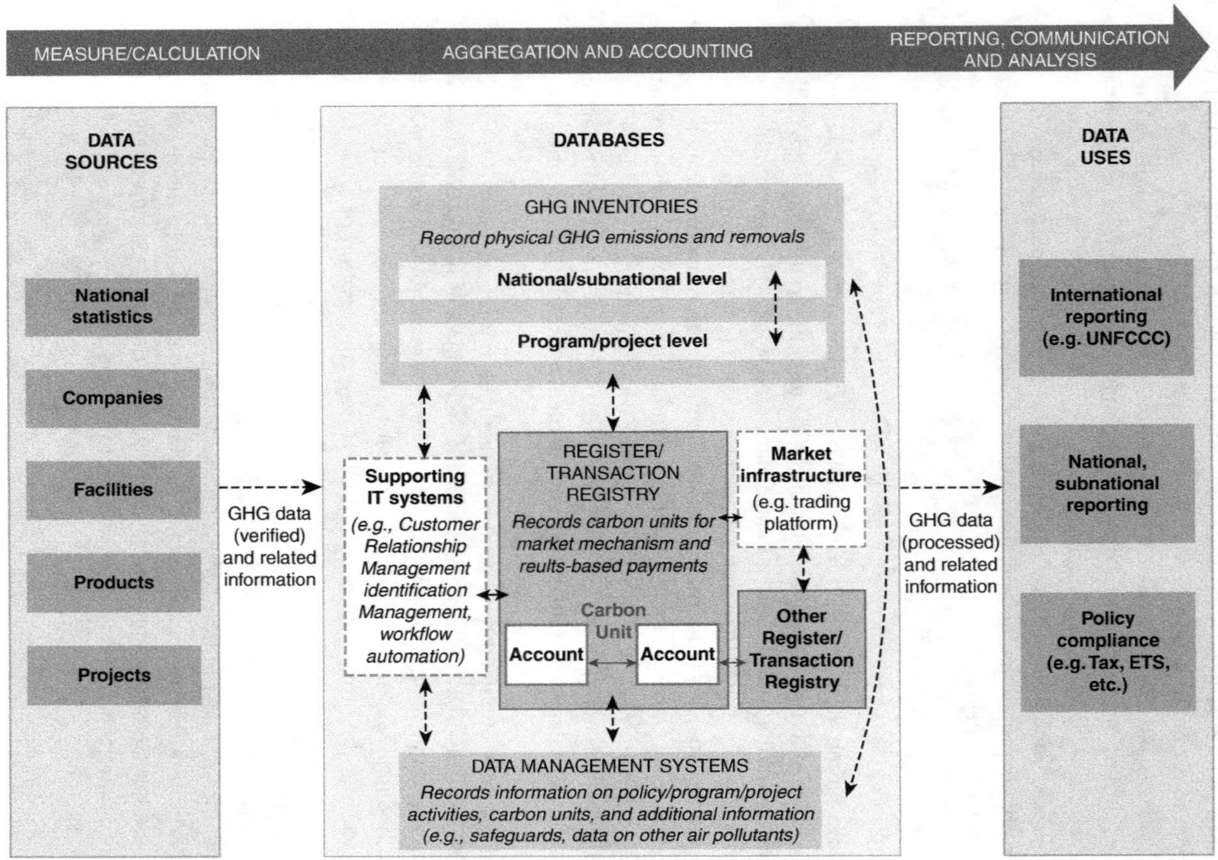

FIGURE 4.2 The registry in its environment: potential connections and interfaces
Source: PMR and FCPF, 'Emissions Trading Registries: Guidance on Regulation, Development, and Administration' (2016).

bottom middlebox 'Data management systems' refers to the systems that record specific information on GHG (and potentially non-GHG) policies, programmes and projects. The central part of the diagram shows the actual registry and other (domestic or international) registries it may be connected to through a central hub or a peer-to-peer connection.[14]

Allowances and credits are the most common types of tradable units in carbon markets. Following the Kyoto Protocol approach, these generally represent one tonne of CO_2, or CO_2–equivalent, depending on the nature of the particular scheme.[15] A functioning climate market requires rules, institutions and infrastructure to enable proper market operation and transparent accounting while ensuring environmental integrity.[16]

4.4.4 *New Market Management Features*

Post-2020 carbon markets will enhance cross-jurisdictional transactions. The World Bank Group's Climate Warehouse Initiative is a response to this paradigm shift. At least three conditions will allow it to take place more easily. The first condition is to maintain the integrity of the information. The second condition is that the data are aggregated in an accepted form. The last is about the necessity of having a proper mechanism that converts climate assets to a standard metric for comparability, such as their mitigation value. Further, any type of market instrument can be so transacted, provided such a metric (as, for example, mitigation value) can be applied. This approach safeguards markets and environmental integrity by preventing double counting concerning climate assets.[17]

Thus, a new architecture is needed to facilitate trading across diverse carbon markets. This approach is dependent on the integration of production data (supported by suitable technology, such as IoT), the next generation of governance that supports digital methods for MRV, larger-scale data analysis (such as big data analytics) and the broad application of DLT. The combination of DLT, IoT and the governance of the next generation of climate markets enables the creation of digital representations of commodities that can be used for existing markets and for transacting across climate markets (see Figure 4.3).[18]

A significant aspect of transactions on the distributed network is the question of dispute resolution between counterparties. Bearing in mind that counterparties can be from different jurisdictions, the issue of how legal disputes between them should be settled may arise. Alternative dispute resolution mechanisms, such as arbitration,

14 PMR and FCPF, 'Emissions Trading Registries: Guidance on Regulation, Development, and Administration' (2016) 47.

15 World Bank (n 7) 8.

16 ibid 9.

17 ibid 12.

18 ibid.

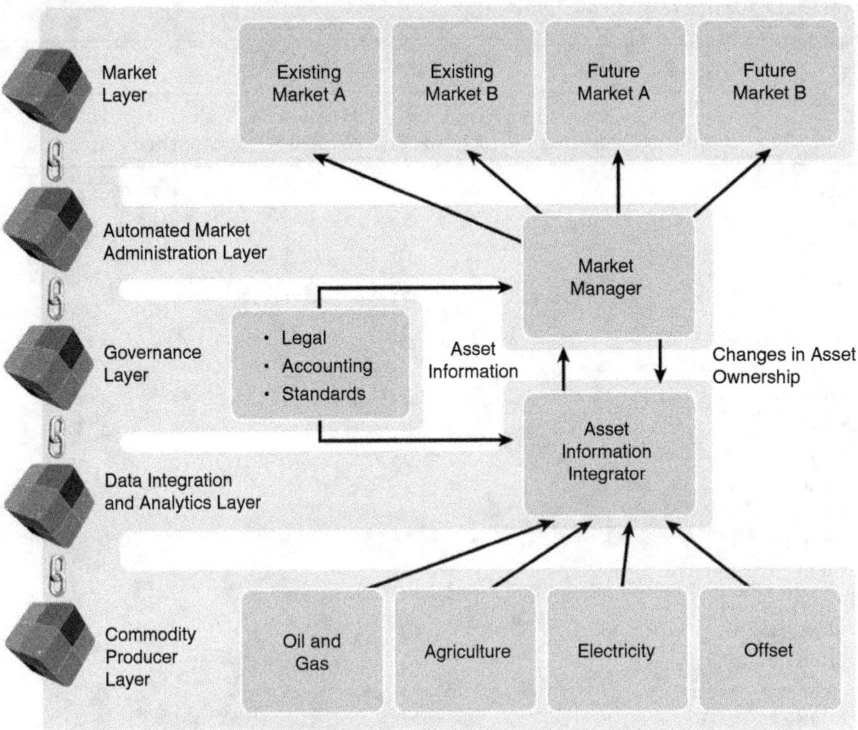

FIGURE 4.3 Architectural vision for the networked climate markets
Source: World Bank, 'Blockchain and Emerging Digital Technologies for Enhancing Post-2020 Climate Markets' (2018).

are a way to solve these conflicts and parties should have agreed, before joining the networked market, to standard terms and conditions. An applicable law would still need to be specified for any arbitration.[19]

Owing to the development of algorithmic dispute resolution,[20] AI could be useful in settling disputes that could arise from carbon market transactions. Algorithmic dispute resolution can be carried out online. Online dispute resolution (ODR) uses technology to facilitate the resolution of disputes between parties and involves negotiation, mediation, arbitration or a combination of all three. It can be fully automated or require human intervention. In ODR, automation is used to bring parties together, for a neutral decision, or to propose a settlement. Table 4.1 summarises these elements of ODR.[21]

19 JD Macinante, 'A Conceptual Model for Networking of Carbon Markets on Distributed Ledger Technology Architecture' (2017) 11 *CCLR* 243, 257 www.jstor.org/stable/10.2307/26245363 accessed 15 April 2020.

20 Jeremy Barnett and Philip Treleaven, 'Algorithmic Dispute Resolution: The Automation of Professional Dispute Resolution Using AI and Blockchain Technologies' (2018) 61 *Computer J* 399.

21 ibid 400.

TABLE 4.1 *Online dispute resolution*

	Negotiation		Mediation		Arbitration	
	Full-automated	Human-assisted	Full-automated	Human-assisted	Full-automated	Human-assisted
Process						
Consumer ODR	✓		✓			
Judicial ODR	✓		✓		✓	
Corporate ODR	✓		✓		✓	
Resolution						
Consumer ODR		✓		✓	✓	
Judicial ODR	✓	✓	✓	✓		✓
Corporate ODR	✓		✓		✓	✓
Mandatory						
Consumer ODR						
Judicial ODR						✓
Corporate ODR	✓		✓		✓	✓

Source: Jeremy Barnett and Philip Treleaven, 'Algorithmic Dispute Resolution-The Automation of Professional Dispute Resolution Using AI and blockchain Technologies' (2018).

While ODR is a way to gain time and save money for the parties, it can also help to avoid paralysis in the carbon market. For example, in some cases, European authorities have been obliged to suspend EU ETS to solve problems.[22]

Moreover, the Covid-19 pandemic has exposed weaknesses of our traditional governance, and justice is not spared. Social or physical distancing makes classical dispute resolution bodies, which require physical presence, obsolete. Apart from the length of the judiciary process, health crises, or climate crises such as hurricanes or floods, can put the carbon market in a challenging situation.

Indeed, AI can help find the most appropriate solution not only for the parties but also for the market. For example, AI-based ODR can help to adjust the carbon price considering the difficulties of a party to meet its commitments. For instance, parties

[22] Silke Goldberg and others, 'TheSuspension of Trading in Certified Emission Reductions: Consequences for EU ETS Trades' (*Lexology*, 20 April 2010) www.lexology.com/library/detail.aspx?g=47ca7d94-22e5-4056-8849-5bd8081d2290 accessed 12 January 2021.

may agree to sell carbon credit at a determined price. Then the buyer, perhaps owing to a force majeure such as Covid-19, might face financial difficulties and become unable to make the payment. In this situation, AI can produce a settlement decision or recommendation according to the evolution of the carbon market and the impact of the crisis. If the carbon credit has already been transferred, and in case of disagreement, AI can suggest to the registry manager to void the carbon credit transfer. Further, the conflictual credits can be marked to prevent any other transmission by the insolvent buyer.

Another way that AI can help carbon markets, at the subnational, national or international level, is in adjusting the allowances' price to avoid a market crash. The Covid-19 outbreak might cause a drop in the carbon price as the amount of GHG emissions has decreased drastically. Carbon markets will need to be able to predict such an event before it happens. Being able to analyse carbon markets crash risks will avoid living a similar event as the stock market crash of 2008. Unlike the stock market, the climate, which is already really harmed, cannot recover so easily. To monitor the market, and make a possible crash forecast, the system will need reliable and real-time data that can, fortunately, be provided through DLTs. As the information will be gathered all around the world, big data analysis provided by AI is advantageous.

4.5 POTENTIAL DLT APPLICATIONS TO ADDRESS SECURITY ISSUES AND POINTS OF FAILURE

The EU ETS and its security failures, especially in the period 2010–11, can be used as an example to highlight the legal and practical issues that can arise with a carbon trading platform. These issues are not unique to the EU ETS; however, the focus will be on the EU ETS for this section as it offers ample examples of security lessons to be learnt. For example, in 2010, hackers stole 475,000 allowances, worth approximately EUR 7 million, from the Czech Republic's registry account. This followed other hacking attacks in Greece and Poland with a cumulative cost to the EU ETS of approximately EUR 30 million for this period.

These hacking incidents led the EC to suspend spot trading of allowances for a period of time in January 2011. This caused a number of adverse effects such as the costs associated with national registries adopting more stringent security measures to prevent system abuse, mistrust among the participants in the system and loss of valuable time in the attempts to reduce carbon emissions through the EU ETS. Using the EU ETS and the hacking issues associated with it as the main example here, it is obvious that there are clear legal and practical issues surrounding the handling of stolen allowances.

The legal and practical issues around the handling of stolen allowances would become irrelevant in a crypto-legal structure primarily because the possibility of theft through hacking or phishing happening in a DLT-supported EU ETS would be close to zero. In the cybersecurity breaches of 2010–11, the major points of failure in the EU ETS included:

(1) the security of the computer server hosting the corporate accounts;
(2) account-opening procedures; and
(3) the transfer approval process.

A DLT-supported carbon market can be outlined as a decentralised autonomous organisation, formed by multiple 'modules' embedded with a complex mechanism of smart contracts. On this smart-contract-centred distributed ledger, national authorities and regulated financial institutions can be the nodes and/or oracles executing modular regulatory logics to be elaborated on in Sections 4.5.1–4.5.3 and forthcoming chapters*. Several legal and operational issues around the handling of stolen allowances (as further explored in Chapter 6, Section 6.2.2) would become irrelevant in a crypto-legal structure primarily because the possibility of theft through hacking or phishing happening in a DLT-carbon market would be negligible. The specific features of DLT could address the main issues related to the transfers of carbon credits, and, while solutions to the single points of failure are introduced in the rest of this section and considered in more depth in Chapter 6, Section 6.2.2 for the EU ETS context, the advantages of adopting DLT are relevant and applicable to any kind of carbon market.

4.5.1 *Doorkeeper Module*

Against point of failure (1) in Section 4.5, the 'Doorkeeper Module' can provide a sophisticated shield defending all subscribing servers and accounts from the kind of virus and malware cyber-attacks that fuelled the cybersecurity breaches in 2010–11. Thus, DLT would form a single cyber-threat detection platform connecting the geographically diverse security experts with the Union Registry and subscribing servers (i.e. computer servers hosting the 'holding and trading' accounts of companies and traders). On this platform, security experts would devise and maintain competing anti-virus/anti-malware software underpinned by 'scanning engines' that rapidly detect the latest threats.

4.5.2 *Know-Your-Customer Module*

In relation to point of failure (2) in Section 4.5, in the spirit of 'code is law', a customised account-opening DLT would be deployed to govern the processes of the EC, as the central administrator, approving new 'holding and trading' accounts in the Union Registry through a sophisticated 'KYC Module'. The KYC Module comprises functions of KYC application and processing on-chain and off-chain. The

* Rather than direct citations, the design of some of these modules was enlightened by the ideas in Liss, Florian. (2018). Blockchain and the EU ETS: An architecture and prototype of a decentralized emission trading system based on smart contracts. (Master's Thesis) Munich: Technical University Munich.

on-chain KYC application function is a permissioned distributed ledger storing identity data of verified companies and traders; identification documents are stored off-chain because foreseeably the method of processing identity proof might evolve in the future.

4.5.3 *Transaction Module*

Against point of failure (3) in Section 4.5, approvals for the sale and purchase of allowances among traders or companies could be executed through the 'Transaction Module' where traders/companies can create buy/sell orders. The principle of carbon allowance transfer here is similar to the logic in Bitcoin transactions on a DLT.

The technical workings of these modules will be described in context in Chapters 6 and 7.

4.6 CONCLUSION

The main selling points of DLT are its uniqueness, validity, consensus, immutability and authentication. These attributes complemented by its decentralised nature and ability to function without a middle operator give DLT an advantage over the current ETSs in place. Also, DLT solutions will create a new and simplified crypto-legal structure that can generate different roles and responsibilities for legal actors within each local, regional, national and international playing field. Thus, DLT usage can simplify the legal process and enforcement and can also lead to automation of the regulatory requirements and decision-making, which, in turn, is likely to reduce the strains on the current legal systems in place in each country. There are further benefits of DLT when integrated with AI and IoT, which can enhance both data and market management within carbon markets. A crypto-legal system would also eliminate the possibility of account-operating and transfer failures and security breaches by using the Doorkeeper, KYC and Transaction Modules referred to here.

5

Transition to a DLT-Supported Governance Framework

Clare Reynolds and Nicola Massella

5.1 INTRODUCTION

For DLT to be successful in carbon markets and to address the challenges discussed in Chapter 2 (such as issues of double counting and theft), implementing appropriate legal, governance and administrative frameworks is essential.

This chapter first provides a brief overview of regulatory approaches to DLT to date; and an overview of the challenges and legal issues associated with its governance. It goes on to explore some general principles necessary for an appropriate 'crypto-legal' structure for DLT in carbon markets, and discuss how the roles of stakeholders in carbon markets might change as a result. It concludes with a short discussion of how such a transition might take place.

5.2 CHALLENGES OF GOVERNING DLT AND EXISTING REGULATORY FRAMEWORKS

5.2.1 *A Very Short History of Existing Approaches to Regulating Crypto-assets and DLT*

To help provide insight into how DLT might be governed in a carbon market context, this section provides a very brief history of the development of key measures and the increasing institutionalisation of DLT and crypto-assets. The detailed evaluation of these measures (in particular their application to financial services) is beyond the scope of this book.

To date, moves towards a direct regulatory framework for DLT have focussed on the primary use cases in financial markets, motivated primarily by concerns relating to the use of cryptocurrencies and crypto-assets for illicit purposes (such as terrorist financing) and the need to protect consumers, businesses and other users from services akin to financial services.

As an initial step, lawmakers in several jurisdictions introduced measures to bring certain services provided in relation to crypto-assets (such as exchanges and custody providers) into the remit of anti-money laundering (AML) and counterterrorist financing (CTF) legislation. This began with interpretative guidance in 2013 from the Financial Crimes Enforcement Network (FinCEN) of the US Department of the Treasury, to clarify the applicability of the money service business regulatory regime to persons creating, obtaining, distributing, exchanging, accepting or transmitting virtual currencies.[1] The Financial Action Task Force spread this approach at the international level, publishing in June 2014 its report on virtual currencies.[2] In Europe, following reports from regulators including the European Banking Authority[3], in 2016 the European Commission proposed amendments to EU AML legislation resulting in the inclusion of cryptocurrency exchanges and custodians operating in the EU within the scope of the EU's Fifth AML Directive 2018/843/UE.[4]

In recent years, the potential benefits of DLT for financial markets appeared more clearly, in particular in relation to efficiency in post-trade processes, transparency and resilience.[5] Beyond the AML and CTF concerns emerged a trend towards the regulation of DLT-based digital assets. With the intention of attracting highly innovative businesses, several small countries established a clear regulatory framework for token offerings. For example, in October 2019 Liechtenstein enacted the Token and TT Service Provider Act[6] and in September 2020 Switzerland issued a law concerning the adaptation of federal legal provisions to the development of DLT,[7] which provides for the existence of transferable securities in the form of DLT tokens.

Recognising the emergence of a fragmented legislative approach to crypto-assets across the various EU member states, the European Commission adopted as part of its 'Digital Finance Package' in September 2020 proposals for two EU regulations in relation to crypto-assets. The first concerns the regulatory regime for markets in crypto-assets that do not qualify as financial instruments under the Markets in Financial Instruments Directive II (MiFID II) and crypto-asset service providers

1 Department of the Treasury Financial Crimes Enforcement Network, 'Application of FinCEN's Regulations to Persons Administering, Exchanging, or Using Virtual Currencies' (Guidance, FIN-2013-G001, 18 March 2013).

2 Financial Action Task Force, 'Virtual Currencies Key Definitions and Potential AML/CFT Risks' (June 2014) www.fatf-gafi.org/media/fatf/documents/reports/virtual-currency-key-definitions-and-potential-aml-cft-risks.pdf accessed 24 December 2020.

3 European Banking Authority, 'EBA Opinion on Virtual Currencies' (Opinion, EBA/Op/2014/08, 2 July 2014).

4 Directive (EU) 2018/843 amending Directive (EU) 2015/849 on the prevention of the use of the financial system for the purposes of money laundering or terrorist financing, and amending Directives 2009/138/EC and 2013/36/EU.

5 European Securities and Markets Authority, 'The Distributed Ledger Technology Applied to Securities Markets' (Report, ESMA50-1121423017–285, 7 February 2017) www.esma.europa.eu/sites/default/files/library/dlt_report_-_esma50-1121423017-285.pdf accessed 24 December 2020.

6 Proposal for a Regulation on Markets in Crypto-assets, and amending Directive (EU) 2019/1937.

7 Swiss Law 'Adaptation du droit fédéral aux développements de la technologie des registres électroniques distribués', Swiss Confederation, 25 September 2020.

(MiCA).[8] The second aims to introduce a pilot regime for financial market infrastructures based on DLT.[9] Taken together, these proposals and wider measures under the EU Digital Finance Package represent a meaningful acknowledgement of the potential of DLT and a significant step towards implementation of this technology in the EU. Their application in the context of emissions markets raises some interesting questions, which are discussed further in Sections 5.5.1 and 5.5.2, and very briefly in Sections 5.3 and 5.4, as well as in Chapter 6.

This is by no means a complete list of measures. Other countries that have adopted DLT and/or crypto-asset legislative measures include Australia,[10] China,[11] Italy,[12] Malta,[13] Russia[14] and Singapore.[15] Legislation has also been adopted in various jurisdictions to address specific aspects such as taxation of crypto-assets.[16]

8 See n 6.

9 Proposal for a Regulation of the European Parliament and of the Council on a pilot regime for market infrastructures based on distributed ledger technology.

10 In 2018, the Australian Transaction Reports and Analysis Centre (AUSTRAC) announced the implementation of more robust cryptocurrency exchange regulations. Those crypto regulations require exchanges operating in Australia to register with AUSTRAC, identify and verify users, maintain records and comply with government AML/CFT reporting obligations. Unregistered exchanges are subject to criminal charges and financial penalties. AUSTRAC, 'New Australian Laws to Regulate Cryptocurrency Providers' (11 April 2018) www.austrac.gov.au/new-australian-laws-regulate-cryptocurrency-providers accessed 24 December 2020.

11 In October 2019, the Standing Committee of the 13th National People's Congress in China passed a cryptography law that will be effective from 1 January 2020, according to a Chinese media report. As reported by Coindesk, www.coindesk.com/chinas-congress-passes-cryptography-law-effective-jan-1-2020 accessed 5 January 2021.

12 With the purpose of enhancing innovation, Italy adopted a positive definition of DLT and smart contract under the provisions of D.L. 14 December 2018 n. 135. Italy also anticipated the EU in expanding the scope of AML regulation to virtual currencies with D.Leg. 25 May 2017 n. 90.

13 In 2018, Malta enacted legislation, comprising three separate bills, which set a global precedent by establishing a regulatory regime applicable to crypto exchanges, ICOs, brokers, wallet providers, advisers and asset managers. The three laws are the Virtual Financial Asset Act, the Innovative Technological Arrangement and Services Act and the Malta Digital Innovation Authority Act.

14 Russian law 'On digital financial assets, digital currency and amendments to certain laws of the Russian Federation' dated 31 July 2020.

15 In January 2019, Singapore passed its 'Payment Services Act', which aims to regulate both traditional and crypto-currency based payments. In July 2020, the Monetary Authority of Singapore published a 'Consultation Paper on New Omnibus Act for the Financial Sector', which includes new licensing requirements for certain types of virtual asset service provider and technology risk management requirements.

16 In 2014, the Internal Revenue Service of the United States (IRS US) issued a notice confirming that virtual currency is treated as property for US federal tax purposes. IRS US, 'IRS Virtual Currency Guidance: Virtual Currency Is Treated As Property for U.S. Federal Tax Purposes; General Rules for Property Transactions Apply' (25 March 2014) www.irs.gov/newsroom/irs-virtual-currency-guidance accessed 24 December 2020. In Singapore, a business that sells goods and services in exchange for virtual currency has to charge Goods and Services Tax. Inland Revenue Authority of Singapore, 'e-Commerce' www.iras.gov.sg/IRASHome/GST/GST-registered-businesses/Specific-business-sectors/e-Commerce/#title5 accessed 24 December 2020.

The regulation of various aspects of DLT is therefore not new, and it is clear that the approach to governance and regulation of DLT will vary depending on the jurisdiction and particular use case.

5.2.2 *Challenges of Governing DLT within Existing Legal Frameworks*

Originally, blockchain technology was conceived for state-remote networks, that is, networks entirely self-governed on the basis of consensus among their users.[17] However, as understanding has increased of the potential significance of blockchain and DLT (as well as the risks, including of use to facilitate illicit activity), so have questions regarding the appropriate legal framework. To understand how DLT might be governed in carbon markets, it is first necessary to explore some of the challenges associated with governing DLT in general. This section therefore explores some of the legal challenges associated with DLT and smart contracts in intentionally general terms and, where relevant, how these relate to the use of DLT in carbon markets.

Both DLT and crypto-assets challenge long-standing regulatory strategies. Traditionally, regulators tasked with supervising a new or unregulated market begin by identifying the relevant parties and intermediaries to regulate as gatekeepers in the relevant jurisdiction; they then issue rules applicable to those gatekeepers to achieve the stated goals of the market. This traditional model of regulatory oversight does not necessarily translate easily to more 'decentralised' DLT ecosystems.

Despite some public misconceptions about blockchain and crypto-assets as a 'lawless' space, this does not mean that DLT operates in a legal vacuum. Many existing legal principles, including company law,[18] contract law,[19] property law[20] and tort,[21] can be applied to DLT systems, although the way in which this is done varies across different jurisdictions and use cases.

[17] Philipp Paech, 'The Governance of Blockchain Financial Networks' (2017) 80(6) *Mod L Rev* 1073–1110.

[18] On 30 May 2018, Vermont Governor Phil Scott signed into law Senate Bill 269: An Act Related to Blockchain Business Development, allowing companies to incorporate in the state using a new type of business entity, a blockchain-based limited liability company. In Malta, there are also proposals to ascribe a new form of legal personality to the decentralised autonomous organisation, an entity enabled by DLT. Max Ganado, Joshua Ellul, Gordon Pace, Steven Tendon and Bryan Wilson, 'Mapping the Future of Legal Personality' (*MIT Computational Law Report*, 20 November 2020) https://law.mit.edu/pub/mappingthefutureoflegalpersonality/release/1 accessed 7 April 2022.

[19] In several jurisdictions such as the UK and Finland, the existing principles that determine whether an agreement constitutes a legally binding contract are also applied to determining whether a smart contract constitutes a legally binding contract.

[20] *AA v Persons Unknown* [2019] EWHC 3556 (Comm), [2020] 4 WLR 35 [59][61]. The case held that 'a crypto asset such as Bitcoin is a property, [as it] meet[s] the four criteria set out in Lord Wilberforce's classic definition of property in *National Provincial Bank v Ainsworth [1965] 1* AC 1175 as being definable, identifiable by third parties, capable in their nature of assumption by third parties, and having some degree of permanence'.

[21] Two California federal court cases indicated that the prospect of negligence claims being directed at cryptocurrencies will be subject to the plaintiff's ability to establish the traditional elements of negligence claims: duty, breach, causation and damages. *Terpin v AT&T Mobility* LLC, 399

Extensive academic literature has addressed the approaches to and challenges of regulating or applying private law to DLT. For the purposes of this chapter, the following provides a short overview of some of these challenges in intentionally general terms:[22]

(1) **Exploring the relationship between code and law**: use of both DLT and smart contracts raises complex questions about the relationship between code (a formalised language that can be interpreted by a machine) and law (as a flexible and inherently ambiguous set of rules). The use of DLT and smart contracts reinforces the tendency to rely on code, rather than the law, to regulate individual actions and transactions.[23] One advantage of 'regulation by code' is that it can enable *ex ante* enforcement of rules (making it difficult for people to breach them in the first place), rather than relying on *ex post* enforcement by third parties (i.e. courts and enforcement agencies).[24] However, regulation by code is always less flexible than regulation by law. In reality, social interactions and bargains are complex and messy; law is intentionally ambiguous so that it can be applied on a case-by-case basis. By contrast, a smart contract may not be able to distinguish between routine situations and edge-cases that might require a different kind of treatment, and will not be able to account for the original intentions of the legislator.

    This means that the use of code to enforce legal obligations needs to be carefully and properly designed, and balanced with more flexible dispute resolution mechanisms where necessary. For any particular use case of DLT, determining which functions or circumstances can be governed by code, and which should continue to be governed by more traditional legal frameworks, is of fundamental importance. This is equally the case for DLT in carbon markets: although code and smart contracts can be used to improve the efficiency and transparency of certain processes, there will remain areas where regulation by more flexible law and guidelines is necessary. An example would be guidelines relating to the credibility and standard granularity of data feeding into the MRV blockchain of carbon units.

(2) **Determining which jurisdiction's laws claim jurisdiction and the relevant applicable law**: DLT ledgers do not have a specific or clearly identified location for each transaction, and each node or validator might be located

F Supp 3d 1035, 1051 (CD Cal 2019) and *Fabian v LeMahieu et al*, 2019 WL 4918431 (ND Cal 4 October 2019).

22 Philipp Hacker and others, 'Regulating Blockchain: Techno-social and Legal Challenges' in Philipp Hacker and others (eds), *Regulating Blockchain: Techno-social and Legal Challenges: An Introduction* (OUP 2019) 9.

23 Samer Hassan and Primavera De Filippi, 'Blockchain Technology as a Regulatory Technology: From Code Is Law to Law Is Code' (2015) 21(12) *First Monday* 10.5210/fm.v21i12.7113 accessed 24 December 2020.

24 Paech (n 17).

in a different jurisdiction. Determining the legal jurisdiction and the applicable law is therefore a significant challenge in decentralised DLT networks across multiple jurisdictions.

In relation to jurisdiction, this challenge is most acute in relation to decentralised autonomous organisations (DAOs) as there is often no clear link to connect a DAO to one national law system;[25] usually, a DAO has no seat, no board, no central point of government and no place of operation relating to the territory of one state.[26] However, this issue is specific to DAOs. In the case of carbon markets, it is more likely that a regulator or administrator would decide to implement a system with centralised governance, including a prior determined legal jurisdiction. The issue with the jurisdiction of DAOs is therefore somewhat theoretical in relation to DLT for carbon markets.

In relation to the applicable law, there is a plethora of possible choice of law approaches for the proprietary effects of transactions conducted using DLT. Applying traditional approaches such as the law of the place where the property or claim to property is situated may not be feasible for some crypto-assets, and different crypto-assets with varying levels of decentralisation may attract different approaches.[27] However, this issue may again be somewhat hypothetical in the case of DLT for carbon markets; where carbon units are allocated and traded as part of a regulatory compliance system, the governing law of the system is usually predetermined by the regulator or administrator and each participant in practice has limited influence over this. For the trading of allowances between participants, there are certain cases (such as individual OTC transactions[28]) where parties have the ability to specify the governing law. In both cases, ideally, the relevant governing law should be one that recognises that a tokenised carbon unit based on DLT can be validly held and transferred in a similar way to one represented on a centralised register.

The challenges for jurisdiction and choice of law associated with DLT more widely may therefore be somewhat hypothetical in relation to DLT's application to carbon markets.

(3) **Specifying the relevant regulatory regimes for different DLT use cases:** From a regulatory perspective, it makes sense to distinguish between different

25 Blockchain communities such as Bitcoin or Ethereum (which can be considered a DAO variant) have never registered themselves in any jurisdiction, not even in a 'blockchain-friendly' jurisdiction.

26 The European Union Blockchain Observatory & Forum, 'Legal and Regulatory Framework of Blockchains and Smart Contracts' (2019) www.eublockchainforum.eu/sites/default/files/reports/report_legal_v1.0.pdf accessed 24 December 2020.

27 ibid.

28 The International Emissions Trading Association (IETA) has established framework trading documentation for OTC emissions markets. Both the International Emissions Trading Master Agreement (IETMA) v1.0 and the EU ETS IETA Emissions Trading Master Agreement (ETMA) v3.0 and v.4.0 are governed by English law, unless parties otherwise elect in the elections to the relevant master agreement.

types of token and crypto-asset in order to delineate which legal obligations should apply.[29] However, the various different approaches to defining DLT and blockchain and the numerous different use cases can make it difficult to form a clear picture of DLT and the surrounding phenomenon.[30] Different jurisdictions may have very different conceptions of what qualifies as DLT or a crypto-asset.[31] Work by the international standard-setting organisations to establish common definitions and use cases for blockchain and DLT (e.g. under ISO/TC 307[32]) can therefore help bring clarity.

Different applications and use cases of DLT will each have their own legal and regulatory challenges. For example, crypto-assets involve specific challenges regarding taxation, as existing approaches to taxation of assets are difficult to apply[33] and designing a tax law framework has many challenges. Other applications of DLT may involve participants storing competitively sensitive information on a distributed ledger, which may raise specific competition law or antitrust concerns.[34]

For carbon markets specifically, regulation of carbon units currently depends on whether the units are classified as financial instruments subject to applicable financial regulations or not. For example, in the EU, allowances issued for compliance with Directive 2003/87/EC are classified as 'financial instruments' under the MiFID II Directive 2014/65/EU, whereas other systems (such as offsetting systems) would fall outside the scope of EU financial regulation. Where regulatory frameworks distinguish between DLT applications that are or are not financial instruments (e.g. MiCA in the EU as discussed in Section 5.2.2), this could potentially lead to different regulatory treatment for different types of DLT-supported carbon market. Policymakers will therefore need to be mindful of the wider regulatory environment applicable to different types of carbon market, including the overlap with financial

29 Philip Hacker and Chris Thomale, 'Crypto-securities Regulation: ICOs, Token Sales and Cryptocurrencies under EU Financial Law' (2018) 15(4) *ECFR* 645–96.

30 Juri Mattila, 'The Disruptive Potential of Distributed Consensus Architectures' (2016) ETLA Working Papers 38 www.etla.fi/wp-content/uploads/ETLA-Working-Papers-38.pdf accessed 24 December 2020.

31 Even within the application of blockchain technology to crypto-assets, there have been various different regulatory approaches to defining different types of crypto-asset in order to determine how they should be regulated. For example, in the EU, the Commission's 'taxonomy' of crypto-assets distinguishes between crypto-assets, asset-referenced tokens and e-money tokens, and crypto-assets qualifying as financial instruments. In the UK, the Financial Conduct Authority has instead categorised crypto-assets as security tokens, e-money tokens and unregulated tokens (made up of exchange tokens and utility tokens).

32 International Organization for Standardization (ISO), ISO/TC 307 'Blockchain and distributed ledger technologies'.

33 Channing Flynn 'Preparing for Digital Taxation in a Blockchain World' (2016) 43(10) *Tax Planning Intl Rev* 24–26.

34 Christophie S Hutchinson, 'The Challenges of Blockchain Technology to Competition Law' (2020) 1 (1) *Legal Issues in the Digital Age* 32–53.

regulation. Except for additional requirements applicable to the use of DLT itself, the legal status of a carbon unit (including under financial services legislation) should not change simply because it is cryptographically secured.[35] In other words, the 'tokenisation' of carbon units should not affect their pre-existing legal status.

(4) **Addressing data protection and privacy issues**: DLT applications need to comply with other areas of indirect, cross-cutting regulations such as data protection and privacy regulation. Data protection and privacy considerations in DLT have gained increasing prominence, in particular following the General Data Protection Regulation (GDPR)[36] entering into force in the EU in May 2018. Whether and how such laws apply will depend on various factors, including the type of data held or processed on the blockchain (i.e. whether it relates to 'personal data'), territoriality[37] and whether data encryption and anonymisation really do mean that parties cannot be identified.[38] For further discussion regarding data protection and privacy considerations in DLT for carbon markets, see Chapters 3 and 4.

(5) **Identifying which parties are the addressees of regulation**: As explored by Paech in relation to blockchain financial markets, applying regulation and private law to DLT networks involves various challenges as the traditional two-party intermediary relationship gives way to a distributed network built on poly-directional relationships among its nodes. Paech therefore suggests that regulation and law could target what replaces the traditional two-party model: the software platform or the nodes, or both.[39] The material scope of existing regulation may therefore need to be extended to cover the new actors in DLT-supported transactions, as the suitable addressees against which to enforce network-wide laws and requirements (such as continuity of service, availability and integrity, rules governing the acquisition of rights, etc,). For DLT networks where participants are geographically dispersed across different jurisdictions, identifying these parties and enforcing applicable regulations against them may not be straightforward.

As discussed in Chapter 1, it is more likely that a DLT-supported carbon market would rely on a permissioned system, in which case this issue of identifying the relevant parties may not be so acute. The roles of different

35 For example, proposals by HM Treasury in the UK in relation to the financial promotion regime for crypto-assets could have the effect of an emission allowance that is cryptographically secured being subject to the UK financial promotions regime, in circumstances where it might not otherwise, were it not cryptographically secured.

36 Regulation (EU) 2016/679 of the European Parliament and of the Council of 27 April 2016 on the protection of natural persons with regard to the processing of personal data and on the free movement of such data, and repealing Directive 95/46/EC.

37 Under Article 3(2) GDPR, data processing that takes place outside of the EU may still fall within the scope of the GDPR to the extent that the data processing relates to data subjects within the EU.

38 Matthias Berberich and Malgorzata Steiner, 'Blockchain Technology and the GDPR – How to Reconcile Privacy and Distributed Ledgers?' (2016) 2 *Eur Data Protection L Rev* 422

39 Paech (n 17).

actors in carbon markets and how these might change as a result of DLT-supported carbon markets is discussed further in Section 5.4. In particular, at least in compliance markets (as opposed to offsetting schemes) the relevant regulator or administrator will continue to play a key role, although new actors including DLT platform providers may also need to be brought within the scope of governance frameworks.

(6) **Making decisions actionable and enforceable for physical assets in the real world**: How might decisions made by a DLT community be legally enforced? Parties to a DLT network need to know that the legal obligations executed on that network or through an associated smart contract can be enforced against the relevant third parties in the real world.[40] Whether and how smart contracts can be legally enforceable depends upon the legal framework of the applicable law under which they are executed;[41] legislators may therefore need to consider whether regional or international legislation is necessary. Similarly, where a token is used to represent ownership of an asset[42] (whether a property, a piece of art or a carbon unit), whether ownership of that token can give rise to a legally enforceable claim against another party in relation to the underlying asset is key. Whether the courts of a particular jurisdiction will accept this argument and whether assets (such as carbon units) held on a blockchain can be treated as property ultimately depends on the nature of those assets and the laws in the relevant jurisdiction.

Aside from the trading of carbon units, an additional enforceability dimension arises for mandatory carbon markets because the units are required for regulatory compliance; covered emitters need to measure and report their emissions and either surrender units commensurate with past emissions (in an emissions trading system (ETS) such as the EU ETS) or establish a baseline and measure and report reductions (in a crediting system such as CORSIA). Any DLT-supported carbon market will therefore need to ensure that a carbon

40 Hong Wu and Guan Zhen, 'Electronic Evidence in the Blockchain Era: New Rules on Authenticity and Integrity' (2010) *Computer L Sec Rev* 36.

41 For example, under English law, a smart contract is at least capable of satisfying the requirements of a contract, that is, two or more parties reach an agreement, intend to create a legal relationship by doing so and involve the provision of consideration; however, this may or may not be the case depending upon the particular smart contract. The position in Finland, Spain and the United States is similar, that is, a smart contract is legally enforceable provided that it satisfies the legal requirements necessary for a legally binding contract. Interestingly, in Italy, Law Decree No. 135/2018 introduces the smart contract, which is defined as 'a computer program based on DLTs which execution is legally binding upon two or more parties with reference to the effects previously agreed by the same parties'. Smart contracts shall satisfy the requirement that a contract be in writing upon electronic identification of the relevant parties, in accordance with a procedure that has yet to be issued by the Agency for Digital Italy. Otherwise, the smart contract may not constitute a contract with legal effects and will instead be no more than a computer program built into the blockchain.

42 For example, gemstones and art (http://everledger.io).

unit held on DLT is equally valid and capable of being used for regulatory compliance purposes as units that do not rely on DLT.

(7) **Managing immutability**: The immutability of transactions recorded on a DLT ledger and the automatic execution of transactions on smart contracts are among the potential security advantages of DLT-supported transactions since transactions cannot be interfered with once they are recorded or executed. However, this also brings about a number of regulatory challenges. For example, there may be exceptional circumstances where a transaction may need to be undone (such as where executable code written into a smart contract results in a breach of the law, or where regulatory requirements require anonymity or the 'right to be forgotten'). In the absence of built-in circuit breakers, the only way to address this would be to create a new contract to reverse and cancel the operations effected by the first contract.[43]

In the carbon market context, a similar issue has arisen in connection with stolen allowances (see further Section 5.3 point (3) in relation to the ownership of emissions allowances).

The immutability of transactions recorded on the blockchain can help add to the security of carbon market systems, but only if the technology is implemented (and verified) in a way that maximises the benefits of DLT to protect against theft. To minimise the risk, the code would need to be verified and the DLT platform subject to some form of oversight.

(8) **Decentralising**: The concept of 'decentralisation' is central to many of the challenges of regulating and governing DLT. However, this terminology, itself one of the central claims of DLT and digital assets, requires further examination. The term 'decentralisation' is often used to denote systems that lack central power centres, in particular in relation to permissionless blockchains. Walch, however, argues that its use in relation to blockchain is often ambiguous, misleading or even incorrect, and can lead to problematic consequences where authorities rely on an unsubstantiated conclusion that a given blockchain or blockchains generally are 'decentralised'.[44]

Most carbon markets are essentially 'regulatory creations' for market-based emissions reductions, with highly centralised governance architectures. It is therefore unlikely that such systems will demonstrate (or strive to achieve) 'decentralisation' as such term is commonly used in relation to permissionless blockchains. Instead, use of DLT for carbon markets will still involve centralised authorities and regulators, except that their involvement in certain aspects of the system will reduce as certain functions shift to the DLT platform

43 Sebastien Meunier, 'Blockchain 101: What Is Blockchain and How Does This Revolutionary Technology Work?' in Alastair Marke (ed), *Transforming Climate Finance and Green Investment with Blockchains* (Academic Press 2018).

44 Angela Walch, 'Deconstructing Decentralization: Exploring the Core Claim of Crypto Systems' in Chris Brummer (ed), *Crypto-assets, Legal, Regulatory and Monetary Perspectives* (OUP 2019).

(see further Section 5.4). As discussed previously, a permissioned (rather than permissionless) DLT system is therefore more likely for a DLT-supported carbon market, in order to enable a degree of centralised governance and regulatory safeguards.

By contrast, purely voluntary emissions trading systems (for example, for individuals or emitting firms not covered by a mandatory system) may be one use case where a permissionless DLT system might be feasible. However, even then, to build trust in the units sufficient for participants to attribute real value to them, a degree of centralised oversight may still be necessary.

Given these challenges and the specific challenges associated with crypto-assets and cryptocurrencies, in particular, Arner and colleagues argue that, from a policy perspective, the most appropriate regulatory approach to DLT is one based upon function, where different instruments and systems are regulated as appropriate given their function. For example, financial regulation would only focus on applications with a currency/payment or investment function, and not on other functions such as donation or reward.[45] According to Arner and colleagues, the rapid development and the wide application of different blockchain technologies make regulation of blockchain technology itself (rather than its applications) 'arduous … and rarely necessary'.[46]

Some commentators therefore suggest that regulators, for the time being at least, should prioritise regulating the principal applications of DLT, focussing first on crypto-assets such as initial coin offerings (ICOs) and cryptocurrencies, rather than devoting substantial resources to regulating the technology itself. Many aspects of the legal, policy and strategic implications of DLT will only crystallise as the technology and its use cases continue to unfold.[47] This is likely to be true for DLT in carbon markets, which have unique regulatory and compliance needs, and the role of carbon units as both a tradable instrument and part of the compliance cycle. However, a number of general principles can be identified as necessary for the development of a 'crypto-legal' structure to deploy DLT for carbon markets.

5.3 GENERAL LEGAL PRINCIPLES FOR A 'CRYPTO-LEGAL' STRUCTURE IN CARBON MARKETS

To leverage the full potential of DLT to address current risks or inefficiencies in carbon trading while balancing against potential new risks, appropriate legal and

45 Douglas Arner and others, 'Policy and Regulatory Challenges of Distributed Ledger Technology and Digital Assets in Asia' in Chris Brummer (ed), *Crypto-assets, Legal, Regulatory and Monetary Perspectives* (OUP 2019).

46 Walch (n 44).

47 Michèle Finck, 'Blockchains: Regulating the Unknown' (2017) 19(4) *German LJ* 689.

governance frameworks are essential. Given the variety of existing carbon markets, there is no one-size-fits-all solution for appropriate governance arrangements or how this transition should take place.[48] However, a number of general principles can be identified for governing DLT in carbon markets:

(1) **Overseeing the providers of the relevant services**: As discussed in Section 5.2.1, the material scope of regulation should be extended to cover the new actors for DLT-supported transactions[49] since certain aspects can be overseen only at the level of the platform provider (such as continuity of service and, in the case of permissioned networks, admission to the network). In a DLT-supported carbon market, in addition to accommodating existing actors in carbon markets (see Chapter 2) and specifying their role and functions in a DLT-supported architecture, the material scope of regulatory oversight should be extended to cover new legal actors such as platform providers and validators of nodes.

To build trust in the DLT-supported carbon market, the relevant DLT platform provider should therefore be a legal person who is subject to at least some degree of certification or oversight. This oversight could be carried out by the entity already administering and overseeing the carbon market (such as the EU Commission in the EU ETS), or alternatively it might take the form of certification under an international certification body or authorisation under laws applicable to DLT and crypto-assets.[50] The roles of these new actors are explored further in Sections 5.4.5–5.4.6.

(2) **Governing the use of DLT within each system**: The rules and regulations of existing carbon markets are geared towards a non-DLT architecture. A number of revisions would therefore be necessary to the rules governing the system in order to enable the relevant carbon units to be 'tokenised' (i.e. transformed into crypto-assets to enable them to be issued, stored and transferred on a distributed ledger). For example, this might include guidelines or regulatory frameworks relating to:

- *Admission to the network*: In permissioned networks, it is possible to select the participants and award them with different licences. Such a DLT-supported network could be suitable for being adapted to the current legal framework for carbon markets. (On the contrary and as discussed earlier, in a permissionless network it is impossible to select the participants but only to fix some requirements that need to be fulfilled,

48 Not least, the necessary governance framework will depend upon whether a system is national, regional or international in scope.

49 Paech (n 17).

50 For example, in the EU, the MiCA proposal would require certain crypto-asset service providers (including those operating a trading platform for crypto-assets) to be authorised in an EU member state.

and therefore the governance mechanism of a permissionless network is ill-suited to existing regulations for carbon trading).

- *Dispute resolution mechanism and choice of law*: New patterns of enforcement and regulation as a result of self-executing smart contracts would require additional rules or frameworks to govern the relevant parameters, as well as what happens when things go wrong. The mechanism for dispute resolution would need to be specified, for example, to process claims for unjust enrichment if carbon units are unlawfully transferred. Similarly, the governing law should be specified centrally.
- *Applicable KYC requirements*: As discussed in Chapters 1 and 4, DLT could enable the automatic verification of applicable KYC requirements for carbon trading, for example, through a permissioned distributed ledger storing identity data of verified companies and traders (with identification documents potentially stored off-chain). However, for this to operate effectively and in a way that reduces the risk of illicit activity, the parameters and rules for KYC applications would need to be established at the level of the system.
- *Rules for interaction with the compliance cycle*: For DLT to streamline and automatise elements of the compliance cycle (such as initial allocation/ issuance of units, measuring and reporting of emissions by entities, verifying of those emissions reports, surrendering units, overseeing and enforcing these steps), guidelines for how it would take place on DLT would need to be specified.

(3) **Establishing ownership of carbon units**: Depending on the definition and scope of the term in specific jurisdictions, carbon units may represent an 'administrative' or 'regulatory' right (as they are issued by public authorities), 'private intangible property' (for being identifiable and tradable) or yet another *sui generis* classification.[51] While different jurisdictions may not share a uniform view on the legal nature of carbon units, they have adopted a similar way to reflect the ownership of units, by way of an electronic registry.

The electronic nature of carbon units identified by a central registry makes them particularly susceptible to technology crimes such as theft through

[51] For example, the EU ETS Directive does not attempt to specify the legal nature of the allowances; it merely imperceptibly states that the allowances are 'transferable'. Article 3(a) EU ETS Directive: '"allowance" means an allowance to emit one tonne of carbon dioxide equivalent during a specified period, which shall be valid only for the purposes of meeting the requirements of this Directive and shall be transferable in accordance with the provisions of this Directive'. It may be that the EU ETS Directive is silent on this point, as Article 345 Treaty of the Functioning of the European Union precludes the EU adopting legislation to clarify the legal nature of the allowances, providing that the Treaties shall in no way prejudice member states' rules governing the system of property ownership.

hacking.[52] As a unit is traded between market participants, the trading history might comprise a mix of validly acquired transfers and those obtained following a defective transfer (in instances such as theft and double counting), making it difficult to differentiate between the two. This raises difficult questions, including as to the legal owner of the 'defective' units and what claims (if any) a victim of carbon unit theft can bring. For example, under the Union Registry for the EU ETS, there is a statutory presumption that the holder of an allowance is the rightful owner, regardless of any prior theft of that allowance.[53] Such a presumption helps protect the legitimate expectations of a bona fide third party purchasing an allowance, at the expense of the original (rightful) owner of that stolen allowance. No simple resolution has been found to this issue in the EU ETS.

DLT cannot resolve legal difficulties such as balancing the interests of the original owner of a stolen allowance with that of a subsequent purchaser. However, use of DLT can enable greater protection against the theft and duplication of carbon units in the first place,[54] thereby reducing the chances of these legal conundrums arising. In particular, DLT can provide mechanisms whereby the relevant digital records cannot be duplicated in such a way as to permit them to be reused more than once or by more than one party. Validity can be ensured through validation of each carbon unit transfer on the blockchain, the cryptographic hash function and the use of AI-based transaction monitoring. For further discussion on how DLT could help reduce the theft of carbon units, see Chapters 4 and 6.

Similarly, the ability to include additional information in the DLT ledger may help address other legal challenges faced when dealing with carbon units, such as identifying units that have been given as collateral for debt or that are held by an entity in the process of bankruptcy.

Governance frameworks for DLT in carbon markets should therefore focus on how DLT can help to resolve some of the existing legal difficulties owing to the specific nature of carbon units. This will need to be carefully implemented to ensure alignment with the legal treatment of carbon units in the relevant jurisdiction(s).

52 Ewa Krukowska and Mathew Carr, 'Carbon-Allowance Thieves Force EU to Boost Security' *Bloomberg* (London, 21 January 2011) www.bloomberg.com/news/articles/2011-01-21/carbon-thieves-force-eu-to-improve-security-close-spot-markets accessed 24 December 2020.

53 A purchaser and holder of an allowance acting in good faith shall acquire title to an allowance regardless of any defects in the title of the transferor (Regulation 389/2013 establishing a Union Registry pursuant to Directive 2003/87/EC of the European Parliament and of the Council, Decisions No 280/2004/EC and No 406/2009/EC of the European Parliament and of the Council and repealing Commission Regulations (EU) No 920/2010 and No 1193/2011, Article 40(4)).

54 UK Jurisdiction Taskforce of the LawTech Delivery Panel, 'The Status of Crypto Assets, Distributed Ledger Technology and Smart Contracts under English Private Law' (Public Consultation, May 2019) www.enyolaw.com/downloads/ukjt-consultation-crypto-assets-smart-contracts-may-2019%20(1).pdf accessed 24 December 2020.

(4) **Using standards**: As discussed above, application of legal principles to DLT systems varies across different jurisdictions and use cases, adding barriers to their global adoption. To address these issues, standards bodies (such as the International Organization for Standardization (ISO)[55]) and private consortiums (such as Hyperledger[56]) have launched industry initiatives with a view to building industry standards. The use of standards can also help reduce compliance burdens for smaller actors, thereby improving competition and market access. Standardisation can also improve interoperability between different applications and technologies that run on different underlying platforms.

In the carbon markets context, standards could play an important role in creating trust in the technology and helping to address concerns relating to security, resiliency and the privacy and data governance aspects of DLT.[57] The use of common standards across different DLT-supported carbon markets could also help support the complex process of linking or networking different national or regional markets, the complexity of which is demonstrated by the time it took to agree to link the Swiss and EU ETSs.

(5) **Managing information communication technology (ICT) and cyber risks**: Given previous instances of security vulnerabilities and cybercrime in relation to carbon markets,[58] building trust that ICT and cyber risks can be managed effectively when using DLT is essential. Although DLT offers a number of potential benefits when it comes to security and cyber risk, these can be realised only if the technology in question is deployed effectively and participants trust it.

In addition to the use of standards, further regulatory requirements for the management of ICT risk may be appropriate. For example, as part of its Digital Finance Package, the European Commission has issued a proposal for the regulation of 'digital operational resilience' in financial services,[59] which would impose additional requirements on (inter alia) in-scope crypto-asset service providers to manage ICT risk. This includes requirements to implement internal governance and control frameworks for effective and prudent management of ICT risks, systems testing requirements, systems monitoring and systems for the identification, management and reporting of

55 For example, ISO/AWI TS 23259 'Blockchain and distributed ledger technologies – Legally binding smart contracts' and ISO/TC 307 'Blockchain and distributed ledger technologies'.

56 www.hyperledger.org/.

57 Advait Deshpande, Katherine Stewart, Louise Lepetit and Salil Gunashekar, 'Understanding the Landscape of Distributed Ledger Technologies/Blockchain: Challenges, Opportunities, and the Prospects for Standards' (2017) https://doi.org/10.7249/RR2223 accessed 24 December 2020.

58 For example, a phishing attack on the German central registry in 2010 saw an estimated 250,000 permits worth more than EUR 3 million stolen.

59 Proposal for a Regulation of the European Parliament and of the Council on digital operational resilience for the financial sector and amending Regulations (EC) No 1060/2009, (EU) No 648/2012, (EU) No 600/2014 and (EU) No 909/2014.

ICT-related incidents such as cyber-attacks. Any DLT-supported carbon market should consider imposing similar digital resiliency requirements to provide further mitigation of ICT and cyber risks.

5.4 INSTITUTIONAL OPTIONS TO OPERATIONALISE THE TRANSITION: EVOLVING ROLES OF STAKEHOLDERS IN CARBON MARKETS

A DLT-supported carbon market would involve changes in the roles of various carbon market stakeholders. In particular, use of DLT represents a degree of the shift away from trading based on a centralised register administered by a centralised administrative body towards a more decentralised system where participants trade their 'tokens' on the DLT network. However, it is important not to overemphasise the shift of power from centralised authorities towards 'decentralised' and 'distributed' DLT networks. Centralised authorities would remain important for administering various aspects of the carbon market, including allocation and verification. The purpose of using DLT within a carbon market is not to exclude public bodies but, rather, to create a more efficient system that enables the effective participation of private stakeholders.

This section provides an overview of how the roles of key actors in the existing carbon markets framework would change under a DLT-supported carbon market. The specifics of a particular stakeholder's role would, of course, depend upon the particular system and the type of DLT; however, certain common themes can be identified.

5.4.1 *Centralised Authorities, Oversight Organisations and Single Centralised Registers*

The inventors of blockchain aimed at creating self-governing and state-remote networks, as epitomised by Bitcoin, where states should not be able to interfere with governance or regulate the network.[60] This would not be the case in a DLT-supported carbon market. For mandatory carbon markets at least, centralised authorities would continue to play a role in overseeing carbon markets, including overseeing the allocation of carbon units, the opening and closing of accounts, the recognition of offset credits and certain operational procedures.[61]

Regulators also have a crucial role to play in adopting the necessary revisions to the existing legislative and regulatory framework governing carbon markets, in order to enable the robust adoption of DLT-supported carbon markets or a pilot. The role

60 Paech (n 17).

61 For example, in the case of emission reporting for the EU ETS, ensuring compliance of annual emissions reports (AERs) with the Monitoring and Reporting Regulation (MRR) (Commission Regulation (EU) 601/2012 on the monitoring and reporting of greenhouse gas emissions pursuant to Directive 2003/87/EC of the European Parliament and of the Council).

of centralised authorities would not dissipate but *change*; their role in certain specific functions would diminish, yet centralised authorities would continue to play an important role overall in the establishment, operation and oversight of carbon units and credit markets.

In a DLT-supported carbon market, DLT could, however, replace many functions currently performed by regulators or implementing authorities, and the role of regulators would need to adapt accordingly. For example:

- *Centralised registry*: Currently, centralised registers of carbon units tend to be controlled and operated by a central body (e.g. the Union Registry in the EU ETS run by the European Commission). In a DLT-supported trading system, the centralised registry could be replaced by a distributed ledger, held across the DLT nodes; data currently inserted in the centralised registry would be shared across the set of DLT, making the administrative functions of the central registry operator somewhat obsolete.
- *Transaction checking and recording*: Secondly, transaction checking and recording, rather than being executed through the system administrator,[62] could instead be executed by the blockchain itself along with cryptographic systems and a web of programmable smart contracts. The blockchain can independently verify transactions, enabling faster and more secure transaction checking and recording, with records held across all nodes, meaning that they cannot be tampered with by hackers in the same way as on unconnected existing centralised registries (see further discussion in Chapters 6 and 7).

5.4.2 *Covered Entities/Emitting Firms*

Firms that emit GHGs and participate in carbon markets rely on the fact that each carbon unit – for example, European Union Allowances in the case of the EU ETS, or New Zealand Units in the case of the New Zealand ETS – represents or allows the discharge of a specific quantity of a specific pollutant over a set period of time. With the exception of voluntary offsetting systems, covered entities are required to hold units equivalent to their emissions, including by buying additional units where required.

At present, these units are represented by entries in the centralised registry. However, in a DLT-supported trading system, each firm would have its own digital 'wallet' in which it would hold 'tokens' representing these units. The holding of emissions units as 'tokens' in a digital wallet, along with the use of AI and self-executing smart contracts, could have a number of benefits for covered entities:

1) Validation of every transaction could reduce fraudulent transactions and the threat of units being 'stolen'. The use of DLT could enable each carbon unit to have its own unique identifier. All the key information relating to that unit (e.g.

62 For example, through the European Union Transaction Log (EUTL) in the case of the EU ETS.

origin, buyer and seller) would be trackable through its cryptographic hash function, with new 'blocks' added to the chain as the unit is traded between covered entities. By creating a consensus network, the traceability of information can be ensured in order to avoid issues such as lost units and repeated transactions.[63] Even where fraud does occur, the information recorded on the blockchain could enable this to be identified and prevent the fraudulent surrender or resale of the units. This would reduce the fraud risk to individual participants.

2) KYC protocols executed using smart contracts could eliminate artificial shell companies from trading. In ETSs such as the EU ETS, many emissions trading accounts have been registered by companies that no longer exist in official records at the time of transactions, or that are using contact details that render them uncontactable.[64] A DLT system could be combined with an extended self-executing KYC protocol to efficiently validate KYC information before approving *every* transaction. This could virtually disqualify illegitimate shell companies from trading, increasing trust in the system by genuine participating firms.
3) The confidentiality of participants' data could be protected using encryption systems. By replacing accounts with a centralised registry with digital 'wallets', each participant would be provided with a digital wallet address and private key to enable secure access. Without this private key, illicit actors would be unable to access the wallet or the encrypted data.

The same advantages would apply if DLT were to be applied to carbon markets between individuals (in which case, the need to protect and authenticate the identity and personal information of the individual would be more acute). For example, Universal Carbon (UPCO_2) is a tradable carbon token on a public blockchain that allows individuals to buy, hold and sell tokenised carbon credits, enabling individuals to offset their carbon footprints where each token is backed by a credit representing one year-tonne of CO_2 averted by a certified REDD+[65] rainforest project.[66]

5.4.3 *Intermediaries (Including Exchanges)*

Much has been written about the potential for DLT to eliminate the need for intermediaries, in particular in financial services.[67] In the context of carbon markets,

[63] Yuting Pana and others, 'Application of Blockchain Carbon Trading' (10th International Conference on Applied Energy, Hong Kong, 22–25 August 2018) https://doi.org/10.1016/j.egypro.2019.01.509 accessed 24 December 2020.

[64] Paech (n 17).

[65] Reducing Emissions from Deforestation and forest Degradation in developing countries.

[66] http://uphold.com.

[67] Benjamin Geva 'Disintermediating Electronic Payments: Digital Cash and Virtual Currencies' (2016) 32(12) *J Intl Bank L Reg* 661–74.

DLT could enable participants to trade units directly, rather than through the current channel based upon a triangular relationship between the transacting market participants and the central registry. However, this would mean that the current role of the central registry and intermediaries of enforcing relevant requirements (such as carrying out KYC requirements) might be diminished. Rather than financial institutions being responsible for verification of the identity of participants, a DLT-supported carbon market would open up other approaches to KYC that would need to be appropriately overseen or subject to appropriate standards.

These changes could also help address current inefficiencies and structural issues in carbon trading exchanges. Transaction fees for carbon emissions trading often generate only a small income for the exchange. For example, in China's regional ETSs, transaction fees generally cover operating costs only.[68] Many exchanges therefore rely on reporting carbon market–related research and consultancy to generate revenue, and the business of carbon trading can fall behind.

Subject to compliance with applicable regulatory requirements, it might also be feasible for carbon units held as digital assets to be traded on existing crypto-asset exchange platforms. The vast majority of them are subject only to AML/KYC obligations.[69] In jurisdictions where carbon units (and likewise the 'tokens' representing carbon units) are deemed to be financial instruments, this may exclude the majority of crypto-asset exchange platforms from offering trading services for tokenised carbon units. Still, as the evolution of DLT-supported digital assets moves towards compliance with financial markets regulation,[70] this limitation may reduce over time to enable wider trading of carbon unit 'tokens' on crypto-asset exchanges.

5.4.4 *Assessors and Compliance Officers*

In a DLT-supported carbon market, officials from public authorities or accredited entities would continue to perform the verification process. This is one example of a process that would continue to be performed 'off-chain'; the verification process would continue in a similar manner to non-DLT carbon markets, except that the relevant information (i.e. verification of a covered entity's GHG emissions against number of allocated or purchased units) would then be inputted into the DLT ledger in accordance with the rules of the DLT network.

In general, the roles of such verifiers and compliance officers would continue in a similar manner under a DLT-supported trading system, except that they would interface with the DLT network, rather than the centralised authority. The current

68 Pana and others (n 64).

69 M Todd Henderson and Max Raskin, 'A Regulatory Classification of Digital Assets: Toward an Operational Howey Test for Cryptocurrencies, ICOs, and Other Digital Assets' (2019) 2019(2) *Columbia Bus L Rev* 443–93. *See also* Hacker and Thomale (n 29).

70 OECD (2020), The Tokenisation of Assets and Potential Implications for Financial Markets, OECD Blockchain Policy Series www.oecd.org/finance/The-Tokenisation-of-Assets-and-Potential-Implications-for-Financial-Markets.htm.

structures, regulations and operational procedures[71] for these roles would continue to apply, but the integration of this verification with the DLT network is where efficiency benefits could be realised.

5.4.5 *New Actors in DLT-Supported Carbon Markets: DLT Platform Providers*

As discussed throughout this chapter, oversight of the relevant DLT platform provider would be crucial for a DLT-supported carbon market to be trusted and successful. As DLT-supported carbon market platforms are yet to be established, we can only hypothesise what such DLT platforms and their oversight might look like. However, based on the experience of currently active decentralised finance (DeFi) platforms and crypto-assets market in general, we can try to imagine possible scenarios.

In the unlikely scenario of a permissionless carbon market platform, Ethereum, Cardano or Polkadot might host such a platform. These DLT networks do not have a business entity behind them; communities of developers or a private entity can propose projects based on these networks, but the major downside is the inability to identify a subject liable for the underlying network's malfunctioning (as the community behind the blockchain network has no legal obligation for its maintenance and correct operation). Permissionless DLT systems are therefore unlikely to enable the level of oversight of the DLT platform provider necessary for a DLT-supported carbon market.

By contrast, in a permissioned DLT system, the relevant regulator could outsource the realisation and maintenance of the system to a suitably skilled and qualified DLT platform provider, while maintaining appropriate oversight of that third party. Oversight might take the form of a licence along with the necessary conditions; and might require the DLT platform provider to be certified under appropriate standards. The DLT provider would then be responsible for the system's correct operation and be liable accordingly. The involvement of private third parties in carbon trading infrastructure is similar to existing practices; for example, in the EU ETS, emission trading services such as auctioning of allowances are provided by, inter alia, the European Energy Exchange AG (EEX), a part of the German stock exchange group, subject to appropriate oversight and conditions.

5.4.6 *New Actors in DLT-Supported Carbon Markets: The Nodes*

As explained in Chapter 1, nodes are vital actors in every DLT network. Although their role is less important in a permissioned DLT system than in a permissionless

[71] For example, in the case of emission reporting for the EU ETS, ensuring compliance of annual emissions reports (AERs) with the Monitoring and Reporting Regulation (MRR) (Commission Regulation (EU) 601/2012 on the monitoring and reporting of greenhouse gas emissions pursuant to Directive 2003/87/EC of the European Parliament and of the Council).

one, their existence is essential to achieving a necessary degree of validation. Nodes need to be encouraged by economic incentives to engage 'non-strategically' to maintain and secure the system so that the data are robust enough to withstand adversarial interference, double spend, censure, counterfeit, collusion, tampering or other types of malicious action.[72]

In a permissioned DLT-supported carbon market, the nodes might be made up either of parties that are already part of the carbon market infrastructure (such as carbon market trading venues) or of other parties that are licensed and overseen by a public authority or international body. In either case, the relevant regulator or system administrator would need to reward nodes for their fundamental role, for example, through remuneration for the transactions the nodes help to process. Carbon market trading venues may be the best-positioned players to participate as nodes of the network because they would be entitled to process transactions directly.

5.4.7 *New Actors in DLT-Supported Carbon Markets: New Opportunities*

A DLT-supported carbon market could open various new opportunities for businesses, for example, provision of custody of private keys for covered entities. The possibilities to participate are difficult to predict and will depend upon the aforementioned 'crypto-legal' structure put in place by regulators. The use of DLT can enable broad participation in carbon markets and offsetting schemes, so long as the technology is implemented in a way that carefully mitigates against the risks. Tokenisation of carbon units and offset units might, in turn, contribute to what has been described as the 'democratization of markets'.[73]

5.5 TRANSITION ROADMAP AND PROCESS

Policymakers and regulators looking to explore the deployment of DLT in climate policy should treat DLT as a platform technology that can be used across a variety of functional areas, including carbon markets. The appropriate regulation and governance of DLT for use in carbon markets will differ compared to other applications of DLT. To this end, policymakers and regulators should seek to better understand individual use cases for DLT; Chapters 6 to 9 provide more detailed case studies in relation to the domestic carbon market, voluntary offset crediting systems, international carbon markets and networked carbon markets for this purpose.

[72] Michel Rauchs and others, 'Distributed Ledger Technology Systems: A Conceptual Framework' (13 August 2018) https://ssrn.com/abstract=3230013.

[73] Jonathan Rohr and Aaron Wright, 'Blockchain-Based Token Sales, Initial Coin Offerings, and the Democratization of Public Capital Markets' (2019) 70(2) *Hastings LJ* 463–524.

5.5.1 *The Importance of Enabling Environments or Regulatory Sandboxes*

Given the legal uncertainty associated with the adoption of DLT, governance frameworks that specifically *permit* or *enable* the application of DLT for specific use cases[74] and subject to certain criteria and safeguards can play a vital role.

For example, in the EU, legislators recognised industry sentiment about the existing EU financial services regulatory framework posing a number of obstacles to the full use of DLT in market infrastructure but also that it was not necessarily easy to pinpoint or address. Unsurprisingly, EU financial services legislation was not designed with DLT in mind and this uncertainty presents a further obstacle to realising the efficiency improvements that DLT could bring to the trading and post-trading environment. As a result, the European Commission's proposal for a pilot regime on market infrastructure based on DLT aims to allow certain market participants to operate DLT multilateral trading facilities and DLT securities settlement systems, provided certain conditions and eligibility criteria are met to ensure that the pilot regime will be operated at a small scale only.[75]

This type of 'regulatory sandbox' approach allows innovators to test their product in an environment that temporarily exempts them from some or all legal requirements, in exchange for operating in a restricted or controlled manner. It is designed to be mutually beneficial for both regulators and the regulated industry, by reducing legal uncertainty while enabling innovation and dialogue with regulators.[76]

Similarly, existing regulatory frameworks for carbon markets were not designed with DLT in mind and there may be provisions in existing legislation or regulation limiting its adoption in carbon markets. Adopting regulatory sandbox approaches could help reduce these barriers and provide a safe space for the development of proposals for DLT-supported carbon markets with oversight from regulators and while mitigating the potential risks.

5.5.2 *The Role of a Pilot Application of DLT in Emissions Trading*

To realise the full benefits of DLT for carbon markets, it is imperative that the transition takes place in a way that is thoroughly tested, involves input from stakeholders and ensures that any risks can be avoided or mitigated. The first step to doing this would be an initial pilot for DLT use in carbon markets, on a small scale and (depending upon the relevant system) with oversight and support from the relevant administrative or regulatory body. Such a pilot is necessary in order to demonstrate

74 By contrast, there have also been examples of legislation that specifically prevents the use of DLT in certain use cases. For example, legislation in Arizona restricts the use of blockchain as a tool for electronic firearm tracking technology.

75 Proposal for a Regulation of the European Parliament and of the Council on a pilot regime for market infrastructures based on distributed ledger technology.

76 Finck (n 47).

feasibility, build trust and address any potential risks. If these pilots are successful, they can then be scaled more widely.

Such a pilot might take a phased approach. For example, the initial stage could begin with establishing a pilot network for the tokenisation of carbon units. Then, to allow the characteristics of that information to execute simple transactions between participants, further layers of complexity and data manipulation may be added at a higher technology stack level, such as to integrate with KYC and identity verification systems.

5.5.3 *Pilot Development and Technology Transfer*

To understand how such a pilot might be developed, the 'technology transfer model' (unpublished) advocated by our colleagues at BCI provides a helpful framework. Adapting this model to a pilot for DLT in carbon markets, the roadmap to develop a pilot DLT-supported carbon market might include:

1. **Idea**: This would involve identifying the key objectives to be achieved by the pilot, in particular to address the current challenges in the carbon markets described in Chapters 2 and 4.
2. **Desk-based assessment**: DLT systems can differ substantially from one to another. A deep understanding and evaluation of the underlying technology is therefore important to ensure that the DLT network selected is appropriate. A critical evaluation of the different options of DLT infrastructure to be used would be required, first as a desk-based assessment and followed by applied assessment. The former would include a comparison matrix of the stated aims of the system, considered against the various DLT profiles and configuration options. This process should involve technical experts within the crypto and blockchain space, for example, through an open call for ideas.
3. **Applied assessment**: To assess the functioning in practice of different DLT infrastructure options, demo systems should be tested. The testing phase should be as open as possible, involving all relevant stakeholders and academic institutions.
4. **Development**: The development of the DLT infrastructure should follow the standard software release life cycle, with particular attention dedicated to beta testing. Participation of relevant stakeholders would be key; for example, rules for the operation of smart contracts should be developed in collaboration with and following consultation with relevant stakeholders and participants.
5. **Product**: As part of the final product launch, the following plans and procedures could help ensure smooth and sound operations and enhance usability:
   - *Operational guide*: A best practice guide could explain how covered entities and other participants practically operate within the DLT infrastructure.

The guide should address security parameters, administrative procedures, requirements for admission to the network, etc. (see further Section 5.3).

- *Regulator guidance*: To help resolve regulatory uncertainty, guidance from the relevant regulator or administrator on how the pilot interacts with the various regulatory requirements (such as applicable financial services, carbon market and technology regulation) might prove helpful.
- *Proof of proper operations*: This would establish the process for checking that the codified rules of the DLT network are geared towards incentivising players to act honestly, limiting the impact of bad actors and disseminating reports in real-time to demonstrate that the system is operating as intended.
- *Technologists team management and succession plan*: Ensuring that the technology is administered and evolves in a way that meets industry-wide standards and mitigates risks will be critical to establishing and maintaining trust in the system. Core to this is a plan for the ongoing management of the technology by appropriately qualified personnel and, where necessary, appropriate succession plans.
- *Compliance monitoring*: Procedures for technology-centric and participant-based reporting should also be established to enable regulators and administrators to monitor and address any issues, incidents and ongoing updates as required.

The thorough development and assessment of a pilot phase would help to ensure that any concerns and risks could be addressed at the pilot stage, before adopting the DLT network for a DLT-supported carbon market on a wider scale.

5.6 CONCLUSION

There are various legal and governance questions associated with DLT, blockchain and crypto-assets. However, when it comes to the use of DLT for carbon markets specifically, some of these hurdles might not prove as challenging as the 'hype' around blockchain and Bitcoin might suggest. Many of the governance challenges of DLT relate specifically to permissionless blockchains; by contrast, the prudent adoption of a permissioned DLT system for carbon markets could still enable the relevant regulator or administrator to implement the necessary controls and safeguards in order to ensure a secure, reliable and efficient carbon market.

Regulators and policymakers in carbon markets should therefore consider DLT as a platform technology that can be used across a variety of functional areas. Its successful adoption for carbon markets will depend upon regulators partnering with technologists to ensure that the technology adopted (most likely a form of permissioned DLT system) is implemented in a way that adequately addresses the unique governance challenges of carbon markets.

6

DLT and the European Union Emissions Trading System

Marco Zolla, Alastair Marke and Michael A. Mehling

6.1 INTRODUCTION: CURRENT GOVERNANCE FRAMEWORK

Launched in 2005, the European Union Emissions Trading System (EU ETS) remains the largest carbon market in the world. It presently operates in 30 countries – all 27 EU member states as well as Iceland, Liechtenstein and Norway – and covers more than 10,000 emitters and around 2 billion metric tonnes of greenhouse gas (GHG), or 45 per cent of EU emissions. This makes the EU ETS a central pillar of European climate policy.[1] Over a dozen directives, regulations and decisions set out the legal framework of the EU ETS, linking it to international offsets, extending the market to new sectors and gases, establishing a common registry, and providing technical guidance and procedural details on design features such as auctioning, and monitoring, reporting and verification (MRV).[2] The governance of the EU ETS has evolved significantly since its inception, with competences in a number of areas – such as allocation of units and registry operation – becoming successively more centralised. Features not yet envisioned in the original directive were added over time in response to observed regulatory gaps and design shortcomings.

During its first trading period from 2005 to 2007, the EU ETS was overshadowed by a widely publicised collapse of carbon prices owing in large part to insufficient or inaccurate data.[3] European Union Allowances (EUAs) witnessed a price drop from originally more than EUR 32 in the spot market in early April 2006 to a figure in the single digits only weeks later. The first set of independently verified emissions reports for the year 2005 had been released earlier that month by the member states,[4] revealing that aggregate emissions were significantly below the annual average

1 Jos Delbeke, 'The Emissions Trading Scheme (ETS): The Cornerstone of the EU's Implementation of the Kyoto Protocol' in Jos Delbeke (ed), *EU Energy Law, Vol. IV: The EU Greenhouse Gas Emissions Trading Scheme* (Claeys & Casteels 2006).

2 Damien Meadows and others, 'EU ETS: Pricing Carbon to Drive Cost-Effective Reductions across Europe', *EU Climate Policy Explained* (Routledge 2015).

3 Regina Betz and Misato Sato, 'Emissions Trading: Lessons Learnt from the 1st Phase of the EU ETS and Prospects for the 2nd Phase' (2006) 6 *Clim Policy* 351, 352–54.

4 European Commission Press Release IP/06/612, EU Emissions Trading Scheme Delivers First Verified Emissions Data for Installations (15 May 2006).

allocation of allowances for the first period.[5] Capacity constraints and an ambitious timeline contributed to this information shortfall, although political incentives for the member states to favour their domestic industries in the allocation process also influenced national allocation decisions.[6] Reports of substantial windfall profits for sectors able to pass through the cost of freely allocated EUAs added to the reputational damage for the EU ETS.[7]

Carbon prices experienced continued weakness over the following two trading periods owing to an economic slowdown across Europe, greater than expected abatement under complementary policies, and extensive use of offset credits from Clean Development Mechanism (CDM) and Joint Implementation (JI) projects.[8] When the value of EUAs fell to new lows early in the third trading period (2013 to 2020), what had been a simmering crisis of confidence erupted in calls for fundamental changes to the European carbon market. After years of resisting such calls for intervention in the carbon market, the European Commission responded by initiating a discussion about structural reform options.[9] Eventually, the European Council and Parliament approved a delay in the scheduled auction of allowances ('backloading')[10] as well as a dynamic supply adjustment mechanism, the Market Stability Reserve (MSR).[11] Carbon prices have since experienced a sustained recovery, strengthened by recent legislative changes for the fourth trading period (2021 to 2030) that introduced a steeper emission reduction pathway and accelerated the withdrawal of surplus allowances into the MSR. Importantly, however, experience under the EU ETS has shown the importance of timely and accurate emissions data, suggesting opportunities for expanded use of innovative technologies to improve the speed and reliability of data flows.

Recent years have also seen a number of criminal activities and efforts to exploit regulatory loopholes in the EU ETS, highlighting a need for stronger market

[5] A Denny Ellerman and Barbara K Buchner, 'Over-Allocation or Abatement? A Preliminary Analysis of the EU ETS Based on the 2005–06 Emissions Data' (2008) 41 *Env and Resource Econ* 267, 286.

[6] Michael A Mehling, 'Emissions Trading and National Allocation in the Member States: An Achilles Heel of European Climate Policy' (2003) 5 *Yearbook of Eur Env L* 113, 156.

[7] A Denny Ellerman, Frank J Convery and Christian de Perthuis, *Pricing Carbon: The European Union Emissions Trading Scheme* (Cambridge University Press 2010) 326; Jos Sijm, Karsten Neuhoff and Yihsu Chen, 'CO2 Cost Pass-Through and Windfall Profits in the Power Sector' (2006) 6 *Clim Policy* 49, 49.

[8] Nicolas Koch and others, 'Causes of the EU ETS Price Drop: Recession, CDM, Renewable Policies or a Bit of Everything? New Evidence' (2014) 73 *Energy Policy* 676.

[9] *Commission Report to the European Parliament and the Council: The State of the European Carbon Market in 2012*, COM(2012) 652 (14 November 2012), https://eur-lex.europa.eu/legal-content/EN/TXT/PDF/?uri=CELEX:52012DC0652&from=EN accessed 11 April 2022.

[10] Decision 1359/2013/EU of the European Parliament and of the Council of 17 December 2013 amending Directive 2003/87/EC Clarifying Provisions on the Timing of Auctions of Greenhouse Gas Allowances, 2013 O.J. (L 343) 1.

[11] Decision 2015/1814 of the European Parliament and of the Council of 6 October 2015 Concerning the Establishment and Operation of a Market Stability Reserve for the Union Greenhouse Gas Emission Trading Scheme and amending Directive 2003/87/EC, 2015 O.J. (L 264) 1.

oversight. Individual market participants and speculators have been periodically reported to influence the price of EUAs and exaggerate price moves, with evidence that individual traders are seeking to move prices. Between 2009 and 2010, value-added tax (VAT) fraud – also known as carousel fraud – in the course of EUA transactions deprived the member states of more than EUR 5 billion in tax revenue.[12] Then, 2010 and 2011 saw scandals involving the sale of recycled certified emission reductions (CERs), phishing attempts on the German national registry, and a series of subsequent cyber-thefts affecting several million EUAs.[13] Such events eroded confidence in the functioning of the market and prompted the European Commission to propose further regulatory reforms.

Aside from a directive extending application of the VAT reverse charge mechanism to emissions trading, the EU also strengthened oversight of carbon market transactions by closing a substantial gap in the existing regulatory framework. Both primary and a majority of secondary market transactions had already been subject to regulatory oversight, but spot market transactions were still largely exempted. Since 2018, a change to the Markets in Financial Instruments Directive (MiFID) mandates trading of derivatives on regulated venues, introduces position limits and reporting requirements for derivatives, and classifies allowances as financial instruments under MiFID, triggering registration and licensing duties, disclosure and reporting requirements, and additional disciplines for the previously unregulated spot market.[14] Additionally, from 2012 onwards, the EU has operated a single European registry for EUAs and other units, the European Union Transaction Log (EUTL), enabling centralised oversight of all transactions.

What all these challenges highlight is the critical role of information. Regulatory decisions on the overall amount of allowances and their allocation have suffered from information asymmetries, a lack of accurate data and uncertainty about fundamental trends, severely undermining the functioning of the European carbon market during its first trading periods. Conventional policy solutions adopted to manage the supply and demand imbalance in the carbon market have taken more than a decade to implement, in part owing to rent-seeking behaviour of affected sectors and the member states. Likewise, incidents of market power and abuse have required a regulatory response, although the additional restrictions – while justified to secure market integrity and restore confidence among its participants – may also

[12] Patrick Keyzer and others, 'Carbon Market Integrity: Integrity and Oversight of the European Emissions Trading System' (Carbon Market Institute (CMI) 2012) 13 www.carbonmarketinstitute.org accessed 12 March 2019; Dominique Guegan, Antonin Lassoudiere and Marius-Cristian Frunza, 'Missing Trader Fraud on the Emissions Market' (2011) 18 *J Fin Crime* 183.

[13] Point Carbon, 'Carbon Market Monitor: A Review of 2012' (Point Carbon 2012) 3 https://archive.annual-report.thomsonreuters.com/2012/_files/pdf/carbon_2012.pdf accessed 22 April 2022.

[14] Directive 2016/1034 of the European Parliament and of the Council of 23 June 2016 amending Directive 2014/65/EU on Markets in Financial Instruments, 2016 O.J. (L 175) 8.

impact market liquidity. Overall, the EU ETS has evidenced various forms of regulatory failure and undergone a difficult process to address design flaws.

Continuous improvements have helped ensure the durability of the EU ETS, which has seen the emergence of a liquid market for allowances as measured in terms of the frequency and size of transactions, the number and type of market participants, and the average size of spreads.[15] By now, the EU ETS has reached maturity, with a number of competing trading platforms – including the European Energy Exchange (EEX) and the Intercontinental Exchange (ICE) – as well as high trading volumes both through exchanges and through over-the-counter (OTC) transactions, a wide range of traded products in the spot and derivative markets, and a diverse set of market participants, including compliance entities and various financial service providers and other intermediaries. Still, as mentioned, the additional layers of regulation have taken time and incurred new trade-offs, such as increased administrative and compliance costs. Unsurprisingly, therefore, the potential to deploy DLT approaches in the operationalisation of the EU ETS has garnered attention in the literature and policy debate. Some potential pathways for incorporation of DLT elements in the EU ETS are outlined in the next sections.

6.2 REGULATORY CHANGES FOR A DLT-BASED GOVERNANCE FRAMEWORK

In the ensuing paragraphs, we intend to explain the requirements and the implications for adopting a DLT model into the existing EU ETS, by providing a practical case-study of the concept of crypto-legal structure introduced in Chapter 5. We analyse the necessary regulatory changes, the possible solutions and the disruptive effects from the adaptation to DLT.

6.2.1 *Transitioning the EU ETS to a Blockchain-Based Architecture*

As outlined in the previous chapters, in an ETS such as the EU ETS, the regulator fixes the total amount of emissions (the 'cap') and issues a corresponding number of allowances, which give its owner the right to emit GHGs equivalent to one tonne of carbon dioxide (so-called CO_2-equivalent, or CO_2e) for a specified period of a calendar year. The European Commission, being the central regulator of the EU ETS, distributes, through benchmark-based free allocation or through auctioning, a predetermined number of EUAs to covered installations that emit GHGs. Then, the operators running such installations are required to annually surrender to the regulator a quantity of allowances equal to their GHG emissions incurred in the previous year. Operators whose emissions exceed their current EUA holdings have to acquire

[15] A Denny Ellerman and Paul L Joskow, 'The European Union's Emissions Trading System in Perspective' (Policy Brief 16, Pew Center on Global Climate Change 2008) www.c2es.org/document/the-european-unions-emissions-trading-system-in-perspective accessed 12 March 2019.

additional EUAs, while those who have reduced emissions below their holdings can sell their surplus allowances.

As currently implemented, the European Commission serves as the system central administrator, while each member state designates a national authority in charge of tasks to render the system operative. Thus, all covered operators in the EU ETS rely on these two layers of public administration for governance functions related to the trading system. As DLT approaches could address several of the inefficiencies experienced in the current system,[16] their introduction into the EU ETS governance architecture could contribute to the more effective achievement of the policy objectives. Transitioning from the current centralised model to a decentralised and distributed one calls for a rethinking of the role of the current actors, however, including the regulator, as these changes will transform the ETS architecture at different levels. Relevant changes will affect the governance of the system as well as its operational, architectural and regulatory aspects.

Blockchain is an evolving technology[17] that can be outlined and operationalised in different ways (i.e. public, private, permissioned, permissionless) based on the needs of its users. A DLT-based EU ETS would be a decentralised autonomous organisation (DAO) composed of several 'modules' and implemented through an intricate web of 'smart contracts' operationalising the crypto-legal structure. A DLT-based infrastructure for the EU ETS would likely combine some properties of a permissioned blockchain (authentication of nodes) with properties of a permissionless blockchain (free access to the blockchain for any user). Therefore, it could be classified as a 'hybrid blockchain', where each node of the blockchain is co-owner of the infrastructure and co-manager of the platform.

The proposed DLT-based ETS would define which entities shall run the nodes of the network and how so that the allocation of nodes meets the criteria of a decentralised and distributed system. Moreover, it would have to identify the properties, together with the set of operational requirements, of each node of the network. The options chosen for the nodes would thus define the responsibilities for being co-owner and co-manager of the infrastructure; a mechanism of shared benefits can ensure that each node has an interest in others being compliant with the applicable regulatory framework. At the same time, the high level of transparency granted by the blockchain infrastructure helps to perform compliance checks among all the nodes.

In a DLT-based system, the current Union Registry database would be replaced by a decentralised and distributed database, where each participant in the network would insert in the blockchain the data that are now contained in the Union Registry. In order to preserve the confidentiality of certain data, an encryption system can be used to ensure that the other participants cannot decode such data. Currently,

[16] See Section 6.1 for discussion of some of these inefficiencies.

[17] Kim Siba and Anuj Prakash, 'Block-Chain: An Evolving Technology' (2017) *Global J Enterprise Info System*.

anyone who intends to acquire EUAs has to open an account in the Union Registry to be able to exchange the allowances with other users who have such an account.[18] In the DLT-based system, the accounts in the Union Registry would be replaced by digital wallets. Each user would obtain a digital address and an access identification key (private key) allowing that user to receive and manage the digital assets.

The transaction checking and the transaction recording – functions that are today performed by the EUTL – could thus be executed by the blockchain itself in a more secure and rapid way by using an efficient cryptographic system. Ultimately, such a mechanism would be able to offer a high level of security, while also enabling easier access to information for defined categories of users.

In a DLT-based architecture, the way the allowances are assigned (through free allocation or auction) would remain unchanged from the current system,[19] with allocation and auction procedures entirely managed within the blockchain platform. Therefore, blockchain does not change the substantive policy design of the ETS and can instead be seen as technological infrastructure, incorporating new governance and operational rules that enable the EU to more efficiently pursue the objectives underlying the current ETS.

6.2.2 *Solutions Offered by a Crypto-legal Structure*

The following three major points of failure in the EU ETS were identified in Chapter 4 (Section 4.4), namely the security of the computer servers hosting the corporate accounts, the account-operating procedures and the transfer approval process. As initially explored in Section 4.4, these points of failure related to transfers of carbon allowances could be addressed in a DLT-based approach through three specific modules: the 'Doorkeeper Module', the 'KYC Module', and the 'Transaction Module'[*]. Each module is described in greater detail in the rest of this section.

Doorkeeper Module: The 'Doorkeeper Module' can provide sophisticated protection against the first point of failure identified above by creating a shield to defend all subscribing servers and accounts from cyber-attacks of virus and malware which fuelled the cybersecurity breaches in 2010 and 2011. As a distributed ledger, the EU ETS blockchain would form a single cyber-threat detection platform, optimising the geographically diverse cybersecurity measures within the Union Registry and subscribing servers (i.e. computer servers hosting the holding and trading accounts of companies and traders). On this platform, security experts devise and maintain

18 A formal distinction is made between the accounts for the operators who have compliance obligations under the EU ETS – referred to as 'operator holding accounts' (OHA) – and accounts for other market participants (e.g. banks), called 'person holding accounts' (PHA).

19 In particular, the free allowances and their progressive reduction of the global EU emissions cap can be transformed into specific functions embedded in the code running the blockchain.

* Rather than direct citations, the design of some of these modules was enlightened by the ideas in Liss, Florian. (2018). Blockchain and the EU ETS: An architecture and prototype of a decentralized emission trading system based on smart contracts. (Master's Thesis) Munich: Technical University Munich.

competing anti-virus/anti-malware software underpinned by 'scanning engines' that rapidly detect the latest threats. Instead of a single anti-virus software to which end-users currently subscribe, all servers hosting EU ETS accounts would subscribe to multiple anti-virus software on a blockchain for collective protection by thousands of scanning engines offering much broader and faster coverage. Different from traditional bug bounty programs, blockchain allows a more collaborative yet competitive cyber-protection network to use 'predictions markets' together with 'proof-of-work'. In the 'Doorkeeper Module', security experts use smart contracts to include 'bets' on whether the artefacts they are evaluating with competing scanning engines are malicious. The threat level of those artefacts would be determined through the consensus algorithm. The scanning engines that provide the best defence for the servers could receive coins/tokens that encourage experts to continuously optimise their engines for competitiveness.

However, movement in the 'Doorkeeper Module' would trigger a smart contract that automatically invalidates the existing login details of the attempted accounts and directs EU ETS account holders to the central administrator's node for resetting their login details (e.g. passwords) with fingerprints reactivating their private keys on the DLT. Thus, the 'Doorkeeper Module' could be regarded as a DLT safeguarding the main EU ETS DLT at its edge. In this smart contract, the 'Transaction Module' (as described later) cannot be activated until the current alert in the 'Doorkeeper Module' is off.

Know-Your-Customer (KYC) Module: The issue regarding the account-operating procedure can be solved by using the KYC Module. Currently, natural and legal persons are not in control of their digital identity other than usernames and passwords assigned by identity providers and third parties. The permissioned DLT storing the identity data is a decentralised identity network that could reform the account-opening protocols in the EU ETS.

The concept of decentralised identity comprises self-sovereign identity and multi-source identity. In a DLT-supported EU ETS, to open a 'holding and trading' account, a covered entity or other market participant would apply for KYC by encrypting its documents with the public key of member states to avoid unauthorised access. It would then upload documents to and answer randomly generated security questions from a node (e.g. the national administrator responsible for administering EU ETS functions in that member state) and the KYC application for 'broadcast' on the blockchain to complete the application process. Afterwards, the corresponding member state would decrypt the uploaded documents with its private key and review them before making the accept/deny decision.

In this part of the distributed ledger, the documentary review process executes the KYC procedures with the concepts of self-sovereign identity and multi-source identity. The national administrator of the member state would verify the details of uploaded documents and responses to the security questions (ideally with the help of artificial intelligence (AI)) against the personally identifiable information (PII) stored in a permissioned decentralised identity network/ledger with data accumulated from multiple entities, including the relevant companies house or official company registry, tax authorities and financial institutions, etc. If all documents and responses from the applicants check out, a smart contract can then be triggered to unlock the account-opening protocols on the server, including an AI-based transaction pattern monitoring facility for active accounts. All of these enhanced KYC procedures are prerequisites for account opening in the crypto-legal structure.

Transaction Module: The issue regarding the transfer of approval process could be solved by the 'Transaction Module'. Firstly, a market participant would select the desired price and volume of allowances to 'broadcast' a 'buy/sell order' on, for example, an Ethereum-based smart contract. Before the transfer approval procedure starts, the 'KYC Module' could be extended as the first 'trigger' of this smart contract. Using the multiple-identity source approach, it would scan whether the PII used by the account holders to apply for their account is still valid in the decentralised identity network. As the second 'trigger', the nodes (computers of relevant authorities) would competitively verify in the distributed Union Registry if the subject account has sufficient funds or allowances through proof-of-work or proof-of-stake ('mining'). If invalid, the buy/sell order would be rejected. Otherwise, the smart contract would allow the regulatory logic to find matching buy/sell orders in the blockchain network and process the accounting of funds/allowances automatically on such a distributed registry. A third 'trigger' would consist in the return of an 'unsuspicious' assessment from the AI-based transaction pattern monitoring system to prevent money laundering and other fraudulent activities. Transfers initiated by new accounts would be subject to a short delay for additional due diligence screening. A fourth 'trigger', finally, could be added to this smart contract to ensure compliance with VAT rules. In a nutshell, an allowance transaction cannot be approved until all these 'triggers' have been activated in the smart contract underpinning the 'Transaction Module'.

6.2.3 *Regulatory Services Delivered by a Crypto-legal Structure*

Compared with the current regulatory framework, such a crypto-legal structure could help the EU ETS prevent unlawful transfers of carbon allowances by delivering five essential regulatory services: (1) uniqueness; (2) validity; (3) consensus; (4) immutability; and (5) authentication. Each of these is described in greater detail below.

Uniqueness: Although each carbon allowance in the current EU ETS has a serial number, the transfers in the 2010–11 cybersecurity incidents occurred so rapidly that the allowances were already 'transferred out' before they could be traced.[20] Allowance buyers were often unaware that they had acquired stolen units. Instead

[20] See n 13.

of forcing national authorities to spend several days to track and recover a percentage of stolen allowances of which serial numbers had been released by the victims, the 'Transaction Module' of the blockchain-supported EU ETS would provide a unique identifier for every carbon allowance, enabling it to be readily traceable through its hashing algorithm. The hash of a carbon allowance contains all its identifiable information in a transaction (e.g. origin, issuer, buyer and seller) and more 'blocks' are added to this chain as the allowance moves across market participants in the EU ETS.

Validity: Intelligent algorithms can be embedded in the 'Transaction Module' to maximise the capacity of blockchain to validate every allowance transfer. In addition to the nodes validating the buy/sell order as such (e.g. ensuring adequacy of funds or allowances in the relevant accounts) by mining to avoid double spends, the EU ETS blockchain could boast a smart contract facility embedded with a 'KYC extension' and an AI-based transaction pattern monitoring system. Thus, AI could detect suspicious transaction patterns (e.g. transfers of unusually large amounts of allowance requested from a new account), enabling the smart contract to offer multiple validation layers against theft, fraud or money laundering.

Consensus: Not only can the blockchain instantly trace the location and status of every (tokenised) allowance with its hash but it can also, as a distributed Transaction Log, determine which version of the allowance file to adopt if there are incompatible copies, for instance, owing to it being hacked from any single point, per its consensus algorithm applicable to all the nodes in the Transaction Module. Likewise, an alarm would be raised by the 'extended KYC Module' whenever hackers' tampering with PII or fraudsters' use of the credentials and biometrics (e.g. fingerprints) of another person to open a new account on the EU ETS blockchain is made impossible owing to its reliance on a decentralised identity network.

Immutability: Since the 2011 cybersecurity incidents, the European Commission has replaced distributed national registries with a single centralised Union Registry in which EUAs are currently stored. In a DLT-supported EU ETS, the Union Registry would be redistributed as a distributed ledger. It would be a trusted repository of carbon transaction data which is transparent and immutable. The transaction checking and recording, both functions that are today performed by the EUTL, would then be executed by the distributed ledger itself in a faster and more secure way thanks to an efficient cryptographic system. Every node in the EU ETS blockchain would then function autonomously with 'good copies' of all the transactional information, preventing hackers from tampering in the way they have in the past with unconnected national registries. The 'Transaction Module' is unlikely to approve any buy or sell orders based on records modified at a single point of the marketplace. The immutability of this distributed Union Registry echoes the proposition that limited market segment fraud and theft are preventable if a real-time database is 'utilised to its fullest'.[21]

[21] R Ainsworth, 'Phishing & VAT Fraud in CO2 Permits: DICE in the EU-ETS; DICE in Power Tomorrow' (BU School of Law 2014) 14–74 https://scholarship.law.bu.edu/cgi/viewcontent.cgi?article=2427&context=faculty_scholarship accessed 11 April 2022.

Authentication: The entire EU ETS blockchain would be governed by layers of interlinked smart contracts or programmable ledgers that could authenticate near-exhaustively every movement of allowances. First, the Doorkeeper Module could even address 'physical' attacks by criminals at the edge of the blockchain with a first-of-its-kind distributed anti-virus marketplace that would be used to activate account suspension and biometric-based resetting processes on that smart contract. 'Snoozing' the alarm raised in this 'doorkeeper' smart contract would itself be a trigger to activate the Transaction Module's smart contracts. Nowadays, the operational rules for ETS accounts are set by the competent authority of each member state; thereby ETS accounts face a very fragmented framework,[22] where several inefficiencies (disciplined information, cherry-picking jurisdiction for opening accounts)[23] are widespread. The blockchain could efficiently execute an extended KYC protocol even before approving every transaction, which virtually precludes illegitimate shell corporations from trading. In the decentralised identity network, the private-key-enabled self-sovereign identity management system means that neither authorities nor institutions have an 'administrator password' to overwrite the PII distributed across all the nodes (forming a 'self-correcting mechanism' in case of cyber-attacks) so that it is unrealistic for cyber-attackers to hack into any node administering the EU ETS.

6.2.4 *Disruptive Effects from the Regulatory Adaptation to DLT*

The self-executing algorithms in a DLT-supported EU ETS would require adapting many of the regulatory and governance functions which the European Commission, in particular, currently performs. First, the governance structure of the DLT-based system should be recognised with appropriate amendments to the legal and regulatory framework underlying the EU ETS. Owing to the decentralised and distributed nature of a DLT-based system, it would be necessary to specify the ownership of this DLT-supported infrastructure and to define relevant supervisory powers over the network. That would enable the European Commission, together with the relevant authorities of each member state, to enforce relevant rules and procedures within the DLT-based infrastructure.

Updating existing rules: A DLT-supported EU ETS with tamper-proof transaction records would be extraordinarily secure against double spending, hacking and

22 The requirements for opening accounts to hold and trade allowances vary from each jurisdiction, thereby allowing participants to choose the most friendly and convenient regulation. The last country to adopt more stringent rules to prevent fraud or elusive practices was the Netherlands where, as of 1 January 2021, every holder of a trading account must be registered in the Dutch Chamber of Commerce.

23 Simone Borghesi and Andrea Flori, 'EU ETS Facets in the Net: How Account Types Influence the Structure of the System' (FEEM Working Paper No 008.2016, 2016); Regina A Betz and Tobias S Schmidt, 'Transfer Patterns in Phase I of the EU Emissions Trading System: A First Reality Check Based on Cluster Analysis' (2016) 16(4) *Clim Policy* 474–95.

theft of carbon allowances. In such a crypto-legal structure, EU ETS market participants would be subject to the extended 'KYC Module' prior to the approval of each and every transaction, which in turn would help address legal challenges usually encountered when seeking to determine the 'good faith' of parties.[24] Theft of allowances would be largely pre-empted so that regulators and courts would no longer be burdened with handling cases of this nature, and legal questions related to the source of funds could likewise lose much of their relevance. Therefore, the relevant articles in the Registry Regulation,[25] for instance, could be simplified, as national administrators in the EU ETS could skip the manual single-point KYC verification exercise. That said, transfers of allowances and money within such a distributed EU ETS should nonetheless be subject to the Anti-Money Laundering Directive 2018/843 and relevant financial regulations,[26] which can be rendered more efficient with the help of AI. By boosting disintermediate interactions and offering higher transparency compared to the current OTC transactions, DLT may unlock trading opportunities among accounts. If the role of intermediaries diminishes, it may no longer be viable to enforce these regulations against intermediaries (e.g. financial institutions), but enforcement would instead shift to the DLT platform providers, who should then bear full legal responsibility for managing access and regulatory matters. This proposed system would open the way for recognising how to conduct KYC checks with datasets in addition to government records in order to materialise the self-sovereign identity and multi-source identity systems on the distributed ledger.

The emergence of new legal elements and actors: A DLT-supported EU ETS would replace the current trading model in which carbon allowances are transferred based on *ex ante* regulation-induced trust and *ex post* court review. Instead, the DLT-supported approach would be a technology-based solution (built on a consensus algorithm) that offers nodes the trust that transfers are executed and recorded accurately. This would require a new legal element in the Registry Regulation that prohibits any party from taking control of the majority of nodes and, hence, of the validating process carried out by the 'Transaction Module'. Thus, the strict liability issue alleged in the *Holcim (Romania) SA* v. *European Commission* case[27] would no longer be relevant.

24 See *Armstrong DLW GmbH v Winnington Networks Ltd*, 2012.

25 Commission Delegated Regulation (EU) 2019/1124 of 13 March 2019 amending Delegated Regulation (EU) 2019/1122 as regards the functioning of the Union Registry under Regulation (EU) 2018/842 of the European Parliament and of the Council, [2019] OJ L177/66 (hereafter 'Registry Regulation').

26 The current EUAs are units of exchangeable value, see art 40 of the Registry Regulation, traded exclusively electronically and classified as financial instruments as of 3 January 2018 owing to the application of Parliament and Council Directive 2014/65/EU of 15 May 2014 on markets in financial instruments and amending Directive 2002/92/EC and Directive 2011/61/EU, [2014] OJ L173/349 (hereinafter 'MiFID II').

27 Case T-317/12 *Holcim (Romania) SA v European Commission* [2014] ECLI:EU:T:2014:782.

In such a system, there may be a future risk of hacking into the AI-based monitoring facilities and other oracles of the smart contracts that authenticate EU ETS users. In addition, given the irreversibility of transactions on a smart contract, there may be a need for new *ex ante* legal elements mandating a dispute resolution mechanism to process claims in contract or for unjust enrichment when allowances are unlawfully transferred. The use of smart contracts in the EU ETS would mirror a wider discussion on their legal status.

New legal questions are therefore emerging around the capacity of smart contracts to meet all legal tests of long-standing principles of contract law. The European Commission may need to consider whether Union-wide smart contract-enabling legislation is necessary,[28] as already exemplified in the States of Arizona[29] and Tennessee[30] in the USA that led the way in passing legislation recognising the binding nature of smart contract transactions. In the next legislative steps, it shall be discussed whether new legal actors, especially coders of smart contracts, should be included in the scope of new/amended regulations. The regulatory changes for the DLT-based system may also open additional business opportunities where new actors can operate; in fact, different kinds of services can be provided to token holders by the emerging roles (i.e. custodian, exchange platforms, traders) that are needed to make the infrastructure working. The adoption of the proposed model can also help optimise the existing transaction costs thanks to a more efficient data collection system.

New patterns of enforcement and regulation: Since a DLT-supported approach could replace many functions (the five regulatory services mentioned earlier) currently performed by regulators or law enforcement agencies, the role of regulators would need to be adapted to the resulting near-automatic compliance environment.[31] The system administrator, which would continue to play a co-ordinating and overseeing role thanks to its supervisory powers, would continue to manage the process of issuing, distributing and overseeing the surrender of allowances, but the underlying process would be simplified by becoming fully automated

[28] Within the EU jurisdictions, Italy has been the first EU country to introduce a legislative definition of a smart contract, defined as 'a computer program that operates on technologies based on distributed registers and whose execution automatically binds two or more parties on the basis of predefined effects' (art 8-ter Law Decree no 135/2018 – Decreto Semplificazioni – converted into law by Law 11 February 2019 no 12, published in the 'Gazzetta Ufficiale' 12/02/2019 n 36). Moreover, according to the same disposition, a smart contract, after a digital identification of the parties involved, meets the requirement to be qualified as a written contract.

[29] Arizona House Bill 2417 (2017).

[30] Tennessee House Bill 1507 (2018).

[31] With a distributed Union Registry, for example, all parties involved in the EU ETS always have a real-time copy of the same record of allowance transfers. Article 110 of the Registry Regulation, which stipulates the confidentiality of account information held on the Registry, would become obsolete because the EC technically cannot control such DLT-based Registry. Rather, it should regulate an 'on-and-off ramp' when value is being exchanged or traded. The 'on-and-off ramp' here could be what data categories should enter into smart contracts and their coding standards.

within the DLT infrastructure, helping reduce management and monitoring costs. Therefore, the digitalisation of these governance functions should reduce the administrative burden placed on the system administrator. As mentioned, the proposed technology would also ensure full transparency of the token management process, since all users would have access in real-time to the data (including all the transactions) entered in the distributed ledger. That would significantly reduce the information asymmetry experienced in the current EU ETS. In addition, thanks to the user authentication system, it would help ensure the ability of the administrator to carry out a check on the identity of the users who participate in the trading.

6.3 LEGISLATIVE ROADMAP

6.3.1 *Aligning the EU ETS with the EU Digital Strategy*

Making Europe fit for the digital age is one of the top priorities spelt out by the European Commission with its latest strategy issued in February 2020,[32] and DLT is one of the technologies for which the European Commission has confirmed an interest in developing and promoting uptake in multiple sectors across the EU.[33] In this context, the Digital Financial Package, a set of legislative proposals adopted by the European Commission on 24 September 2020,[34] sets out the first broad digital financial strategy[35] to ensure that the EU embraces the digital revolution, making the benefits of digital finance available to European consumers and businesses. The package contains a proposal for a regulation on

[32] European Commission, Shaping Europe's Digital Future, COM(20) 67 final.

[33] A co-ordinated effort to deliver public services through the use of blockchain technology is envisaged by the European Blockchain Services Infrastructure (EBSI), a joint initiative between the European Commission and the European Blockchain Partnership (EBP) that is a Declaration signed by twenty-eight member states, Liechtenstein and Norway to co-operate in the delivery of cross-border digital public services, with the highest standards of security and privacy. The ESBI infrastructure is a network of distributed nodes across Europe, where blockchain technology will ultimately enhance the way citizens, governments and businesses interact. https://ec.europa.eu/cefdigital/wiki/display/CEFDIGITAL/EBSI accessed 9 January 2021.

[34] European Commission, Digital Finance Strategy for the EU, COM(20) 591 final https://ec.europa.eu/info/publications/200924-digital-finance-proposals_en accessed 9 January 2021.

[35] This proposal represents the outcome of an extended analysis that has been carried out by the European Securities and Markets Authority (ESMA) since 2016 with the publication of a discussion paper titled 'The Distributed Ledger Technology Applied to Securities Markets' dated 2 June 2016. In the document, ESMA pointed out various potential benefits concerning clearing and settlement, the record of ownership and safekeeping of assets, reporting and oversight, counterparty risk, efficient collateral management, security and resilience, and costs. The discussion paper also mentioned the potential conflicts between the EU-level regulatory regime and the application of DLT to securities markets. This topic has been further addressed in the report published on 7 February 2017. However, the in-depth analysis came only with the Advice to the EC on Initial Coin Offerings and Crypto-Assets, published by ESMA on 9 January 2019, that addresses the regulatory implications when a crypto-asset qualifies as a financial instrument.

markets in crypto-assets,[36] the proposal for a pilot regime for market infrastructures based on DLT[37] (hereinafter, 'DLT markets infrastructure proposal') and a proposal for digital operational resilience.[38] The Digital Financial Package draws on observations made by the European Securities and Markets Authority (ESMA) and proposes establishing a regime for DLT market infrastructure, with various exceptions and temporary derogations to current EU financial markets law. More specifically, the DLT markets infrastructure proposal aims to create an EU framework that enables the tokenisation of traditional financial assets and thus a secondary market for crypto-assets that qualify as financial instruments under MiFID II. The DLT markets infrastructure proposal defines two types of DLT markets infrastructure: a DLT multilateral trading facility (DLT MTF) and a DLT securities settlement system. On the one hand, these would fall under a special regime that allows the implementation of DLT; on the other hand, both would still be subject to most of the requirements for traditional multilateral trading facilities and central securities depositories. Furthermore, the proposal is intended only to allow innovation and experimentation while preserving financial stability. Thus, the type of transferable securities admitted to trading on a DLT MTF or recorded in a central securities depository (CSD) operating a DLT securities settlement system is limited to shares and bonds that are not liquid.[39] This approach provides a clear example of how it would be possible to advance a legislative process capable of introducing – within a long-established and highly regulated system, such as the EU financial market rules – a new infrastructure accommodating new types of assets.

Another recent step initiated by the EU to incentivise the adoption of DLT in the European market is contained in the Report on a New Industrial Strategy for Europe, approved by the European Parliament in November 2020[40] and forwarded to the European Commission and the Council; this report stresses the strategic role that new emerging technologies, such as the Industrial Internet of Things (IIoT), AI, DLTs, hyper-performance computing and quantum computing, will play in future

[36] European Commission, Proposal for a Regulation on Markets in Crypto-assets, and amending Directive (EU) 2019/1937, COM(20) 593 final https://eur-lex.europa.eu/legal-content/EN/TXT/?uri=CELEX%3A52020PC0593 accessed 9 January 2021.

[37] European Commission, Proposal for a regulation on a pilot regime for market infrastructures based on distributed ledger technology, COM(20) 594 final, https://eur-lex.europa.eu/legal-content/EN/TXT/?uri=CELEX%3A52020PC0594 accessed 9 January 2021.

[38] European Commission, Proposal for a regulation on digital operational resilience for the financial sector and amending Regulations (EC) No 1060/2009, (EU) No 648/2012, (EU) No 600/2014 and (EU) No 909/2014, COM(20) 595 final, https://eur-lex.europa.eu/legal-content/EN/TXT/?uri=CELEX%3A52020PC0595 accessed 9 January 2021.

[39] The market capitalisation (or a tentative market capitalisation) of the shares' issuer shall be less than EUR 200 million and convertible bonds, covered bonds, corporate bonds and other bonds, with an issuance size of less than EUR 500 million. Also, DLT market infrastructures are prevented from admitting to trading or recording on the distributed ledger sovereign bonds.

[40] European Parliament resolution of 25 November 2020 on a New Industrial Strategy for Europe [2020] www.europarl.europa.eu/doceo/document/TA-9-2020-0321_EN.html accessed 9 January 2021.

European industrial policy;[41] more specifically, the Report calls on the Commission and the member states to promote investment measures in several promising areas of technological development,[42] including DLT.

These various legislative and policy initiatives could pave the way for advancing a mandatory, DLT-supported European carbon market, by enabling greater confidence in the regulatory framework, its available remedies and the routine operation of the market. The pathway towards a DLT-supported EU ETS could be included in the European Industrial Strategy proposed with the Green Deal,[43] where the European Commission has coined the notion of a 'twin transition' of Europe's industry towards digitalisation and climate neutrality. The definition of measures and allocation of resources needed to realise this twin transition poses substantial challenges, which have only increased as a result of the Covid-19 pandemic. Europe can only play a leading role in implementing this twin transition, however, if the resources allocated are consistent with the required investments. Despite widespread recognition of the importance of the digital and green objectives, their pursuit appears full of obstacles. The debate around which level of governance (the EU or the member states) shall outline the strategy to reach climate neutrality and enhance digitalisation is still open,[44] as is the methodology that should be used when evaluating the projects and the measures submitted by the member states to operationalise the twin transition. While some stakeholders seem to prefer a standardised perspective, others have expressed a preference for a flexible approach by the European Commission in evaluating the relevant projects and measures submitted by the member states. What appears certain, in any case, is that the legislative changes required for use of blockchain in the EU ETS will necessitate a co-ordinated effort between the member states and European institutions, among which the European Commission will play a leading role. Importantly, however, DLT adoption under the EU ETS will depend on the active involvement of all ETS stakeholders, private and public, to create the enabling environment for operationalisation of the new infrastructure.

6.3.2 *New Legislative Approach for Blockchain*

There is a significant appetite in European markets for a new regulatory framework to facilitate and accelerate a transition towards digital finance, specifically the use of DLT and crypto-assets. This appetite has found its formal reflection in the DLT markets infrastructure proposal, mentioned in Section 6.3.1. This section will

41 Letter N of the Report.
42 Point no 32 of the Report.
43 European Commission, the European Green Deal, COM(19) 640 final.
44 Interview with Mr Paolo Borchia, MP sitting in the ITRE committee of the EU Parliament (Brussels, 9 October 2020).

consider some of the key articles of that proposal and how these can promote and maintain the efficiency of a new DLT market.

The first consideration relates to how this proposal can provide legal certainty to the parties involved in a transaction. To this end, Article 9 of the proposed regulation ensures co-operation between the DLT market infrastructure creators and controllers, the competent authorities and ESMA, and imposes a requirement for DLT market infrastructures to let authorities know if there have been any material changes to business plans, evidence of fraud and hacking, technical or operational difficulties in delivering activities or services, and any further issues regarding market integrity or financial instability. This level of transparency is more likely to lead to an environment of trust, in which experimentation with DLT can take place and necessary corrections can be made.

The second argument in favour of the approach chosen in the proposal is that it has, in its Article 3, incorporated parameters such as the requirement for a transition strategy if the total market value of the DLT transferable securities reported has reached EUR 2.25 billion. There are multiple benefits to this approach: first, the limit ensures that the security of financial markets is not compromised when implementing the system, and limits the risk and extent of potential damage to overall financial markets relative to implementation without a cap on the value of traded DLT transferable securities. Second, the transition strategy sets out what procedures should be followed and how the relevant players should be treated in the event of a failure to achieve the requirements set out in Article 3. This is likely to strengthen confidence in the DLT-supported trading system.

There is a third benefit of the new proposal, as set out in Article 40, which is that there is an in-built requirement for ESMA to monitor the system and provide a report on the current system after a five-year period. This will help provide clarity as to the significance and usefulness of the DLT pilot scheme and whether a further period of time can be agreed for additional experimentation. Over the medium to long term, this can help create a new and safe financial market for crypto-asset transactions, bolstering the overriding objective of the EU ETS, namely the reduction of European GHG emissions.

There are additional considerations which the proposed regulation itself does not touch upon, and which may prove critical for a functioning system. For example, one initial legal question is whether two entities entering into a contract have the relevant capacity to do so. It is likely that DLTs will work by recording the sale of an emissions credit from the seller to the buyer on a single block. While, in a contractual situation, the sale of an allowance may involve a physical or electronic signature identifying the transacting parties and their authorised signatories, DLTs are likely to function slightly differently, for example, by disposing of a transaction by simply digitising the private key (an alphanumeric code) in the possession of the account holder. In such a scenario, issues regarding mental capacity may arise, and there will be a need to provide clarity and confidence regarding the parties' ability to enter into the transaction. Future legislation can solve this issue by providing the basis for assessing parties' capacity, for instance by outlining a procedure for both verifying the signatories' authority to bind the parties entering into the sale and establishing the signatories' mental capacity to instruct the technology to complete the transaction. Such additional safeguards are likely to provide greater clarity for all parties involved and to build additional trust in the system.

6.4 CONCLUSION

The EU ETS offers a useful case study for the potential integration of a DLT-supported infrastructure in an already existing ETS. This chapter has outlined some ways in which such a crypto-legal structure and the governance functions it would support can be adapted to the existing regulatory framework of the EU ETS. It has also identified some of the challenges alongside the benefits. One of the main objections raised against policies promoting the transition towards greater deployment of disruptive technologies is the risk that entities with more limited political and economic power (i.e. the lower-income member states, smaller market participants) will benefit less from the transition measures because of their reduced capacity to attract the envisaged benefits.[45] For that reason, the proposed transition has to be built with particular attention to avoid disadvantaging those market participants and other stakeholders that may have limited access to emerging technologies. Therefore, ensuring a proper balance between the different interests at stake is crucial to delivering efficient solutions and to securing progress on the twin goals of the digital and green transition. Eventually, the transition towards a crypto-legal structure, outlined here for the EU ETS, requires a cross-cutting perspective and inclusive political action to drive a sustainable and broadly accepted systemic change.

[45] Interview with Mr Eduardo Besa, Chilean Diplomat and Climate Negotiator (20 November 2020).

7

DLT and the Voluntary Carbon Markets

Nicholas Scott, Sai Nellore and Alastair Marke

7.1 INTRODUCTION

Carbon trading is widely used in conjunction with sector- or region-wide emission caps or baselines in order to achieve climate mitigation targets in the most efficient way. Carbon markets, however, are not limited to trading systems in which covered entities face mandatory compliance obligations. Voluntary carbon markets involve governments, companies and even individuals choosing to reduce their emissions through trading carbon units, without necessarily being subject to any binding obligations to do so. Even where entities have compliance obligations, the voluntary carbon market can provide an alternative compliance option if the applicable rules allow.

Carbon offsetting is a key concept in the context of voluntary carbon markets. It represents a variant of the baseline-and-credit approach to carbon markets, and involves an actor – typically an emitter, such as an organisation or an individual – paying for emissions reductions that occur elsewhere and then counting those emissions reductions as its own. This may include funding renewable energy development, paying farmers to shift to more sustainable practices or paying for the preservation of forests. Buyers in the voluntary carbon market will typically choose to fund such practices where that is more efficient or cost-effective than directly reducing their own emissions; sellers and project developers, meanwhile, gain a source of carbon finance and thus a financial incentive to engage in emissions-reducing activities. Table 7.1 lists countries with the highest volume of carbon offsetting projects and countries with the most voluntary carbon market buyers by volume. Figure 7.1 shows the total volume of voluntary carbon offset transactions worldwide from 2015 to 2019, as measured by the Ecosystem Marketplace Reports.

The most established international governance structure for carbon offset crediting is the Clean Development Mechanism (CDM), which allows developing countries to earn certified emission reduction (CER) credits that are equivalent to the reduction of one tonne of CO_2 emissions. Under the Kyoto Protocol, these credits can be purchased by industrialised countries with quantified emissions

TABLE 7.1 *Countries with the highest volume of carbon offsetting projects and countries with the most voluntary carbon market buyers by volume*

Largest producers and buyers of voluntary carbon offsets			
Country	Volume of carbon offsets produced ($MtCO_2e$)	Country	Volume of carbon offsets bought ($MtCO_2e$)
India	23.1	United States of America	12.1
United States of America	14.4	France	10.1
China	10.2	United Kingdom	5.9
Indonesia	7.0	Germany	1.9
Peru	5.8	Switzerland	0.9

Source: Stephen Donofrio and others, 'State of the Voluntary Markets 2020: The Only Constant Is Change' Forest Trends (19 December 2020) www.forest-trends.org/publications/state-of-the-voluntary-carbon-markets-2020-the-only-constant-is-change/ accessed 11 April 2022.

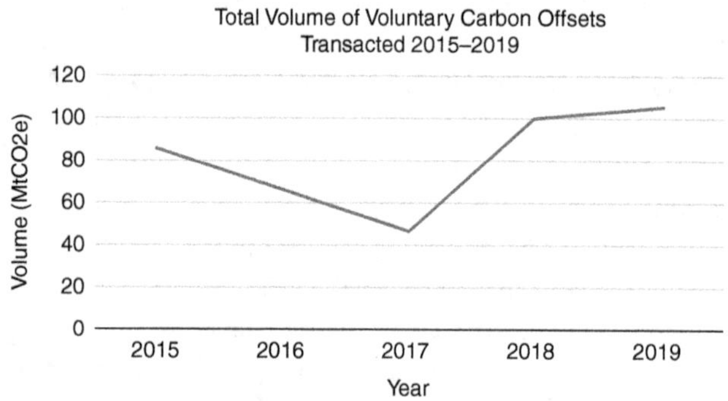

FIGURE 7.1 Total volume of voluntary carbon offset transactions worldwide from 2015 to 2019, as measured by the Ecosystem Marketplace Reports
Source: Stephen Donofrio and others, 'Financing Emissions Reductions for the Future: State of the Voluntary Carbon Markets 2019' Forest Trends (December 2019) www.forest-trends.org/wp-content/uploads/2019/12/SOVCM2019.pdf accessed 11 April 2022; Donofrio and others, 'State of the Voluntary Markets 2020: The Only Constant Is Change' Forest Trends (19 December 2020) www.forest-trends.org/publications/state-of-the-voluntary-carbon-markets-2020-the-only-constant-is-change/ accessed 11 April 2022.

limitation and reduction objectives (QELROs) to meet part of their emission reduction obligations. From the outset, however, the CDM has primarily served as an alternative source of carbon credits for compliance under domestic and regional emissions trading systems (ETSs), such as the EU ETS, which conditionally defined the fungibility of CERs for compliance purposes. More recently, CERs have also become a carbon unit sold in retail carbon markets for individuals or companies looking to voluntarily reduce their carbon footprint. As such, the CDM demonstrates how a carbon offsetting regime with a centralised and public governance framework can become relevant both for compliance and for purely voluntary carbon markets.

In parallel to the CDM, private voluntary markets have emerged to enable individuals and corporations to reduce their carbon emissions using similar principles. A number of separate private organisations have developed standards and methodologies for carbon offsetting projects. These organisations verify emissions reductions from projects around the world before issuing credits that are sold to either individuals or corporations looking to offset their emissions. Although a number of competing standards exist, the Verified Carbon Standard (VCS) administered by the non-profit organisation Verra is the most widely used voluntary standard.

This chapter will use the VCS carbon offsetting standard as a case study to evaluate how voluntary markets can benefit from distributed ledger technology (DLT) and other emerging technologies, and also explore potential actions that public and private stakeholders might take to facilitate emerging technologies in voluntary markets. After describing the voluntary carbon market landscape and examining how DLT and other technologies can enhance these systems, this chapter will give a short explanation of platforms that have combined DLT with carbon crediting. Finally, it will offer broad recommendations about how regulators and voluntary standards themselves might compel this change on a national and international level.

7.2 OVERVIEW OF CURRENT VOLUNTARY MARKETS

7.2.1 *The CDM*

According to Article 12 of the Kyoto Protocol, the CDM aims 'to assist Parties not included in Annex I in achieving sustainable development and in contributing to the ultimate objective of the Convention, and to assist parties included in Annex I in achieving compliance with their quantified emission limitation and reduction commitments under Article 3'.[1] By developing different methodologies for emissions-reducing projects in the developing world, verifying reductions and issuing CERs, the CDM offers a global and centrally administered platform for carbon offset credits that can be traded in the voluntary carbon market. The CDM's registry is managed by the CDM Executive Board of the United Nations Framework Convention on Climate Change (UNFCCC) Secretariat. The registry operates on

[1] Kyoto Protocol to the United Nations Framework Convention on Climate Change (adopted 11 December 1997, entered into force 16 February 2005) 2303 UNTS 161 (Kyoto Protocol) 12.

a centralised electronic database that tracks the issuance, ownership and acquisition of CERs.

Countries that fall under Annex I of the UNFCCC ('Annex I countries') are industrialised countries that have historically contributed the most to climate change.[2] They include both members of the Organisation for Economic Co-operation and Development and countries with 'economies in transition'. The principles of equity and 'common but differentiated responsibilities' mandate that Annex I countries take the lead in addressing the issue of driving climate action with the aim of reducing their greenhouse gas emissions to 1990 levels.

Under the UNFCCC, Annex I countries are required to submit regular reports, known as 'national communications', elaborating the different policy measures that they have undertaken during the reporting period.[3] They also are required to submit an emissions inventory that is subject to in-depth review by a team of experts. All of this is managed through different registries that compile the necessary information pertaining to the emission reductions. These registries communicate with each other to ensure that the integrity of the broader system is maintained at all times. The maintenance and servicing of the registry involve costs that are currently recovered from the project developers who are registering their projects with the CDM.

The CDM verifies projects across a multitude of sectors including renewable energy, energy distribution, chemical industries, transportation, waste handling, forest conservation and agriculture. Pursuant to Article 12 of the Kyoto Protocol and subsequent policy documents adopted by its parties, projects registered under the CDM are expected to benefit not only communities in developing countries at a local level but also environmental integrity at a global level. Agriculture, forestry and land use (AFOLU) projects pose particular challenges and opportunities as they can often have an acute impact on poor local communities and delicate ecosystems. Thus, while there is a risk that these impacts are negative, if carried out carefully AFOLU projects can help bolster development and biodiversity. Ultimately, however, revenues from ecosystem-based projects tend to be low in comparison to projects that are undertaken in other sectors. This is partly owing to the fact that reductions in emissions need to be permanent, a requirement that poses particular challenges in projects involving forest carbon stock, as carbon stored in trees will be released into the atmosphere if those trees are later cut down or burnt. Thus, any area where deforestation has been prevented, or that has been reforested, needs to

[2] United Nations Framework Convention on Climate Change (adopted 9 May 1992, entered into force 21 March 1994) 1771 UNTS 107 (UNFCCC).

[3] New reporting obligations have been included in subsequent treaties, most recently the Paris Agreement, which calls on all parties to submit biennial transparency reports (BTRs); see Paris Agreement on Climate Change (adopted 12 December 2015, entered into force 4 November 2016) UNTC XXVII-7.d art 13.

maintain its forest carbon stock over a number of years in order to yield an absolute reduction in global emissions.

To address the underlying non-permanence risk, the CDM has two special approaches for the allocation of CERs for forestry projects: temporary CERs (tCERs) and long-term CERS (lCERS). The tCERs have a shelf-life of five years, after which the buyer must replace them with permanent credits to meet their compliance requirements.[4] In this scenario, they attract a lesser value as the buyers will have to replace them in due course. The second credit type, lCERs, must be replaced on completion of the project's lifetime, which usually varies between thirty and sixty years depending upon the project. These special types of CER recognise the potentially transitory nature of forestry emissions reductions but also reduce the profitability of forest carbon projects.

Transaction costs including registry fees and administrative charges reduce revenues further,[5] thereby impacting the long-term sustainability of many projects. Specialised professionals are essential to monitoring, reporting and verification (MRV) processes, and help project developers accurately set a proper baseline level of emissions and measure actual emissions or changes in carbon stock to determine ultimate emissions reductions. However, paying these professionals also incurs a cost to project developers. In small-scale agricultural projects, the complexity of monitoring increases as the smallholder farmers' lands are spread across diverse landscapes and over large areas, thus cost-effective MRV processes, potentially involving dealing with groups of farmers rather than individuals, are important.[6] Reduced profits affect not only project developers but also the often-underprivileged local communities involved with offsetting projects.

A final two important challenges facing CDM projects are carbon leakage and double counting. Carbon leakage refers to the risk that economic activity will merely shift location in response to offsetting projects, thus not actually reducing global emissions. Double counting describes the potential that emissions reductions from one project will be counted towards two countries' emissions reductions, often the country in which the project is based and the country that purchases the resulting CERs.

Summing up, the CDM faces three distinct challenges: (i) the risk that emissions reductions are not accurate or permanent, or are counted twice; (ii) high transaction costs that can affect carbon project developers; and (iii) potential harm to local

4 UNFCCC, 'Report of the Conference of the Parties Serving as the Meeting of the Parties to the Kyoto Protocol on Its First Session, Held at Montreal from 28 November to 10 December 2005' (2006).

5 Bruce P Chadwick, 'Transaction Costs and the Clean Development Mechanism' (2006) 30 *Natural Resources Forum* 256; Matthias Krey, 'Transaction Costs of Unilateral CDM Projects in India: Results from an Empirical Survey' (2005) 33 *Energy Policy* 2385; Axel Michaelowa and others, 'Transaction Costs of the Kyoto Mechanisms' (2003) 3 *Clim Policy* 261.

6 Johannes Woelcke, 'More Than Just Hot Air: Carbon Market Access and Climate-Smart Agriculture for Smallholder Farmers' IFC Smart Lessons Brief (World Bank 2012) https://openknowledge.worldbank.org/handle/10986/17106 accessed 11 April 2022.

communities or ecosystems. The second commitment period of the Kyoto Protocol has ended, and the fate of the mechanism is largely uncertain. Nonetheless, it serves as a useful illustration of problems affecting project- and program-based carbon crediting markets, and offers a useful point of departure for an analysis of the potential applications of DLT and other technologies.

7.2.2 *The VCS*

As the most widely used voluntary carbon standard, the VCS is a useful case study for voluntary markets more generally. The VCS sets criteria to assess the integrity of voluntary carbon offsets. Developed by a number of carbon market experts and administered by Verra, the VCS is a voluntary standard that issues verified carbon units (VCUs) that are equivalent to one metric tonne of CO_2 that is either avoided or sequestered. These units may be traded between project developers and individuals or corporations looking to offset their own carbon emissions by funding emissions reductions elsewhere. Compliance markets may allow their participants to meet their emissions targets through offsetting, but VCUs are increasingly being purchased for both reputational and ethical reasons by companies and individuals not legally bound by any emissions limits.[7] Further, VCUs may be issued for a number of different emissions-reducing projects including renewable energy development and AFOLU initiatives.

By setting standards for offset projects, the VCS aims to ensure the integrity of VCUs, giving purchasers certainty that they are actually funding the emissions reductions purported by each offset. In turn, the standard gives project developers and sellers the chance to prove the quality of their offsets. The VCS sets out eight broad criteria that a project must meet before being issued a VCU. Emissions reductions must be: (i) real, (ii) measurable, (iii) permanent, (iv) additional, (v) independently audited, (vi) unique, (vii) transparent and (viii) conservative.[8]

To receive VCUs, project developers must be able to prove that emissions reductions have actually taken place and that they have been measured using specific tools with a realistic emissions baseline. To address permanence for AFOLU projects, the VCS uses a pooled AFOLU buffer account that holds non-tradable buffer credits to cover the non-permanence risk associated with such projects. For reductions to be 'additional', they must not have occurred in the 'business-as-usual' scenario if the project had not taken place. The VCS's independent auditing and transparency requirements aim to ensure that projects are open, accessible and free from bias or corruption. Reductions are deemed 'unique' if they

7 Stephen Donofrio and others, 'Financing Emissions Reductions for the Future: State of the Voluntary Carbon Markets 2019' Forest Trends (December 2019) www.forest-trends.org/wp-content/uploads/2019/12/SOVCM2019.pdf accessed 11 April 2022.

8 Verra, 'Verified Carbon Standard Program Guide' v4.1 (20 January 2022) https://verra.org/wp-content/uploads/2022/01/VCS-Program-Guide_v4.1.pdf accessed 22 April 2022.

are accounted within a single VCU, rather than being double counted across multiple units or credits. Finally, the VCS requires conservative emissions estimates.

The foregoing criteria indicate that numerous challenges make accurate emissions offsetting difficult. After Verra and third-party verification bodies confirm that a project meets the VCS's criteria, that project is then placed on a centralised and accessible registry that tracks all projects and VCUs. Thus, the VCS has created a governance framework for voluntary carbon markets that makes this standard attractive both to project developers and to buyers. Still, it bears noting that the VCS competes with a number of other carbon certification programmes. Though its competitors do not necessarily threaten directly the VCS's integrity, the lack of a single cohesive governance framework for voluntary carbon markets raises certain issues. Without a single centralised registry, there is a risk that emissions reductions are double counted and sold under multiple certification schemes. Recognising this risk, the VCS and other carbon standards have taken a number of actions to ensure that projects are not sold under multiple certification schemes.

Market segmentation with multiple standards and narrowly focussed offsetting initiatives can also usher in risks of carbon leakage. Though the VCS does set out standards and guidelines for how projects may mitigate leakage, it is difficult to fully ensure that emissive economic activity does not shift elsewhere. Henders and Ostwald have recognised that the VCS leads other standards in leakage prevention, but it still struggles to account for leakage across international borders.[9] Partially in response to these risks, there is a strong push to implement the UNFCCC's 'REDD+' forest management framework on a jurisdictional, rather than an individual project, level.[10] Verra has responded to this with its own Jurisdictional and Nested REDD+ (JNR) accounting and verification framework.[11]

It is also worth noting that compliance with the VCS relies on a project having access to sufficient resources for MRV. Measuring emissions reductions is difficult, particularly in AFOLU. To accurately ensure that AFOLU emission reductions are additional and permanent, a project might need to monitor the carbon stock of large swathes of forest. The VCS also charges fees for registration, methodology approval and consulting assistance. Project developers must therefore have the technological and financial resources to ensure accurate MRV procedures. Thus, there are clear barriers to entry for individuals or groups looking to reduce emissions in exchange for VCUs.

Though the VCS primarily focusses on the integrity of emissions reductions, it also dictates that projects cause 'no net harm' to local communities or the native

9 Sabine Henders and Madelene Ostwald, 'Forest Carbon Leakage Quantification Methods and Their Suitability for Assessing Leakage in REDD' (2012) 3 *Forests* 33.

10 Donofrio and others (n 7).

11 Verra, 'Jurisdictional and Nested REDD Framework' (2020) https://verra.org/project/jurisdictional-and-nested-redd-framework/ accessed 16 August 2020.

environment.[12] Further, Verra administers separate standards that support projects that offer additional societal or socio-economic co-benefits. These include the Climate, Community and Biodiversity (CCB) standards and the Sustainable Development Verified Impact Standard (SD VISta). Empirical evidence suggests that buyers are attracted to standards that offer the potential co-benefits of mitigating these risks – in 2018, projects registered under both the CCB standards and the VCS saw the highest spike in demand across the entire voluntary carbon market.[13]

On balance, the VCS is an example of a comprehensive framework through which project developers can verify the integrity of offsets sold to voluntary purchasers. However, as voluntary carbon markets continue to grow, it is important to address a number of potential issues. There are potential accessibility and cost barriers associated with measuring and registering emissions reductions. Further, buyers may still lack certainty that units represent real emissions reductions. Emerging technologies may therefore play an important role in creating more effective and efficient voluntary markets.

7.3 HOW DLT AND OTHER EMERGING DIGITAL TECHNOLOGIES CAN SOLVE TECHNICAL ISSUES AND REGULATORY GAPS IN VOLUNTARY MARKETS

As earlier chapters have set out, blockchain and other emerging technologies could offer significant benefits to carbon markets. Voluntary markets are no exception, but they face unique challenges and opportunities when implementing new technologies. Technology can play an important role in voluntary markets at two key stages: when undertaking emissions-reducing projects for verification with a standard, and when trading credits. This section will examine how voluntary markets such as the CDM and the VCS may benefit from deploying a range of emerging technologies.

7.3.1 *MRV Processes*

The first stage at which emerging digital technologies may have a significant impact is in the MRV of offset projects, particularly AFOLU projects. As explained, carbon markets face serious risks that offsets do not represent real emissions reductions. Emerging digital technologies may allow project developers to more accurately measure their emissions reductions. This improves the integrity of offsets and ultimately ensures that voluntary carbon markets play an important role in the global fight against climate change. Carbon offsetting has been criticised based on fundamental reliability issues,[14] so solving these underlying issues is imperative to voluntary markets' efficacy and political viability.

[12] Verra (n 8) at 38.

[13] Donofrio and others (n 7).

[14] See, for example, the European Union's removal of international carbon credits from its ETS past 2020.

Chapter 4 examined possible links between the Internet of Things (IoT), systems in which a network of physical objects collect and convey data, and DLT. This technology has promising applications in a number of emission abatement contexts. Sensor technologies, such as Continuous Emission Measurement Systems (CEMS), have become an established feature in a number of industrial compliance settings, but evolving capabilities and declining costs make such technologies increasingly viable for a broader set of applications. One example is the type of projects that aim to prevent deforestation: sensors can be attached to trees to collect an array of data related to a forest's growth cycle and broader environmental factors.[15] Being able to collect this information in real-time could reduce the need for site visits while providing accurate and timely information on forest carbon stocks. This technology can also play a key role in protecting biodiversity so that offset projects minimise negative externalities and reap co-benefits. Though IoT deployment in the context of forest management is mostly new or small-scale, falling costs are making this option increasingly viable for project developers.[16] Aside from ensuring greater accuracy of offsets and improving biodiversity, collecting forest data remotely could also reduce the cost to project developers who would otherwise need to organise site visits. Cost reductions can increase accessibility and improve outcomes for project developers, which supports voluntary markets' broader sustainable development efforts. Ultimately, although it is still in its early stages, using IoT technology offers a number of potential benefits for carbon offsetting and removal projects.

Artificial intelligence (AI) is another emerging digital technology that could enhance forest monitoring and carbon offsets. When combined with data collected from remote sensors or satellites, machine learning can identify changes in forest areas over time. These processes may be further improved through the use of drones, which can provide more detailed images of tree populations. This technology may make an impact on two key areas. First, it may streamline carbon stock estimation processes to give project developers more relevant and accurate information at a cheaper cost.[17] Second, it may be used to predict and detect forest fires and other risks that are hazardous and counterproductive to offset projects.[18] These functions serve to mitigate permanence risks discussed earlier, ultimately increasing the efficiency and accuracy of offsetting projects. Like IoT remote sensing, machine learning has yet to see widespread deployment in offset projects. Nonetheless, using

[15] Jennifer Gabrys, 'Smart Forests and Data Practices: From the Internet of Trees to Planetary Governance' [2020] *Big Data & Soc* 1.

[16] Barbara Hock and others, 'The Internet of Things for Forestry: New Concepts, New Opportunities' (2016) 60 *NZ J Forestry* 27.

[17] Rosiane De Freitas and others, 'Estimating Amazon Carbon Stock Using AI-Based Remote Sensing' (2020) 63 *Comms ACM* 46.

[18] Nikos Aspragathos, 'From Pillars to AI Technology-Based Forest Fire Protection Systems' in Yang (Cindy) Yi (ed), *Intelligent System and Computing* (IntechOpen 2020) https://doi.org/10.5772/intechopen.86904 accessed 11 April 2022.

AI for forest preservation is being actively explored in both research and industry, indicating that it may proliferate in the coming years.

7.3.2 *Trading Credits Using DLT*

Emerging technologies clearly offer a range of functions for projects implemented under voluntary standards. Like other carbon markets, however, such voluntary standards may also implement emerging technologies into their underlying structure. Voluntary standards can implement DLT to move away from a centralised ledger and to execute transactions using smart contracts. Decentralisation generally offers two key benefits to market participants – transparency and accessibility. Activities in markets such as the VCS are already fairly transparent: information on VCU issuances and retirements is publicly accessible on the Verra registry. However, DLT could record the activities of a carbon unit over the course of its life without requiring a centrally managed registry. This information would be easily accessible to prospective buyers looking to ensure that an offset complies with a certain standard, or to choose offset projects that meet individual preferences such as location or project type. A study of the Scandinavian aviation industry, for instance, found that there was consumer demand for increased transparency regarding airlines' offsetting activities.[19] Although it is unclear how this demand would ultimately affect carbon market activities, the study concluded that DLT could be important in terms of affording carbon offsetters and their customers greater transparency. Another key advantage of the increased access to real-time data provided by DLT would be the elimination of information asymmetries. Carbon markets thrive when information is shared among project developers, intermediaries and offsetters, and DLT's ability to influence this change may play a key role in broader global climate policy.

Another benefit is that DLT offers the opportunity to address certain criticisms of the CDM. A common perception is that the CDM resulted in a process that was too bureaucratic and not flexible enough to serve the needs of individual parties.[20] Some project developers and members of the industry have suggested that the CDM Executive Board's approach to project approval has been too strict, emphasising 'rigour at the expense of pragmatism' and thus affecting potentially beneficial projects.[21] While adherence to stringent standards is certainly needed to ensure the integrity of offset crediting systems, the transaction costs associated with lengthy

[19] Betina H Gudim and Yvette Carolan, *Blockchain in Voluntary Carbon Markets: A Case Study in the Scandinavian Aviation Industry* (Copenhagen Business School 2020).

[20] Andrei Marcu, 'Governance of Article 6 of the Paris Agreement and Lessons Learned from the Kyoto Protocol' (2017) www.cigionline.org/publications/governance-article-6-paris-agreement-and-lessons-learned-kyoto-protocol accessed 11 April 2022.

[21] Charlotte Streck, 'The Governance of the Clean Development Mechanism: The Case for Strength and Stability' [2007] *Env Liability* 91 www.gppi.net/media/Streck_2007_The_Governance.pdf accessed 18 April 2022.

approval and review procedures could be lowered through the use of DLT and its ability to substitute elements of current, centralised governance processes.

Though shifting to a DLT-based architecture would not necessarily influence the requirements underlying current standards, it would change the mechanism with which credits are issued and traded. Automating verification and registration processes using DLT could allow for more reasonable transaction costs, which Bushnell identifies as a key consideration in carbon markets.[22] This offers clear benefits to both offset buyers and project developers, and could ultimately result in a higher number of credits being issued and traded. Further, Schletz, Franke and Salomo (2020) have noted additional benefits to efficiency and reliability when combining emerging technologies used in MRV processes with a DLT-based trading architecture.[23] Taken together, these innovations could lead to more efficient and less expensive voluntary standards, reducing the resources required to access these markets and therefore increasing accessibility. Given the competitive nature of the broader voluntary market landscape, this should also benefit standards that choose to shift to a DLT-based market. Increased transparency, accessibility and efficiency should be attractive to potential market participants, which might give voluntary standards an edge over their competitors. These qualities should not only influence the particular standards or platforms that buyers and sellers choose but, more importantly, have the potential to attract completely new voluntary market participants.

As has been explored in other parts of this book, DLT has the potential to improve the accounting and tracking of carbon units; it can help counteract risks such as double counting. By automating double-entry bookkeeping, DLT can create a transparent network that protects against emissions reductions being counted twice at any stage in the offsetting process. This has clear benefits for both those administering private voluntary standards and centrally governed standards such as the CDM or any potential successor mechanism. Companies that voluntarily purchase carbon credits can be more certain that they are the only party funding a certain emissions reduction. Perhaps more importantly, preventing double counting is vital to ensuring that national governments do not claim the same emissions reductions. Thus, a DLT-based standard with global scope that countries can use to reach their emissions targets would offer significant benefits over the model underlying the CDM, and ultimately align better with the aims of the Paris Agreement.

On balance, new technologies have the potential to produce efficient and accurate carbon measuring that could be combined with cheaper, more transparent DLT-based carbon markets. Thus, a broad shift towards modernisation and innovation in carbon markets is likely to benefit voluntary standards and those that use them to buy

22 James B Bushnell, 'The Economics of Carbon Offsets' in Don Fullerton and Catherine Wolfram (eds), *The Design and Implementation of US Climate Policy* (University of Chicago Press 2012) ch 12.

23 Marco Schletz, Laura A Franke and Søren Salomo, 'Blockchain Application for the Paris Agreement Carbon Market Mechanism – A Decision Framework and Architecture' (2020) 12 *Sustainability* 5069.

or sell carbon credits. Section 7.4 outlines potential issues with utilising these techniques in the CDM and the VCS to give a broad picture of how voluntary markets might shift in response to emerging technologies.

7.4 EXAMPLES OF VOLUNTARY CARBON MARKET ACTIVITIES THAT USE DLT

Established voluntary markets have yet to adopt DLT-based approaches to carbon trading. However, the voluntary market landscape is also in a unique position to pioneer the implementation of these technologies, as verification bodies are private entities that can be established without assistance from the government. This section provides brief explanations of a number of private initiatives that have integrated, or are currently integrating, DLT in their carbon trading activities.

7.4.1 *Carbonex*

Carbonex is an enterprise that seeks to help solve global warming by creating a trusted, open, efficient and reliable global market on which to trade carbon credits.[24] Through its platform, Carbonex aims to use blockchain to simplify and improve access to the entire carbon credit life cycle through the creation of a verifiable carbon credit register, thereby forcing inclusion, uniformity, liquidity and compliance, and so solving pre-existent issues of transparency, market fragmentation and inadequate environmental enforcement. This is achieved by using DLT to minimise the administrative burden, operational inefficiencies and audit expenses, resulting in increased transparency of the current system. The expectation is that the application will predominantly be used by corporations to acquire carbon credits in order to offset the costs of compliance with targets and policies set by local governments to achieve their country's NDC (nationally determined contribution) targets.

In addition, the platform will integrate with existing ETSs. The network is expected to be structured with a node in all countries that have ratified the Paris Agreement. In addition, there is the potential for countries to have an independent platform owing to local constraints, although this could create its own inefficiencies and reduce jurisdictional emissions displacement.[25] The main entities that may require access to the blockchain are the United Nations Framework Convention on Climate Change (UNFCCC), local governments and recognised supranational organisations. Based on these identified participants, 'write access' is expected to

[24] Carbonex, 'Whitepaper: The Complete Carbon Credit Network Solution' (2018) https://ico.carbonex.co/static/static/documents/carbonex-whitepaper.en_2Pqi9.pdf accessed 11 April 2022.

[25] Mengya Zhang, Yong Liu and Yunpeng Su, 'Comparison of Carbon Emission Trading Schemes in the European Union and China' (2017) 5 *Climate* 70.

be limited. Conversely, 'read access' should be open as public accountability is a fundamental tenet of the platform.

7.4.2 *IBM Energy Blockchain Labs*

Tech giant IBM has partnered with Energy Blockchain Labs to tackle the issue of climate change by creating a general distributed energy ledger platform.[26] This is a carbon asset development platform that is based on IBM's blockchain technology and has been used by organisations to meet legislative carbon emissions reduction quotas. The carbon trading platform created by IBM aims to close the gap between the green economy and finance by compiling carbon asset development methodologies into smart contracts and thereby automating the calculation of carbon quotas for higher-emission organisations. This facilitates information sharing, transparency, monitoring by regulators and accountability in the carbon market. This project uses Hyperledger Fabric, a foundation for blockchain applications.[27]

The IBM Blockchain Energy Labs project works by combining the carbon asset development ledger with a universal distributed ledger to collect the environmental data for all participants. The blockchain technology allows for the secure storage of information and provides transparency to all participants. Easy access to the data available allows participants to track their emissions and adjust their practices to achieve the desired environmental goals while also keeping all relevant private and public bodies informed of any changes.

7.4.3 *ClimateTrade*

ClimateTrade is another online service provider that uses DLT to create a platform that assists with the tracking and sale of carbon credits.[28] Through DLT, every transaction and its associated value are visible to anyone who accesses the platform.

ClimateTrade works by allowing the offset of emissions through carbon credit purchases from voluntary or mandatory carbon markets directly in ClimateTrade. Using DLT allows the storage of all the information associated with each transaction to be visible to the purchaser. The ClimateTrade markets are linked to projects verified by large standards such as the CDM, the VCS and the Gold Standard. The projects focus on all areas of climate change from renewable energy production to carbon capture and storage. Users of the platform also calculate the carbon footprint,

[26] IBM, 'Energy Blockchain Labs Inc.' *IBM* (2018) www.ibm.com/case-studies/energy-blockchain-labs-inc accessed 9 January 2021.

[27] Elli Androulaki and others, 'Hyperledger Fabric: A Distributed Operating System for Permissioned Blockchains' (Proceedings of the Thirteenth EuroSys Conference (EuroSys '18), art 30, April 2018) 1–15 https://doi.org/10.1145/3190508.3190538 accessed 11 April 2022.

[28] 'ClimateTrade' (2020) www.climatetrade.com/ accessed 10 January 2021.

offset the emissions, prepare sustainability reports and guide others on the communication strategy.

7.4.4 *Nori*

One of the initiatives to tackle the problem of excess carbon emissions is to invest in farming regenerative practices that return excess carbon dioxide from the atmosphere to the soil. Nori is a company that uses blockchain to create a market for carbon removals, for the moment focussed on soil carbon projects, and allows participants to offset their emissions. Nori distributes Ethereum-based carbon removal tokens that represent one tonne of carbon dioxide that has been removed from the atmosphere for a minimum of ten years.[29]

Nori works by linking data management in the farming sector with financial incentives. The first step in the process takes place when farmers remove carbon from the atmosphere and store it in the soil. The second step involves an independent third-party verifier quantifying and verifying the carbon removals. The third step involves the party wishing to offset their emissions by purchasing carbon removals from the farmers and receiving a certificate from Nori to prove this. The information regarding the carbon removals, the farmers and the fields where the carbon is stored is all kept in a blockchain database controlled by Nori. Additionally, the use of blockchain technology in the MRV process mitigates the use of double counting, since the public distributed ledger is immutable.

7.4.5 *Moss.Earth*

Moss was established as the first environmental fintech company to help address climate change with the specific aim of eliminating deforestation in the Amazon rainforest. Moss has created a digital platform for selling carbon credits to individuals and companies, also using Ethereum.[30] The carbon credits are linked to local projects including the Ituxi and Juma projects in Amazonas, Brazil.

The Moss platform serves as an accessible and simple virtual space for individuals to buy, store and use their carbon credits. Moss buys carbon credits from various projects in Brazil that prevent carbon dioxide emissions or capture them from the atmosphere. It allows individuals to buy carbon credits directly from Moss on its digital platform and then carry them in a digital wallet for future compensation.

[29] Nori, 'A Blockchain-Based Marketplace for Removing Carbon Dioxide from the Atmosphere' (2019) https://nori.com/resources/white-paper accessed 18 April 2022.

[30] Luis Filipe Adaime, 'Moss Carbon Credit MCO2 Token White Paper' (2020) https://mco2token.moss.earth/ accessed 18 April 2022.

7.5 IMPLEMENTING DLT AND OTHER NEW TECHNOLOGIES IN VOLUNTARY CARBON MARKETS

As we have seen, DLT can bring clear benefits to voluntary markets and carbon offsetting, but deploying this technology in markets requires careful consideration of existing rules and future risks. Currently, there is a lack of clarity regarding the future of the CDM or any potential successor mechanism under the Paris Agreement. It is therefore difficult to confidently state an implementation strategy for including DLT within an international carbon offsetting market established under the UNFCCC. When deciding on the path forward for the CDM or a successor mechanism, policymakers should aim to at least leave open the possibility of deploying DLT and other emerging technologies. As for private standards in the voluntary carbon market, stakeholders can take a number of steps to deploy DLT. This section will again use the VCS as a case study to reveal potential opportunities and hurdles when implementing DLT in voluntary standards. It will then offer broad recommendations for policymakers looking to facilitate DLT-based voluntary markets.

7.5.1 *Solutions Offered to Voluntary Carbon Markets by a Crypto-legal Structure: CDM as a Case Study*

To address issues discussed in Section 7.2, the entire CDM could be coded modularly to form a crypto-legal structure mitigating both the issuance of CERs to substandard offsetting projects and double counting with other carbon markets. Thus, DLT could provide the same regulatory services to the CDM as those discussed in Chapter 6 with regard to the EU ETS. Using the same design principles of the EU ETS blockchain, the CDM blockchain could use a data-driven approach to leverage multiple approval procedures through running smart contracts on a permissionless blockchain storing the CDM registry. In doing so, the CDM could make use of the key modules DLT provides:

KYC and Doorkeeper modules: The CDM blockchain could begin with a 'KYC' or 'Doorkeeper' module similar to the EU ETS blockchain. The targets against which to enforce would be all project developers as well as independent auditors, known as designated operational entities (DOEs), at the points of account opening, CER issuance and transfer requests.

Issuance Module: The 'Issuance Module' would be pivoted on a smart contract that does not approve the issuance of CERs until all CDM requirements are met. For instance, an afforestation project in a developing country would not be issued CERs until all the oracles provide CDM methodology-compliant information that triggers the smart contract. Ideally with the help of AI and IoT, these oracles could upload environmental data from satellite imagery and remote sensors, as well as audit reports from DOEs, local non-governmental organisations (NGOs) or financial institutions that certify that project developers can maintain sufficient funds for the project. During validation and verification, the project developers could release a public key to be matched with the private key of the DOE so that only the authorised DOE can sign off the offsetting project. The token-convertible carbon credits could then be stored on a distributed CDM registry on a permissionless blockchain for public scrutiny.

Export Module: The smart contract in the 'Issuance Module' could trigger another smart contract supporting the 'Export Module'. When the project developer places a 'transfer order' to other carbon markets, the regulatory logic would ask the nodes to collectively scan the hashes of the CER/token against the cancellation record on the distributed CDM registry, the import record of the other markets' registry and the national inventories of the hosting country. This would help detect 'extremely similar' offsetting projects. To avoid double counting, the export of CERs to other carbon markets would not be allowed until the Executive Board confirms that the 'extreme similarities' are justified through additional verification.

7.5.1.1 Regulatory Services Delivered by DLT

In this crypto-legal structure, a DLT-supported CDM could avert the illegitimate issuance and sales of CERs. This would help deliver the five regulatory services outlined in Chapter 1:

(1) **Uniqueness**: In the 'KYC' and 'Issuance' modules, adopting blockchain public and private keys in lieu of a password deviates from the current CDM registry account-opening and credit-issuance procedures. Project developers using a public key and DOEs a unique private key would ensure that the validation and verification process is secure. Only the authorised DOE can use its private key to confirm that project data are accurately filed with no changes since the time of submission, signalling that it agrees that the project has complied with CDM rules. Hacking into a DOE's server to alter project data remotely would be very difficult.

(2) **Validity**: The CDM blockchain provides multiple layers of validation through the smart contract underpinning the 'Issuance Module'. With the help of AI and IoT, the smart contract, which validates the outputs by corroborating the data from many more sources than DOEs using legacy mechanisms, could significantly reduce the validation cost and shorten the validation period – there are currently seven steps in a CDM project life cycle with six actors performing validation/verification services for different phases. With more than 200 different approved methodologies in the CDM, it is beneficial to have blockchain private keys embed the metadata into each record to prove the validity and uniformity of sensitive project data and

confirm conditional contributions required to trigger the smart contract issuing the CERs.[31]

(3) **Consensus**: The consensus service offered by the CDM blockchain is the same as the EU ETS blockchain proposed in Chapter 6. In the 'Export Module', for example, the robust consensus algorithm makes it extremely difficult to gain fraudulent or illegitimate access to any single registry and tamper with CER transfer records. All nodes with the same good copies of registry records will not accept any corrupted copy as a basis of carbon credit transaction.

(4) **Immutability**: The CDM blockchain features a distributed CDM registry that could be linked with other markets' registries and potentially national inventories. This satisfies the requirement in Appendix D of Decision 3/CMP.1 that 'the CDM registry shall be in the form of a standardized electronic database which contains, inter alia, common data elements relevant to the issuance, holding, transfer and acquisition of CERs'.[32] The consensus algorithm and modular security features mentioned above help create an immutable distributed ledger for CDM project data.

(5) **Authentication**: The CDM blockchain offers KYC and Doorkeeper modules that authenticate every user at the point of account registration and credit transfers. Currently, a serial-numbered certificate is issued to evidence the cancellation of credits on the CDM registry. If the CER is tokenised, any stakeholder can verify the authenticity of the certificate on the permissionless blockchain, enhancing public trust in the CDM.

7.5.1.2 Disruptive Effects on Regulatory Enforcement

The CDM blockchain could replace or modify some regulatory functions being executed by the Executive Board. These disruptive effects can be framed using the three propositions of Chapter 2, Section 2.2.2.

(1) **Simplification of existing substantive law**: The multiple validation sources against which the DOEs' validation results are corroborated in the 'Issuance Module' smart contract may already be a fair monitoring of the DOEs' performance as per paragraph 21 of Decision 3/CMP.1(2005).[33] Therefore, implementation of paragraph 22 regarding the manual identification of significant deficiencies in the DOE's validation, verification or certification

[31] S Dunkel, 'How a Blockchain Network Can Ensure Compliance with Clean Development Mechanism Methodology and Reduce Uncertainty about Achieving Intended Nationally Determined Contributions' in A Marke (ed), *Transforming Climate Finance and Green Investment with Blockchains* (Academic Press 2018).

[32] UNFCCC Secretariat, 'Decision 3/CMP.1 (Appendix D)' (2006).

[33] UNFCCC Secretariat, 'Decision 3/CMP.1' (2006).

reports may no longer be necessary, and the Executive Board could directly consider its performance at the triennial re-accreditation process pursuant to paragraphs 53 and 20(d). As no CERs can be issued to offset projects not 'ticking all the boxes' on the smart contract, paragraph 22 mandating the acquisition and transfers of 'make-up' carbon savings by the subject DOE would become superfluous. The DOE performance monitoring-related regulations could be duly simplified.

(2) **Emergence of new legal elements and actors**: The CDM crypto-legal structure would introduce a breakthrough to the validation process of offset projects. In addition to reports by traditional DOEs, oracles could create an automated yet trusted verification platform for CDM projects, which may implicate a range of actors including NGOs, researchers and even local farmers. These new legal elements and actors should be covered in the material scope of the new CDM rules post-2020.

(3) **New patterns of enforcement and regulation**: The Executive Board would not control the distributed CDM registry for crowd management on the blockchain. The role of the Board would gradually shift from administering the registry to enhancing and maintaining the coding standards and AI algorithms so that they can regulate the project data type, format and quality feeding into the oracles that trigger the smart contracts in all modules. However, the Board should continue tackling cases dealing with issues such as additionality, which cannot be directly addressed by using DLT.

7.5.2 *Foreseeable Changes within the VCS and Other Voluntary Standards*

Although they are not legal instruments, standards like the VCS operate under strict rules and requirements that would need to be either complied with or modified when implementing new technologies. As outlined in Section 7.3, emerging technologies have the potential to shape carbon offsetting by optimising monitoring processes, particularly in AFOLU projects. At the monitoring stage, the extent to which projects utilise this technology depends largely on project developers themselves, rather than carbon standards. If monitoring forest loss through IoT or combining satellite data with AI proves accurate and efficient, the technology will likely disseminate among project developers regardless of any changes to the VCS. Thus, if it chooses to capitalise on these new methodologies, Verra should ensure that projects can effectively use these methods within the VCS's current rules and requirements.

Project developers must choose from specifically approved methodologies to have their offsets verified under the VCS. The list of approved methodologies is growing, and strategies that involve emerging technologies have already been approved.[34] The

[34] Terra Global Capital, 'VT0006 Tool for Calculating LULC Transitions and Deforestation Rates Using Incomplete Remote Sensing Images' (2016) https://verra.org/methodology/vt0006-tool-for-

extent to which the VCS adapts to DLT or AI monitoring techniques is therefore dependent on these technologies' ability to gain approval. In its *Methodology Requirements* document, the VCS sets out comprehensive requirements that methodologies must meet before gaining approval.[35] This is unlikely to prove a significant barrier to DLT or AI, but it does require fairly comprehensive data and information relating to the methodology. After assessing each methodology against these requirements, Verra opens up a thirty-day public consultation period during which stakeholders can comment on the methodology's viability.[36] Next, Verra will request an eligible validation or verification body to assess the methodology as it is implemented by a specific developer. After reviewing all relevant documentation, Verra will then grant the methodology final approval. Both DLT and AI-based methods have the potential to gain approval under the VCS provided that methodology developers follow this process.[37] Importantly, the time required for preparing to meet methodology requirements and following the multi-staged process means that emerging technologies' implementation into the VCS may cause a lag between a technology's development and its eventual deployment in VCS-accredited projects.

Both AI and DLT monitoring methods can be implemented within the VCS's current methodology approval framework, but DLT may also cause more fundamental changes to the standard's architecture. As discussed, registering and transacting carbon credits on a distributed ledger can make voluntary markets more accessible and efficient. As the VCS currently records all issues and retirements centrally on the Verra registry, the shift to DLT-based registration may be disruptive. As one of a number of large standards, the VCS faces particular challenges from this technological shift. In lieu of widespread adoption by any major standard, a number of smaller verification bodies that aim to utilise DLT have emerged. If distributed ledgers do make carbon registries significantly more efficient, both sellers and buyers may be attracted to these newer endeavours and the VCS's significant market share might decline. For instance, Aldyen Donnelly, head of carbon economics at Nori, is sceptical about large incumbent standards' ability to adapt to these technological changes and points to the lower cost of verification as a key advantage to Nori's service.[38]

Shifting to DLT-based approval and registration will not necessarily change the VCS's underlying function, but it could significantly affect its procedures. Every step from a project's initial submission through to a VCU's eventual retirement may be recorded on a distributed ledger, broadening the registry's transparency. This would

calculating-lulc-transitions-and-deforestation-rates-using-incomplete-remote-sensing-images-v1-0/ accessed 11 April 2022.

35 Verra, 'VCS Methodology Requirements v4.1' (20 January 2022) https://verra.org/wp-content/uploads/2022/01/VCS-Methodology-Requirements_v4.1.pdf accessed 22 April 2022.

36 ibid.

37 Note also that any methodology developed under the CDM may be used in VCS projects. For a webpage containing all currently approved methodologies, see https://verra.org/methodologies/ accessed 11 April 2022.

38 Interview with Aldyen Donnelly, Head of Carbon Economics, Nori (2 December 2020).

likely affect the VCS's registration and issuance process. To register a project, offset buyers and project proponents must submit a number of documents to Verra, including legal agreements that show the offset credit's transfer between the buyer, seller and any intermediaries.[39] If these transactions occur on a distributed ledger and are executed as smart contracts, Verra might be able to reduce the volume of documentation required during an issuance and registration request. This would streamline Verra's 'completeness review' process, as more relevant information would be easily accessible.[40] After any necessary accuracy reviews, projects would then automatically be registered on a distributed ledger. Relevant information such as a project's geodetic co-ordinates, which are currently used to avoid overlap, could be stored using DLT. Even registration fees themselves may eventually be payable through smart contracts, and VCUs could be issued and recorded similarly – through a transaction that could also be executed automatically with DLT.

The foregoing explanation indicates the wide-ranging effects of moving the VCS to a DLT-based standard. This largely reflects the potential of DLT as a whole. The extent to which the VCS will actually embrace DLT, however, is uncertain. Unlike employing IoT or AI techniques in MRV processes, creating a fully DLT-based VCS will require fundamental restructuring. It should also be noted that the Verra registry already has some qualities similar to those advantages offered by DLT. Information relating to every project is publicly available, and certain parts of the registration process are computer automated. Although DLT can offer transparency and efficiency benefits beyond this, given the relative youth of the Verra registry in its current form, a shift to a fully DLT-based approach may not be viable in the very short term. Still, as alluded to previously, if emerging competitors do prove cheaper and more efficient than the large incumbent standards, the VCS and other standards may be forced to implement some of these changes.

On the whole, implementing IoT and AI methodologies for carbon monitoring should be possible within the VCS's current framework. Moving the standard and registry to an entirely DLT-based platform, however, may require significant reform to current processes and requirements. Given that each voluntary standard operates under its own set of rules, it is difficult to assess the precise outcomes of this technological shift. Nonetheless, market participants would benefit from keeping abreast of changes to large voluntary standards, as well as of new markets run using DLT. Investors can play a unique and influential role in this arena by scrutinising companies' choice of carbon offset mechanism, which could result in a gravitational pull towards DLT-based standards if these prove more effective and less costly. Indeed, as was found in the aviation industry, consumers may also play a role in changing company behaviour in this regard.[41]

39 Verra, 'Registration and Issuance Process' (20 January 2022) https://verra.org/wp-content/uploads/2022/02/Registration-and-Issuance-Process_v4.1.pdf accessed 22 April 2022.

40 ibid.

41 Gudim and Carolan (n 19).

7.5.3 Governance Responses to Facilitate the Deployment of Emerging Technologies in Voluntary Markets

Although regulators do not directly control standards such as the VCS, national and international public bodies may nonetheless play a role in utilising emerging technologies in these markets. Intergovernmental bodies such as the UN's Climate Technology Centre and Network (CTCN) can provide capacity building services to local governments through technical assistance. The CTCN has already indicated its eagerness to help facilitate a combination of remote sensing and DLT for climate action in developing countries.[42] Increased access to and awareness of these technologies could make it easier for voluntary standards to use DLT and other technologies.

Another important international framework is REDD+. Here, an international shift towards the use of DLT would compel changes in the VCS and other standards that certify REDD+ projects. In a study on smart contracts and REDD+, Hoogenberk concludes that smart contracts are well-suited to executing results-based payments under REDD+, but cautions that knowledge gaps between the developed countries and the developing world may make implementation more difficult.[43] Thus, the CTCN's technical assistance may complement changes to REDD+ as it raises awareness of new technologies. Finally, certain compliance market regulators could influence voluntary standards where those standards' credits are traded on compliance markets. For example, the International Civil Aviation Organization's (ICAO) CORSIA framework, which will be analysed in detail in Chapter 8, accepts VCUs provided that they follow certain approved methodologies. By accepting VCUs using innovative methodologies, and perhaps even requiring certain innovation should these methods become accessible and prove effective, trading systems such as CORSIA could accelerate the use of new technologies under voluntary standards. Finally, domestic regulators may aid voluntary markets by supporting carbon project development. Donnelly warns against subsidising the verification processes themselves, as markets need to be resilient in the event of potential funding cuts, instead suggesting that resources are best spent on comprehensive soil carbon testing.[44]

At this point, it is worth noting how the aforementioned changes may interact with the wider effects of a new crypto-legal structure described in Chapters 3 and 5. Though private voluntary standards cannot directly influence the law, they may certainly benefit from a potential simplification of existing substantive law. Similar to regulated markets, voluntary standards using DLT could benefit from increased

[42] Woo Jin Lee and Rose Mwebaza, 'The Role of the Climate Technology Centre and Network as a Climate Technology and Innovation Matchmaker for Developing Countries' (2020) 12 *Sustainability*.

[43] Tim Hoogenberk, *Saving Forests with Smart Contracts: Implementing the REDD+ Mechanism under the Paris Agreement with Blockchain-Enabled Smart Contracts* (Tilburg University 2018).

[44] Interview with Aldyen Donnelly, Head of Carbon Economics, Nori (2 December 2020).

security, transparency of property rights, and automatic enforcement mechanisms, ultimately reducing the number of disputes between parties that need to be mediated or resolved. Voluntary standardisation bodies will also need to stay aware of the changing nature of legal actors and liability as aspects of their markets become self-executing. Depending on the jurisdiction, those responsible for coding a DLT-based market could be liable for an unintended outcome. This would likely result in the verification body itself being responsible for flaws in its system, requiring strong internal precautions against such failings. On the other hand, DLT would allow voluntary markets to take full advantage of new, efficient patterns of enforcement and regulation. Voluntary markets may therefore benefit from a permissive crypto-legal structure that recognises DLT's ability to transform carbon markets, while protecting against potential new challenges posed by emerging technologies.

7.6 CONCLUSION

Carbon offsetting gives companies, countries and individuals the chance to reduce their emissions while helping to sustainably finance mitigation in important and sometimes neglected sectors, such as AFOLU, and regions, notably in the developing world. Thus, a number of public and private initiatives have established voluntary carbon markets in order to verify emissions reductions that can then be traded as credits between different market participants. As this chapter has outlined, however, a number of technical and governance issues can impede the effectiveness and efficiency of these voluntary markets. Emerging technologies have the potential to improve MRV processes, and DLT could create more affordable and accessible markets.

Examining the VCS and the CDM elucidated a number of key points about implementing new technology in private voluntary markets. Remote sensing, AI and IoT applications can all help improve offsetting MRV processes, and standards such as the VCS may accommodate this through existing methodology approval processes. Operating trading platforms themselves using DLT is a more fundamental shift that could enhance the voluntary markets' transparency, accessibility and efficiency. The VCS would need to alter its methods fairly significantly in order to make this change, so it is unclear when established voluntary standards might use DLT in this way. In any case, a number of new platforms have recently emerged that offer DLT-based carbon markets, so broader change across the voluntary market landscape may be on the horizon. To create the best conditions for this change, international organisations and co-operative initiatives could help build technological capacity in the developing world, push for the use of DLT to support international programmes such as REDD+ and accept credits that effectively use these technologies in compliance markets.

8

The Carbon Offsetting and Reduction Scheme for International Aviation (CORSIA)

Dessanin Ewèdew Thierry Awesso

8.1 INTRODUCTION

The Paris Agreement, under the United Nations Framework Convention on Climate Change (UNFCCC) adopted in 2015, does not cover emissions from international shipping or aviation. To reduce the international aviation impact on climate change,[1] the International Civil Aviation Organization (ICAO) has designed a global carbon market-based measure (MBM) for offsetting emissions from international flights, namely the Carbon Offsetting and Reduction Scheme for International Aviation (CORSIA). Section 8.2 aims to provide an overview of the current governance framework.

8.2 CURRENT GOVERNANCE FRAMEWORK AND GAPS/CHALLENGES IN CORSIA

8.2.1 *Current Governance Framework*

Adopted through ICAO's Assembly Resolution 39–3,[2] CORSIA aims to achieve ICAO's global aspirational goal of carbon-neutral growth from 2020. It is the first global MBM for any industry sector. The offsetting programme will be phased in over fifteen years, with a pilot phase running from 2021 through 2023, during which all of the 193 ICAO countries can opt in or out, then a second voluntary phase from 2024 through 2026, and a final phase running from 2027 through 2035 that is mandatory for all ICAO countries. Exemptions are given to member states that contribute minor amounts to overall CO_2 emissions (as determined by their international aviation activities in revenue tonne kilometres in the year 2018) and to least

[1] David S Lee and others, 'Aviation and Global Climate Change in the 21st Century' (2009) 43 *Atmospheric Env* 3520; Susanne Becken and Brendan Mackey, 'What Role for Offsetting Aviation Greenhouse Gas Emissions in a Deep-Cut Carbon World?' [2017] *J Air Transp Manag* 71; Char-lee J McLennan and others, 'Voluntary Carbon Offsetting: Who Does It?' [2014] *Tourism Manag* 194.

[2] ICAO, Resolution A39-3: Consolidated statement of continuing ICAO policies and practices related to environmental protection – Global Market-based Measure (MBM) scheme 2016.

developed, small island developing and landlocked developing member states that opt not to participate in the scheme. Pre-Covid-19, the ICAO agreed that, during the pilot phase, the average emissions over the period 2019 to 2020 should be used as a baseline measure. In practice, aeroplane operators have begun monitoring emissions since January 2019 and will then cap emissions at 2020 levels beginning in 2021.[3] However, the Covid-19 outbreak has resulted in a dramatic decrease in the aviation industry's emissions for the year 2020, which has led to the ICAO's decision to use only 2019 emissions as the baseline period for calculating compensation requirements.[4] The ICAO Council (the Council) has confirmed that 2019 emissions shall be used for 2020 emissions during the pilot phase. Even though CORSIA will only be a voluntary scheme until 2027, it is interesting to analyse such an essential instrument for the global carbon market.

Periodic review will allow the Council to make informed recommendations to the ICAO Assembly on whether it is necessary to adjust the scheme's next phases. A periodic review of CORSIA will be undertaken by the Council every three years from 2022. A special review will take place by the end of 2032 to decide the scheme's termination, its extension, or any other improvements of the scheme beyond 2035.[5]

In brief, CORSIA is a route-based system that applies only to routes that connect participating member states. The aim of this is to provide equal treatment to all aircraft operators on the same route. Besides, monitoring, reporting and verification (MRV) will be crucial for successfully implementing CORSIA, which requires reliable information on CO_2 emissions, and compliance with offsetting requirements. The ICAO CORSIA CO2 Estimation and Reporting Tool is an ICAO tool to help aircraft operators estimate and report their international aviation emissions (Annex 16, Volume IV, Appendix 3). The International Air Transport Association (IATA) has created a platform known as FRED+ (Fuel Reporting and Emissions Database) to facilitate the reporting of CO_2 emissions for aircraft operators and member states subject to CORSIA. This tool can also be used by authorities to administer CORSIA and facilitate the secure communication of information between aeroplane operators and their administrating authority. Operators can also use FRED+ independently of their administering authority to compile their emissions report, undergo the verification processes, and export

3 Melissa Gallant, 'International Airlines Are Shaping Up As Big Force in Carbon Offsetting – Ecosystem Marketplace' (2018) www.ecosystemmarketplace.com/articles/international-airlines-are-shaping-up-as-big-force-in-carbon-offsetting/ accessed 15 March 2020.

4 Greenair, 'EU and US to Back CORSIA Baseline Change Proposal despite Warnings of Unintended Consequences on GreenAir Online' (2020) www.greenaironline.com/news.php?viewStory=2706 accessed 18 June 2020. Council of the European Union, 'Aviation Emissions: EU Adopts Its Position on Adjusted CORSIA Baseline to Take Account of the Consequences of COVID-19 Pandemic – Consilium' (2020) www.consilium.europa.eu/en/press/press-releases/2020/06/09/aviation-emissions-eu-adopts-its-position-on-adjusted-corsia-baseline-to-take-account-of-the-consequences-of-covid-19-pandemic/ accessed 18 June 2020.

5 ICAO, 'Session 1: Overview of CORSIA Introduction to the CORSIA and Resolution A39-3 ICAO Secretariat', *ICAO Regional Workshop on CORSIA* (2018).

the verified emissions report and supporting documentation for submission to their administrating authority.[6] An independent third-party verifier operates the platform. It connects the airline operators with their state authority to ensure the accurate transmission of data regarding fuel, emissions and operational efficiency.

All ICAO member states, regardless of whether or not they participate in CORSIA, with aircraft operators conducting international flights, producing more than 10,000 tonnes of CO_2 annually, are required to monitor, report and verify CO_2 emissions from these flights every year from 2019. Additionally, ICAO member states taking part in CORSIA need to ensure that their aircraft operators comply with CORSIA's offsetting requirements every three years, starting in 2021, in addition to annual CO_2 MRV. Monitoring of CO_2 emissions is done with either a fuel use monitoring method (there are five currently acceptable methods) or the ICAO CORSIA CO_2 Estimation and Reporting Tool (CERT). Following this, CO_2 emissions are reported from aircraft operators to their state authority and from the state authorities to ICAO.

Independent verification aims to check whether CO_2 emissions information is accurate and free of errors.[7] The aircraft operator must engage an accredited and independent verification body to verify its annual emissions report. The verification body must then conduct verification according to ISO 14064-3:2006[8] and the CORSIA requirements described in Annex 16, Volume IV, Appendix 6.[9] Verification is an essential part of CORSIA; it ensures the accuracy of the information related to the amount of CO_2 emissions from international flights, the purchase of emissions units from eligible programmes to address offsetting requirements, and the cancellation of eligible units.

One crucial element of CORSIA will be the Aviation Carbon Exchange (ACE), a centralised marketplace for CORSIA-eligible emission units where airlines and other aviation stakeholders can trade CO_2 emissions reductions for compliance or voluntary offsetting purposes. The Exchange will work by providing a secure platform where airlines can access real-time data with full price transparency. This platform's potential benefit is that the system will probably be more efficient and trustworthy as a result.

To ensure the offsetting programme's success, the 39th ICAO Assembly requested the Council to set up a consolidated central registry, under the auspices of ICAO, for operationalisation no later than 1 January 2021:[10] the CORSIA Central Registry (CCR). The CCR is an information management system that allows states to submit CORSIA-relevant information to ICAO, and ICAO to store this information,

6 ICAO, 'Agenda Item 17: Environmental Protection-Carbon Offsetting and Reduction Scheme for International Aviation (CORSIA). IATA Support for the Implementation of Corsia through FRED+' www.iata.org/FRED. accessed 6 September 2020.

7 ICAO, *Annex 16 – Environmental Protection – Volume IV – Carbon Offsetting and Reduction Scheme for International Aviation (CORSIA)* (ICAO 2018) ch 2 www.icao.int/environmental-protection/CORSIA/Pages/SARPs-Annex-16-Volume-IV.aspx.

8 ISO 14064–3:2006 Greenhouse gases – Part 3: Specification with guidance for the validation and verification of greenhouse gas assertions.

9 ICAO, *Annex 16* (n 7).

10 ICAO Resolution A39-3 (n 2) para 20 g.

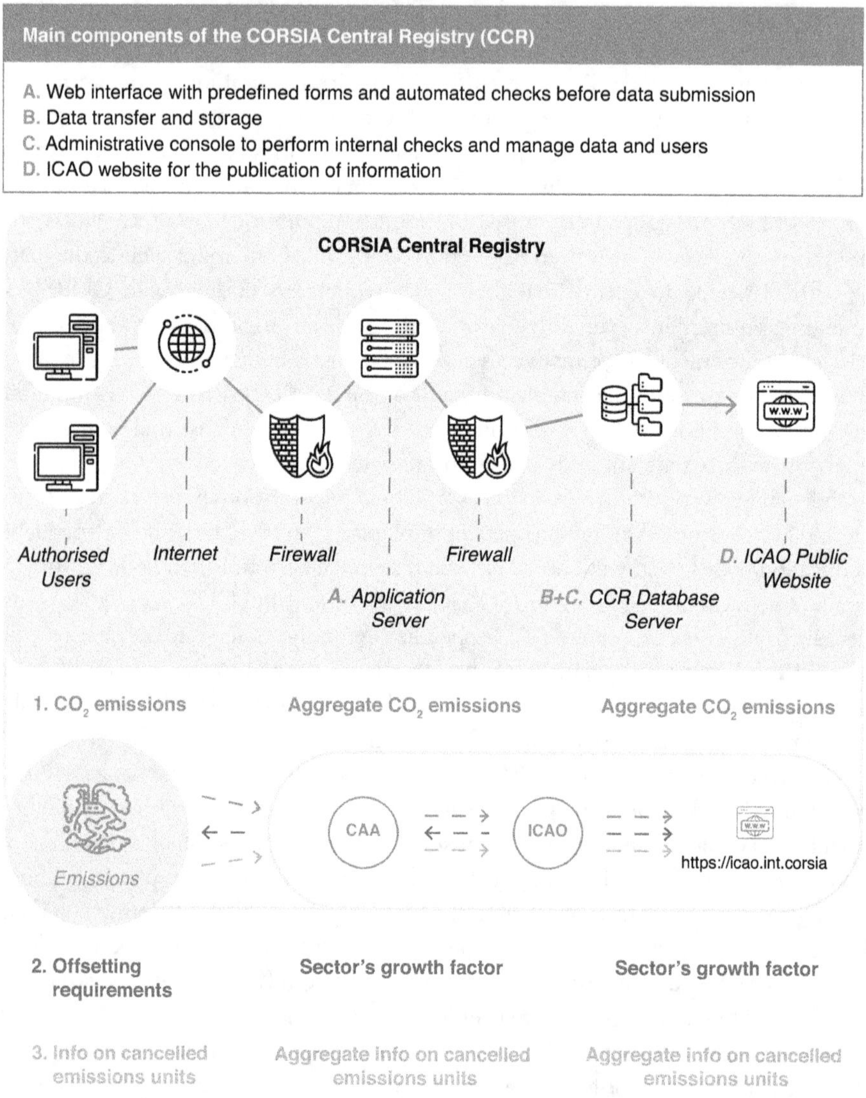

FIGURE 8.1 Main components of the CORSIA Central Registry
Source: Adapted from the CORSIA at a Glance Series, Leaflet No 6 (2019) www.icao.int/environmental-protection/CORSIA/Documents/CORSIA%20Leaflets/CorsiaLeaflet-EN-6-WEB.pdf accessed 22 April 2022.

perform calculations, report data back to member states and make aggregate information publicly available[11](see Figure 8.1).

11 ICAO, 'CORSIA Central Registry' *CORSIA At a Glance Series* http://icao.int.corsia accessed 14 March 2020.

As regards governance of the CCR, the Council will oversee its functioning with support provided by the standing Technical Advisory Body (TAB) and the Committee on Aviation Environmental Protection (CAEP) as needed.[12] The ICAO Council will determine the CORSIA-eligible units, considering the recommendations of the TAB.

The operator shall meet its total final CO_2 offsetting requirements for a given compliance period by cancelling CORSIA-eligible emissions units within the CORSIA-eligible emissions unit programme registry.[13] Cancelling means the permanent removal and single use of an eligible emission unit such that the same unit may not be used twice. Each programme registry must make visible on the public website information on each operator's cancelled CORSIA-eligible emissions units,[14] after which ICAO will compile and publish the emissions units information via the CCR (see Figure 8.2).

8.2.2 *Gaps and Challenges*

As CORSIA is just at its pilot phase, it is maybe too soon to suggest that its governance framework presents gaps. However, we can enumerate some challenges that the architecture could face in the future, although it is important to note that some of these are already, whether totally or partially, being considered by the ICAO Council. There are two main monitoring and enforcement challenges for the success of the ICAO offsetting programme: the accuracy of the information, such as the reporting of CO_2 emissions or emissions unit cancellation, and double counting avoidance.

A key element for every offsetting programme is MRV, to enable tracking of improvements and making information-based decisions. Thus, MRV is at the centre of the CORSIA. One of the main concerns raised regarding MRV has been the potential lack of real-time data collection. However, platforms such as FRED+ and the one created by ACE will help alleviate this problem as they will ensure that data are collected and provided in as close as possible to real-time. There is also a concern that irregular operations, data feed issues or critical system failures can result in significant gaps in emissions-related data. Another potential data gap may arise where airline operators use secondary sources to determine fuel use (e.g., where operators use actual data from fuel invoices and technical logs owing to a problem with data collection while using the Aircraft Communication Addressing and Reporting System). Already, IATA intends to tackle this issue by providing that operators should use CERT to help them estimate and report their international aviation emissions (see Figure 8.3). All aeroplane operators can use CERT to fill such data gaps up to a certain number of flights. Additionally, CERT requires only three elements of input: an aeroplane type, an origin and a destination.[15]

[12] ICAO Resolution A39-3 (n 2) para 20 i.

[13] ICAO, *Annex 16* (n 7) pt II. See Chapter 4 (Section 4.3) in this book.

[14] ibid II. See Chapter 4 (Section 4.2) in this book.

[15] ICAO, 'Session 3: ICAO CORSIA CO 2 Estimation and Reporting Tool (CERT)', *ICAO Seminar on the Carbon Offsetting and Reduction Scheme for International Aviation (CORSIA)* (2018).

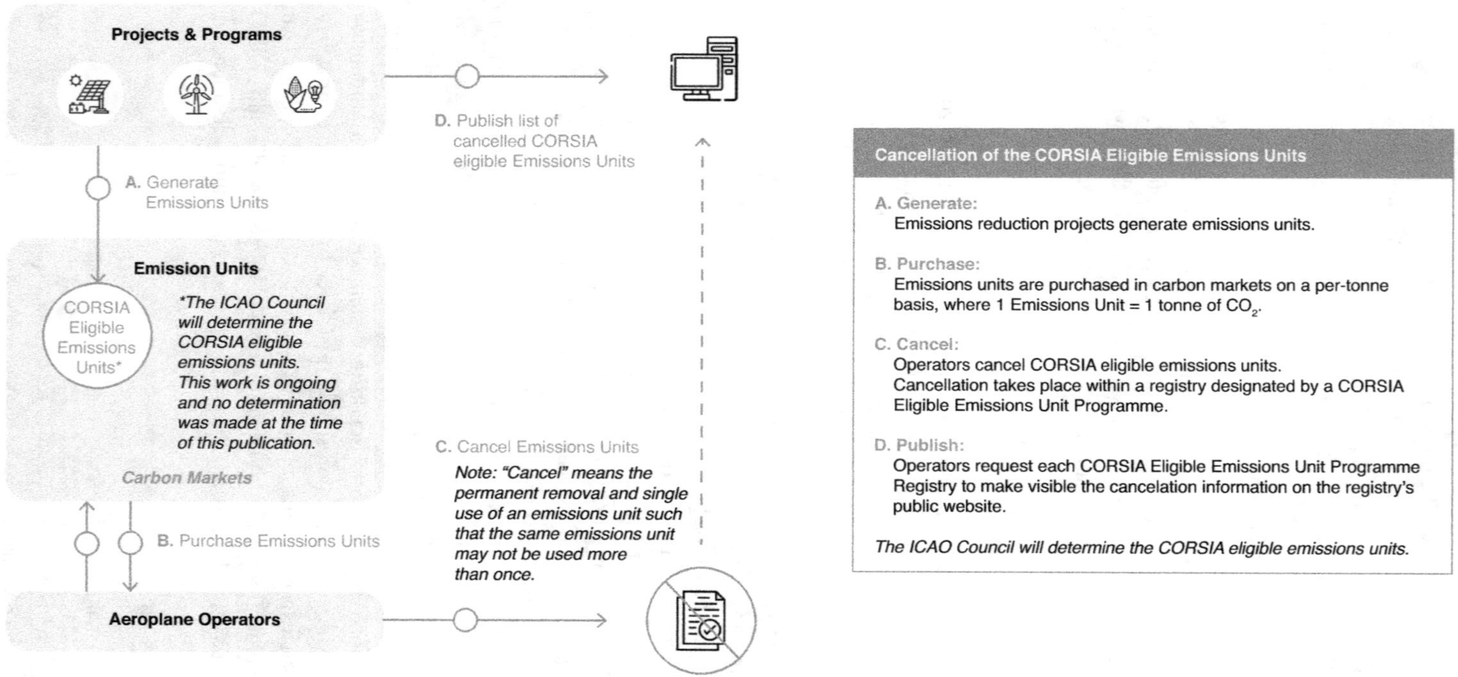

FIGURE 8.2 Cancelling CORSIA-eligible emissions units: carbon markets and CORSIA
Source: Adapted from the CORSIA at a Glance Series, Leaflet No 5 (2019) www.icao.int/environmental-protection/CORSIA/Documents/CORSIA%20Leaflets/CorsiaLeaflet-EN-5-WEB.pdf accessed 22 April 2022.

Input*				Output*		
ICAO Aircraft Type Designator	Origin Airport	Destination Airport	Number of Flights	**Great Circle Distance** (in km)	**CO_2 Emissions** (in tonnes of CO_2)	**Flight(s) subject to Scope of Applicability of CORSIA**
DH8D	EGKK	EVRA	100	1,697	969	Yes
A320	MMMX	MUHA	100	1,772	2,119	Yes
E190	KJFK	KMSY	100	1,903	1,843	No (Domestic)
B789	HKJK	LFPG	100	6,481	13,197	Yes
MD11	SBGR	OMDB	100	12,217	37,053	Yes
AT72	NFFN	NVVV	100	968	473	Yes

***Illustrative numbers/data**

FIGURE 8.3 How does the CERT work?
Source: adapted from ICAO, 'Session 3: ICAO CORSIA CO 2 Estimation and Reporting Tool (CERT)', ICAO Seminar on the Carbon Offsetting and Reduction Scheme for International Aviation (CORSIA) (2018) https://www.icao.int/Meetings/CORSIAHQ18/Documents/3_ICAO_CORSIA_CERT.pdf

Another solution proposed by IATA is to allow data gaps that affect up to 5 per cent of international flights in the 2019–20 period (provided that the data gaps do not affect more than 5 per cent of international flights subject to offsetting requirements in 2021–35). The 5 per cent threshold will be assessed based on the number of flights, not in relation to fuel use or CO_2 emissions. Operators exceeding this threshold will be required to remedy their actions.[16]

Data gaps can be identified at various stages: during data transmission from the aircraft; by the aircraft operator when preparing its emissions report; by the verification body when receiving the report submitted by the aircraft operator; by the state while checking the reports submitted by the aircraft operator and the verification body.[17]

Another critical challenge for CORSIA is the reporting of emissions unit cancellation. Its failure can lead to double counting of emissions reduction. When aircraft operators purchase or cancel emissions units for compliance, they should request that the eligible emissions units' cancellation is communicated on the respective eligible emissions units' programme registries. But with the current architecture of offsetting programs, it is difficult to ensure that such cancellations will be made or announced in real-time.

It is important to note that CORSIA's interconnection with UNFCCC and other programmes is essential for its success, while also keeping in mind, however, that, at present, it is proving technically impossible to connect CORSIA with the Clean Development Mechanism (CDM) registry. The ICAO Assembly has decided that emissions units generated from mechanisms established under the UNFCCC and the Paris Agreement are eligible for use in CORSIA, provided that they align with the Council's decisions and with CAEP's technical contributions, including on avoiding double counting.[18]Thus, if aircraft operators can use various offsetting programmes, responding to ICAO criteria, they will need a reliable and transparent system that allows them to transfer and access data across those different programmes.

8.3 REGULATORY CHANGES FOR A DLT-BASED GOVERNANCE FRAMEWORK

8.3.1 *Overview of DLT Compatibility with the Current Framework*

Using a distributed ledger technology (DLT)-based governance framework to tackle the CORSIA challenges could be part of the solution, although, as we will discuss in Section 8.3.2, it could also demand some regulatory changes. First, however, while considering the current framework, we can highlight some points of convergence with

16 IATA website – An Airline Handbook on CORSIA www.iata.org/contentassets/fb745460050c48089597a3ef1b9fe7a8/corsia-handbook.pdf accessed 19 August 2020.

17 ICAO, *Annex 16* (n 7). See also Chapter 2, Sections 2.5 and 2.6.

18 ICAO, Resolution A40-19: Consolidated statement of continuing ICAO policies and practices related to environmental protection – Carbon Offsetting and Reduction Scheme for International Aviation (CORSIA) (2019) para 20.

TABLE 8.1 *General functional requirements of the CCR*

- **Security/protection of data**
- **Data backup/disaster recovery**
- **Data IT protocols/standards, as applicable**
- **Flexibility** *(modifications/future refinements and upgrades)*
- **Availability**
- **Maintenance and support**
- **Authorised system audit**: *Audit of all system functionalities for technical accuracy according to design, and audit of the accuracy of data entering, being stored in and passing through the CCR, over time and by any user, as relevant*
- **Storage and processing of up to several billion data values**
- **Localisation**
- **Data collection and submission**: *To include system administration and automated error checks*
- **Data analysis and management**: *To include eligibility checks*
- **Data publication**: *Presentation of information on the ICAO CORSIA website for public access*
- **Controlled access:** *Each state will have one account on the CCR and only authorised (limited) users, nominated by a state, will have access to that state's account*
- **Secure web interface** *(password protection/authentication protocol)*
- **Simple web application/portal to upload and submit information**: *Data entry through predefined forms, facilitating submission of new information and updating of previously submitted information*
- **A time-stamp of all operations:** *Actions will be time-stamped (including the electronic signature of the user who initiated the action) and recorded to ensure traceability and data integrity. In case of a resubmission, the previous version of the modified information will be archived*

the features of DLT. This section therefore provides an overview of DLT's compatibility with the current CORSIA framework.

In June 2018, at its 214th session, the ICAO Council approved functional requirements for the CCR. It should be integral to any comparable data management system and, specific to the CCR, divided into three categories: data collection and submission, data analysis and management, and data publication. These functional requirements formed the basis for elaborating the terms of reference for CCR development. Table 8.1 summarises the main functional requirements of the CCR.[19]

The good news is that DLTs, particularly blockchain, can certainly meet these requirements. Blockchain as a secured, shared, distributed and decentralised ledger can be used to achieve the Council's requirements on elements such as security, data backup and flexibility. These features can prevent double counting risks and ensure the integrity of datasets. Combining DLT with Internet of Things (IoT) and artificial intelligence (AI) can add more features to the new framework: flexibility, data analysis, backup. Machine forecasting models based on machine learning can

[19] ICAO, 'Session 6: CORSIA Offsetting Requirements ICAO Secretariat ICAO Regional Workshop on CORSIA', *ICAO Regional Workshop on CORSIA* (2019).

be applied to increase blockchain technology efficiency. Machine learning could help aircraft operators to determine in near-real-time the number of emissions units they need and project the cost of purchase based on the emissions data collected on the distributed ledger and pricing trends in the global carbon market.

Besides, to reduce and control the number of authorised access to the CCR, regarding States Parties and designated users, it is possible to use a permissioned blockchain (see Figure 8.4). Permissioned blockchains are usually privately owned or at least set up by a collaboration of parties so that only trusted or checked participants can participate in control and maintenance.

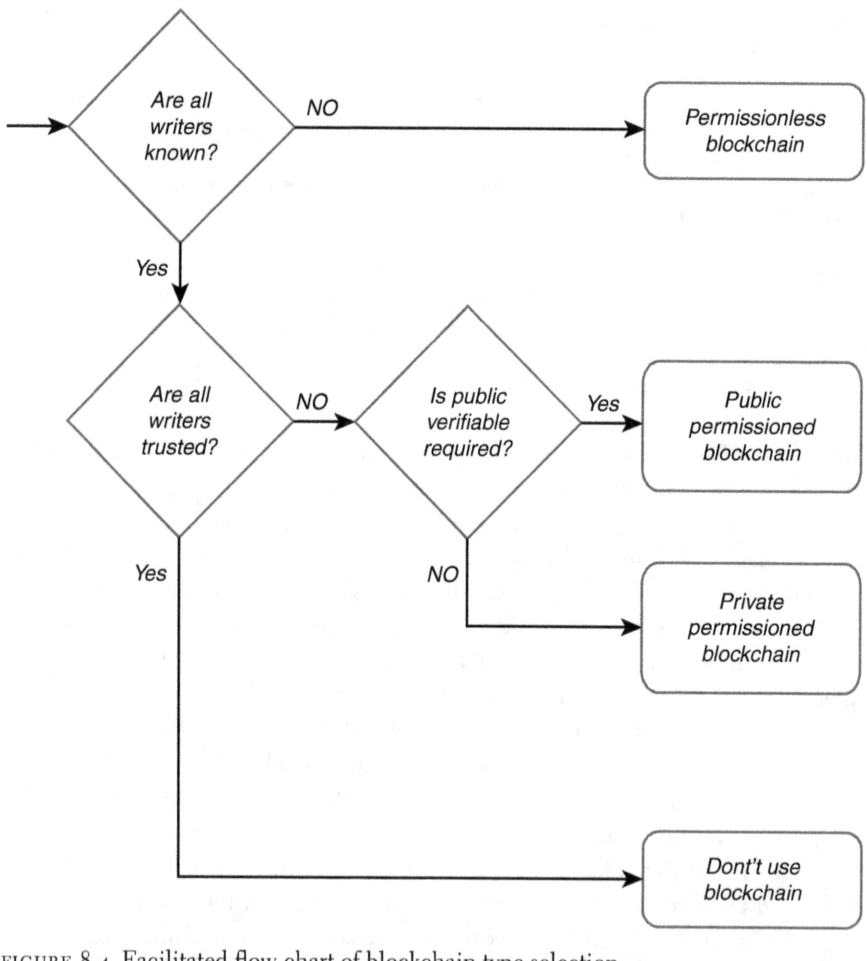

FIGURE 8.4 Facilitated flow chart of blockchain type selection
Source: Mohammad Maroufi, Reza Abdolee and Behzad Mozaffari Tazekand, 'On the Convergence of Blockchain and Internet of Things (IoT) Technologies' (2019).

According to the current CORSIA architecture, the ICAO compiles and publishes the information on the CCR. With access management, DLT can guarantee that it is only this entity, and those authorised such as member states, that can upload or modify the information.[20]

Thus, a DLT is ideal for a multitude of purposes, among them preventing double counting, reducing transactions times and lowering transaction costs:

- **Double counting avoidance**: Establishing an accurate and legitimate baseline measurement improves the ICAO's ability to reduce overall greenhouse gas emissions. A blockchain platform provides a multi-layered database of reported emissions data on a global scale. When a transaction of data occurs on a blockchain, there is no possibility of that data set residing anywhere else than the intended destination within the distributed ledger on which all parties agree.
- **Shorter transaction times**: Another advantage of managing carbon offsetting credits on a distributed ledger is integration speed. With the current framework, it can take weeks of co-ordination to validate emissions data. The process of creating and exchanging emission credits can be performed and near instantaneously confirmed using a blockchain. Emission data created and logged in a blockchain data-stream can also be expanded to be chain-agnostic and cross-reference other carbon emission schemes without the need for additional validation steps or waiting periods. Therefore, blockchain will significantly reduce the process length. With smart contracts, when the transaction occurs, the data contained on a distributed ledger platform are processed to the CCR and deducted from the eligible programme registries.
- **Lower transaction costs**: A pre-constructed smart contract would remove the need for the first two steps in the report validation process: internal pre-verification by the concerned aircraft operator and third-party verification before reporting to the state authority. Blockchain-related automation, referred to as smart contracts, would provide a predictable reporting structure and reduce transaction costs. Many processes rely on the timely yet accurate issuance of credits, compliance with agreements, and validation of emissions data. On-boarding becomes more manageable and less costly with each validation period as use of the distributed ledger grows.

8.3.2 *Overview of the Required Regulatory Adjustments*

The emerging crypto-legal structure, reinforced by the application of DLT (see Chapter 5), will require some changes in the current CORSIA legal framework. However, the adjustments needed to adopt DLT-based governance depend, in part, on the compatibility of the current regulation with the changes induced by DLT

[20] ICAO, *Annex 16* (n 7) pt II. Chapter 2 (Sections 2.5 and 2.6).

introduction. Owing to the convergence between DLT features and current ICAO Council requirements, it should not be necessary to make important changes. Therefore, this section will focus on some of the main points that should require attention.

The choice to adopt a DLT-based governance framework can be made through agreements among the ICAO member states taking part in the offsetting programme. In each case, the agreement should determine which type of DLT will be used and the applicable law, to settle any disputes that may arise. However, as with the current framework, the ICAO Council will still supervise the new framework's functioning based on DLT.

Following the current framework, aircraft operators will need to acquire eligible emissions units, on carbon markets, to comply with their offsetting requirements. With the duty to ask for the cancellation of emissions units and to report to the state authority, after first submitting to a verification body for assessment, the process is lengthy.

After the purchase and the cancellation of emissions units, the operator and the verification body provide emissions unit cancellation reports to the state, which checks them and informs ICAO. With a DLT-based framework, the aircraft operator's state no longer needs to send any report manually, which should shorten the process. A network established between the carbon markets' registries, offering CORSIA-eligible emissions units, and the CCR will allow collection in near-real-time of information about emissions unit cancellations (see Figure 8.5). The proposal that follows is based on DLT but is not intended to replace the actual framework. It should complement the current framework in which member states' authorities submit reports to ICAO to respect their sovereignty. If the carbon market is based on blockchain, then the emissions unit cancellations in its registry can be automated with smart contracts. With all cancellation information sent directly to ICAO, ICAO will be able easily to compare the data provided by operators, member states and carbon markets. Owing to there being various sources of data collected in real-time, and transmitted using DLT, the ICAO Council should be able to monitor the progress of the offsetting programmes better and look for errors or misstatements in the reports received from member states through FRED+.

At the national level, member states, depending on their legislation, will have to admit proof made through DLTs, particularly smart contracts, at least for CORSIA implementation. For example, the law can presume that a fact or record verified through a valid application of blockchain technology is authentic. The established presumption could be, among other things, applied to a fact or record maintained by blockchain technology to determine:

- contractual parties, provisions, execution, effective dates and status;
- ownership, assignment, negotiation and transfer of money, property, contracts, instruments and other legal rights and duties;

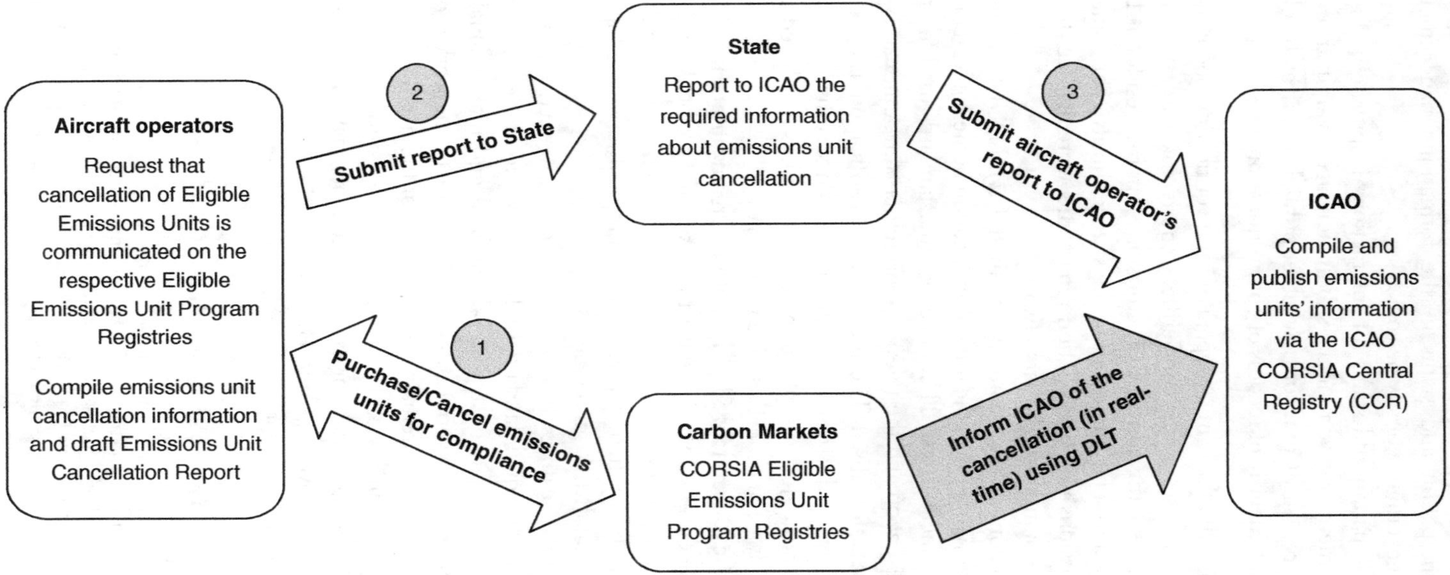

FIGURE 8.5 Linking carbon markets to the ICAO Central Registry using DLT

- identity, participation and status in the formation, management, record-keeping and governance of any person;
- identity, participation and status for interactions in private transactions and with a government or governmental subdivision, agency or instrumentality;
- authenticity or integrity of records, whether publicly or privately relevant; and
- authenticity or integrity of records of communication.[21]

Such regulation will allow aircraft operators and verification bodies to exchange emissions reports, for assessment, and verified reports. Likewise, the same process can be used for the submission of CO_2 emissions reports. Besides, a DLT-based network can be used to send the reports to the state authority. Thus, after assessing the operator's emissions unit cancellation report, the accredited verification body can submit it to the state through that network.

However, regulations changes could be required if, with DLT-based governance, it is decided to remove or reduce the roles of verification bodies, at least for the report of emissions unit cancellations. The process of the standards used for assessment, such as ISO 14064-3:2006 and the relevant requirements in Annex 16, Volume IV, Appendix 6, will be automatised. The automation of verification using AI and smart contracts could allow rapid assessment of aircraft operators' compliance. Hence, the system could determine, for example, if the emissions units purchased are eligible and have not already been cancelled (See Figure 8.6).

In this regard, the Decentralized Autonomous Organization's Integral Platform for Climate Initiatives (DAO IPCI)[22] states that a specific protocol for CORSIA has been developed and proposed for ICAO consideration. It would allow aircraft operators' reports to be verified by a verification protocol following the evaluation algorithms adopted and MRV guidelines.[23]

As concerns the DLT features, ICAO member states will need to define standards or implement an international standard, such as ISO 22739 (under development), to uniformise the different systems at sectoral, national and international levels. In either case, this will require a verification body to ensure the network's compliance. As the ICAO Council should remain the supervisor of the new DLT-based framework, there is an argument that it should be the one to request and/or approve the correction of any technical issues, for example, the modification of an erroneously coded smart contract. However, if the DLT used at the national level is different from the one used to submit reports to ICAO, it is our view that the member state

[21] See, for example, 12 VSA § 1913 Vermont Statutes Title 12 – Court Procedure Chapter 81 – Conduct of Trial Subchapter 1: Generally § 1913 Blockchain enabling 2016.

[22] The DAO IPCI is a digital environment built on smart contracts designed to minimise transaction costs and to make the issuance and transfer of mitigation units – including internationally transferred mitigation outcomes (ITMOs) – highly reliable, transparent and protected from manipulation. DAO IPCI, 'Decentralized Autonomous Organization. Integral Platform for Climate Initiatives. White Paper 5.0' (2018) https://ipci.io/wp-content/uploads/2018/06/WP_5.0-2.pdf accessed 12 April 2022.

[23] ibid 29–30.

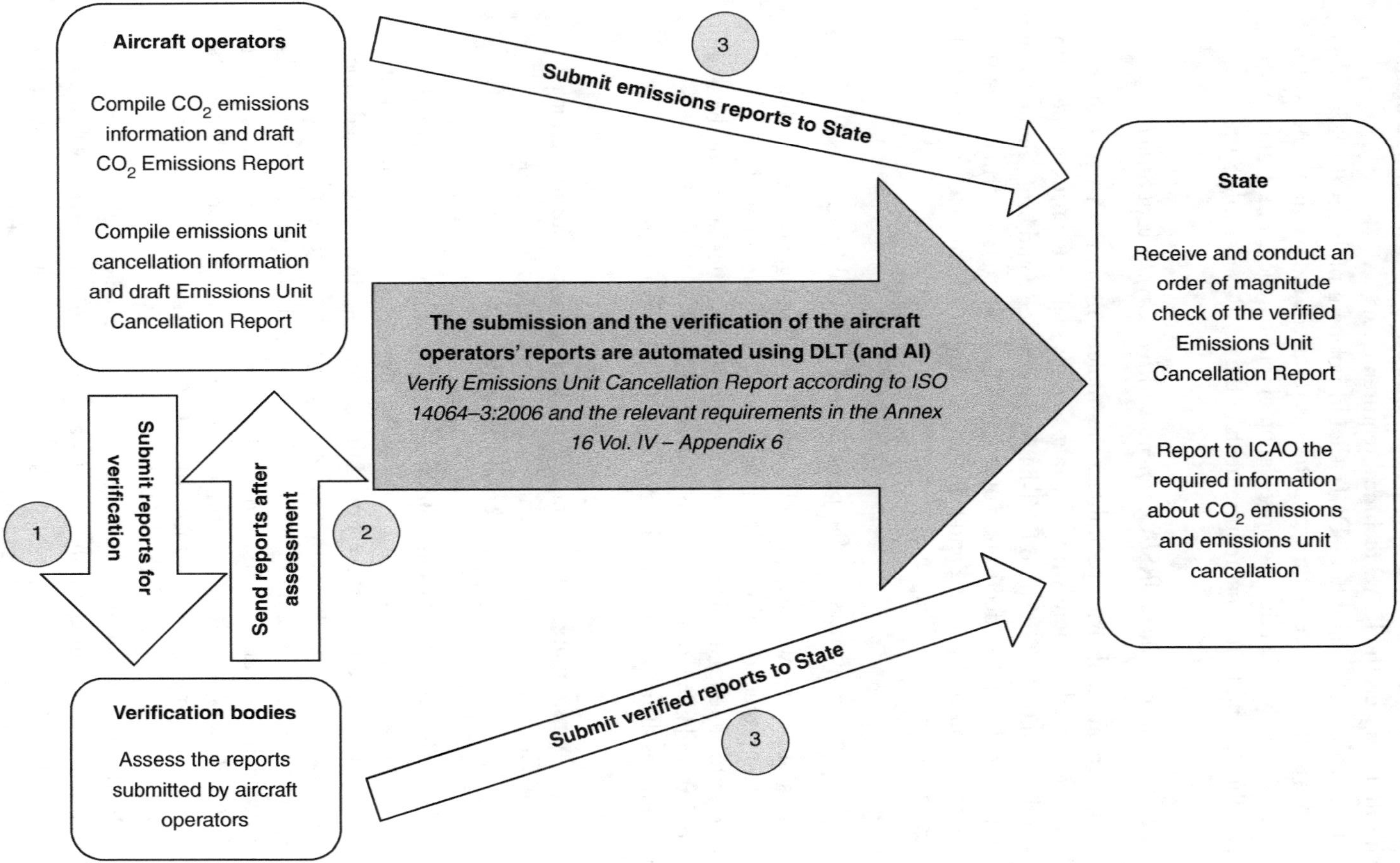

FIGURE 8.6 Linking aircraft operators to the state authority using DLT

should be the one to take the decision. The verification body will ensure that the modification respects the ICAO technical requirements.

Moreover, the immutability of DLTs should not be a problem. In fact, every operation will be registered; if a transaction is reversed, the previous one will be automatically 'archived', allowing preservation of transparency. This feature corresponds to the general functional requirements of the CCR (see Table 8.1).

8.3.3 *Overview of the CORSIA Framework with a 'Crypto-legal Structure'*

Adopting a crypto-legal structure induces the implementation of its general legal principles described previously (see Chapter 5). This section focusses on the main changes that a shift of CORSIA to DLT-based governance could bring about. They concern particularly: the effectiveness of the legal framework; transformation of the current framework architecture; and exploitation of new patterns of enforcement of the legal framework (see Chapter 4).

8.3.3.1 Effectiveness and Simplification of the Legal Framework

Crypto-legal structures will help to resolve some important legal issues regarding, for example, data protection. With a DLT framework, only the allowed persons can have access to stored data. These security features will reduce suspicion between stakeholders and allow the application of contract law (see Figure 8.7). This situation simplifies the application of the existing CORSIA legal framework.

8.3.3.2 Transformation of the Framework Architecture: Transformation of Current Actors, Introduction of New Actors and Emergence of New Legal Elements

Transformation of the current actors: As explained, the ICAO Council will remain the administrator of the DLT-based framework. Its principal objective will be to regulate the system. For example, on a private permissioned blockchain (see Figures 8.4 and 8.7), it will act as the central organ with the ability to determine the access rights of every node; for example, the member states. The recorded information can be modified only by the central organ, which is ICAO. Besides, the ICAO Council must define, among other things, the offsetting programmes that meet the CORSIA criteria and the minimum technical characteristics of the DLT framework.

Introduction of new actors and emergence of new legal elements: The technical feasibility of interconnecting the various compensation programs at CORSIA will require the intervention of new legal actors: the coders. In executing the Council's instructions, they will have to program, for example, the smart contracts

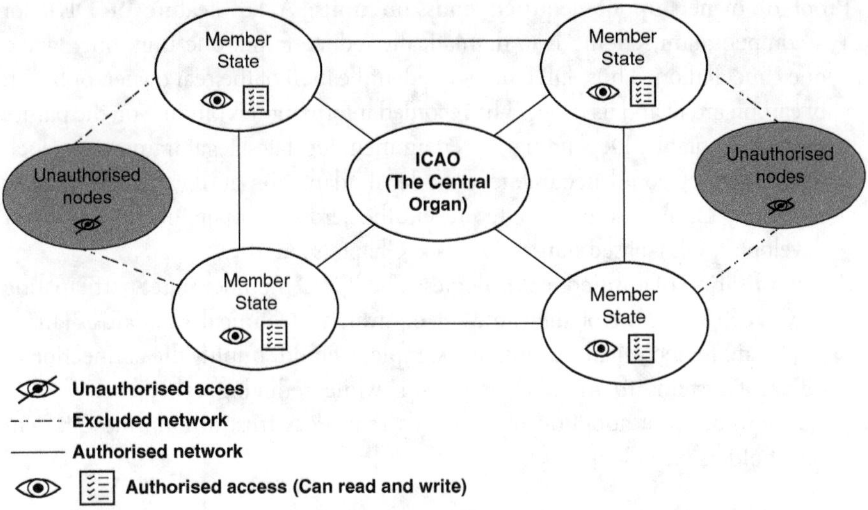

FIGURE 8.7 Overview of the CORSIA DLT framework architecture

that will realise the transactions of 'tokenised' carbon credit for the aeroplane operators (see Chapter 5), inform ICAO of the cancellation of eligible carbon units (see Figure 8.5) and, perhaps, automate verification of the reports (see Figure 8.6). The need to guarantee that the DLT framework used for CORSIA meets ICAO requirements will also require external auditors' involvement. Their mission will be to assure ICAO, the member states and other stakeholders of the system's compliance. Moreover, the decentralised and distributed nature of DLTs will allow the stakeholders – those that have been authorised – to have access to the same information, in near real-time, as the central body.

8.3.3.3 Exploitation of New Patterns of Enforcement of the Legal Framework

The CORSIA legal framework, as well as the legal frameworks of member states, will also be impacted by the transition to a DLT-based framework owing to the application of a crypto-legal structure. It mainly concerns identification of sellers of carbon units, proof of ownership of acquired emission units, and technological standardisation.

Identification of the relevant carbon unit providers: The aeroplane operators cannot buy compensation units from programs other than those identified by ICAO. Coding ICAO criteria can prevent aeroplane operators from acquiring emissions units that do not fulfil CORSIA minimum requirements. Even if the units are acquired, their cancellation cannot be validated during the report's assessment.

Proof of ownership of acquired emission units: A key feature of DLT for a compensation scheme is to dramatically reduce fraud: one unit, one owner, one cancellation. Thus, DLT provides identification of the real owner, or buyer, of carbon credit and its issuer. The recorded information is binding on the parties and is immutable. Depending on certain member states' legal frameworks, such functionalities could necessitate some legal adaptation and/or the enabling of regulatory sandboxes so as not to prevent the aeroplane operators from using or developing DLT-based transactions (see Chapters 4 and 5).

Standardisation of applied technologies: The ICAO member states participating in CORSIA will adopt the same, or equivalent, technical standards. This is important for technical reasons: for example, it could simplify the connection of different systems to the ICAO network while reducing cybersecurity risks. Furthermore, the adoption of standards reinforces trust among the different stakeholders (see Chapter 5).

8.4 IMPLEMENTATION ROADMAP OF NEGOTIATIONS AND IMPLEMENTATION

8.4.1 *ICAO Council and CAEP Role*

The ICAO Council is going to play the most critical role in the transition to a DLT-based governance framework. Under the provisions of Article 49(c) of the Convention on International Civil Aviation, the Assembly has the powers and duties to examine and take appropriate action on the Council's reports and decide on any matter referred to it by the Council.

It is crucial to bear in mind that, according to Article 52 of the Convention on International Civil Aviation, decisions by the Council shall require approval by a majority of its members. Besides, Article 54 of the Convention provides that the Council can adopt international standards and recommended practices. Therefore, for the implementation of CORSIA, the ICAO Assembly, in its resolution A40-19,[24] requested from the Council the following actions:[25]

- to develop and update the ICAO CORSIA documents referenced in Annex 16, Volume IV related to the CORSIA CO_2 Estimation and Reporting Tool (CERT) and the CORSIA Central Registry (CCR);[26] and

24 Resolution A40-19, together with Resolution A40-17: Consolidated statement of continuing ICAO policies and practices related to environmental protection – General provisions, noise and local air quality and Resolution A40-18: Consolidated statement of continuing ICAO policies and practices related to environmental protection – Climate change, supersede Resolutions A39-1, A39-2 and A39-3 and constitute the consolidated statement of continuing ICAO policies and practices related to environmental protection.

25 ICAO Resolution A40-19 (n 18).

26 ibid para 19 b.

- to establish and maintain the CORSIA Central Registry (CCR) under the auspices of ICAO.[27]

Considering these provisions, the ICAO Council, with the assistance of TAB[28] and CAEP, has the means to lead the implementation of a DLT-based governance framework. Pending further studies on this issue, the following points appear to be essential to operationalising CORSIA's transition to DLT-based governance:

1. analysis of the compatibility of the current MRV system with DLT features to determine the advantages and challenges;
2. establishment or adoption of DLT standards and the criteria for retaining a verification body to ensure compliance;
3. exploration of the feasibility of performing verification of aircraft operators' reports using DLT and AI;
4. establishment or adjustment of the rules for conflict resolution, to settle any disputes that may arise.

These are the main points that need to be studied before adopting a new regulatory framework operating through DLT-based governance. In this sense, the Council will be assisted by CAEP's Working Group 4, which was established as a successor of CAEP's Global Market-Based Measure Technical Task Force (GMTF). The group is currently working as per its approved Work Programme for the CAEP/12 cycle (2019–22).[29]

Generally, CAEP's Working Group 4 deals with technical issues relating to the implementation of CORSIA, including maintenance of the related Standards and Recommended Practices (SARPs) contained in Annex 16, Volume IV to the Convention on International Civil Aviation and related guidance contained in the Environmental Technical Manual (Doc 9501), Volume IV. Its current work concerns, among other things:

- improvement of CERT;
- development of further guidance on MRV in CORSIA;
- development of recommendations related to the management of emissions units in CORSIA;
- technical analysis to support deliberations on CORSIA in relevant ICAO bodies.[30]

The previous development demonstrates that the ICAO Council has both the powers and the capacity to lead CORSIA's transition to a DLT-based governance

27 ibid para 19 d.
28 In line with the Assembly request, TAB's mandate TAB is to make recommendations to the Council on the eligible emissions units for use by CORSIA.
29 ICAO, 'CAEP Working Group 4 – CORSIA' www.icao.int/environmental-protection/pages/CAEP-WG4.aspx accessed 1 June 2020.
30 ibid.

framework. However, such a shift will require a thorough feasibility study beforehand. This study will help determine the advantages, and the challenges, to the use of DLTs for the offsetting programme. It will also allow the ICAO to determine the required regulatory changes. Besides, the changes will also need the involvement of the ICAO member states.

8.4.2 *ICAO Member States' Role*

The ICAO member states also have an essential role to play to guarantee the transition to a DLT-based framework, such as implementing the current governance framework. Their implication mostly concerns establishment of registries and a regulatory framework.

Concerning establishment of registries, paragraph 22(d) of the Assembly Resolution A39-3 provides that member states shall build partnerships among themselves to co-operate to establish individual state or group registries, and possibly to pilot their implementation.

Besides, paragraph 20(h) provides that member states shall develop necessary arrangements for establishing their individual state or group registries or for participating in other registries according to the ICAO guidance.

Regarding the regulatory framework, paragraph 20(j) of the Assembly Resolution A39-3 provides that member states shall take necessary action to ensure that national policies and regulatory frameworks are established, for compliance with and enforcement of the scheme.

In accordance with these provisions, ICAO member states can determine the standards and rules for dispute resolution at the national level. However, member states should ensure that their regulatory framework complies with the one adopted, or recommended, by the ICAO Council.

8.5 CONCLUSION

So far, ICAO has created CORSIA to reduce the carbon emissions of the aviation industry. It will operate as a voluntary scheme during the initial pilot phase and will later become mandatory for all participating countries, except for those granted exemptions. Two of the most significant challenges regarding the implementation and success of CORSIA are MRV and double counting of real-time data. A solution to the first challenge is FRED+, which facilitates the exchange of real-time data between airline operators and each relevant state authority. For the second challenge, DLTs, particularly blockchain, offer a solution as they are secured, shared, distributed and decentralised ledgers that can be used to achieve the Council's requirements on elements such as security, data backup and flexibility. They can also reduce the transaction times and costs involved in the data collection, management and distribution process. As recorded in this chapter, IATA, airline operators and member states have all invested a significant amount of time and effort to create a platform to reduce the aviation industry's contribution to CO_2 emissions going forwards.

Even though it is impossible to predict the effect that CORSIA will have on the aviation industry, there is a healthy appetite for participation in CORSIA. As of July 2021, over one hundred member states are included in the scheme, counting certain least developed member states such as Cameroon, Ghana, Ivory Coast and Benin. Since CORSIA is limited to the airline industry, it is important to think about the impact that DLTs can have on the operationalisation of the Paris Agreement. Paris Agreement Article 6 has been highlighted as containing some of the key provisions of the global agreement. It outlines the co-operative approaches that parties can take to achieve their nationally determined contributions. In doing so, it helps establish the Paris Agreement as a framework for a global carbon market.

9

DLT and Networked Carbon Markets

Justin D. Macinante[*]

9.1 INTRODUCTION

Further to the previous chapters, which focussed on the applicability of distributed ledger technology (DLT) in an individual emissions trading market, this chapter goes on to introduce the concept of networking of carbon markets and how the application of DLT can help to operationalise a networked carbon markets framework.

9.2 PARIS AGREEMENT AND HETEROGENEITY

9.2.1 *Current Context*

The Paris Agreement[1] moves away from the homogeneity of the Kyoto Protocol[2] by recognising that jurisdictions will take different approaches that will have different outcomes. This has been ascribed to a general trend away from specific categories differentiating parties in terms of commitments towards self-differentiation, in response to the continuing demands by developed countries for developing countries to take on commitments and developing countries' continuing resistance.[3] The deal struck in Paris 'allows parties to define their own commitments, tailor these to their national circumstances, capacities, and constraints, and thus differentiate themselves from each other'.[4] The Paris Agreement 'establishes a new paradigm in international climate policy. While the Kyoto Protocol was essentially based on the so-called "targets & timetables" the Paris Agreement is based on the so-called

[*] This chapter draws on and reproduces with permission sections of the author's recently published book: Justin D Macinante, *Effective Global Carbon Markets: Networked Emissions Trading Using Disruptive Technology* (Edward Elgar 2020). This section reproduces in part ch 4 thereof.

[1] FCCC/CP/2015/10/Add.1, 29 January 2016 http://unfccc.int/resource/docs/2015/cop21/eng/10a01.pdf accessed 13 March 2017.

[2] Kyoto Protocol, 11 December 1997, 2303 UNTS 162 (2005).

[3] Daniel Bodansky, Jutta Brunnée and Lavanya Rajamani, *International Climate Change Law* (Oxford University Press 2017) 29.

[4] ibid.

"pledge & review" paradigm.'[5] The differences in responsibility for, and in actual capacity to address, climate change are implicit to this approach and evidenced through the nationally determined contributions (NDCs) that parties to the Paris Agreement have lodged. There is a considerable amount of variation in the levels of ambition disclosed, types of contribution, and target years or periods.[6]

An inevitable consequence is that the mechanisms, including pricing mechanisms, applied by jurisdictions will demonstrate substantial variations as well. The introduction by the Paris Agreement of internationally transferred mitigation outcomes (ITMOs) ties the units traded to the results of the mitigation actions taken. This raises a number of issues, such as an appropriate measuring unit and accounting unit, how they should be represented (e.g. by a certificate), whether they could support a secondary market, whether they would all be equal and fungible and, most importantly, what exactly is meant by a mitigation outcome?[7] While there are similarities between the Mitigation and Sustainable Development Mechanism, introduced in Article 6, paragraphs 4–7, and the CDM under Article 12 of the Kyoto Protocol,[8] the concept of mitigation outcomes departs from the Kyoto Protocol concept of centrally sourced and allocated units of equal value. At the time of writing, there are still many issues yet to be addressed including, for example, accounting for these diverse mitigation outcomes and how environmental integrity will be assured.

Key aspects flagged in relation to accounting under this new approach include, for instance, quantifying mitigation targets and progress towards them; quantifying mitigation outcomes; avoiding double counting of reductions; accommodating different metrics for outcomes and targets; accounting for time period factor variations in outcomes and targets; and other factors affecting outcomes (e.g. non-permanence).[9] In relation to environmental integrity, in the context of ITMOs, there is support for the view that it means that the transfer does not result in an increase in global aggregate emissions.[10] Four factors identified as influencing it are the robustness of accounting for international transfers; the quality of the units, which in turn depends on cap setting and monitoring; the ambition and scope of the transferring country's mitigation target; and incentives or disincentives for future

5 Martin Cames and others, 'International Market Mechanisms after Paris' (Discussion Paper, German Emissions Trading Authority (DEHSt) for German Environment Agency, November 2016) 7 https://newclimate.org/2016/11/17/international-market-mechanisms-after-paris/ accessed 14 May 2017.

6 ibid 15; also, for example, see Lambert Schneider and others, 'Robust Accounting of International Transfers under Article 6 of the Paris Agreement' (Discussion Paper, German Emissions Trading Authority (DEHSt) for German Environment Agency, September 2017) www.dehst.de/SharedDocs/downloads/EN/project-mechanisms/Differences_and_commonalities_paris_agreement_discussion_paper_28092017.pdf?__blob=publicationFile&v=2 accessed 29 September 2017.

7 Cames and others (n 5) 12.

8 ibid 17: see table of similarities.

9 Schneider and others (n 6) 18–19.

10 Lambert Schneider and Stephanie La Hoz Theuer 'Environmental Integrity of International Carbon Market Mechanisms under the Paris Agreement' (2019) 19(3) *Clim Policy* 386.

mitigation action.[11] More jurisdictions have begun to develop emissions trading as part of domestic measures to achieve greenhouse gas (GHG) reductions: '2019 saw the largest number of carbon pricing initiatives launched in a single year'.[12] The World Bank reported that there are now sixty-one carbon pricing initiatives implemented or scheduled to be implemented, covering 22 per cent of global GHG emissions.[13] More frequently, they are engaging in discussions aimed at facilitating inter-jurisdictional trading, for example, by linking with each other.[14] The more this happens, the more apparent it will become that such schemes do not all generate equivalent outcomes, thus necessitating consideration of different approaches.

9.2.2 *The Networked Market*

The networked market proposed is one such alternative. It can be viewed not as a single market but rather as a connection facilitating transactions between individual, separate markets, each of which will continue as an autonomous operation in its own jurisdiction, while participating in the network created by the connection. As proposed, this encompasses the digital infrastructure needed to provide the connection between these markets, as well as the legal and administrative structures that will operate, manage and oversee the network. This chapter sets out some of the theory and concepts underpinning that proposal.[15]

Section 9.3 introduces the market proposed in terms of its bifurcated nature; sets out the argument in favour of networking in preference to linking as a way to connect diverse carbon pricing schemes; and introduces the technology proposed to facilitate doing so.[16] Conclusions are then drawn concerning the application of the technology.

9.3 NETWORKED CARBON MARKETS ON DLT

9.3.1 *Two Elements of the Proposed Market*

The proposal is for a network of carbon markets, on DLT architecture.[17] Thus, it consists of two distinct elements: first, networking of carbon markets; and second, that networking being carried out using a specific type of digital information technology (IT) architecture, namely a distributed ledger (or ledgers) (DL).

[11] ibid 389–92.

[12] World Bank, *State and Trends of Carbon Pricing 2020* (May 2020) 19 https://openknowledge.worldbank.org/bitstream/handle/10986/33809/9781464815867.pdf accessed 11 April 2020.

[13] ibid 9.

[14] ibid 22.

[15] For a fuller elaboration see Justin D Macinante, *Effective Global Carbon Markets: Networked Emissions Trading Using Disruptive Technology* (Edward Elgar 2020) especially chs 5–7.

[16] Section 9.3 draws on and reproduces in part Macinante (n 15) ch 6.

[17] Although DLT is sometimes referred to as 'blockchain', blockchain is just one implementation of the broader DLT.

In addition to these two elements, the proposal can be seen to proceed along two independent, but interrelated, arms. The first aims to facilitate and stimulate an inter-jurisdictional market, so that it operates efficiently, encourages private sector engagement, promotes a stable carbon price and fosters the effective application of carbon finance. This first arm is directed towards, and supports, the second arm, but also provides a stand-alone outcome in its own right. The second arm promotes the objectives of climate policy, evidenced by the terms of the Paris Agreement, including higher ambition, greater transparency, accuracy, accountability and security of information sharing and management.

Currently, there is no trading network or market such as that which is proposed. Networking carbon markets is a concept originally introduced by the World Bank;[18] however, there are no existing examples, nor are there market networking models in other areas with which to draw comparisons. There are DLT use cases being developed in the financial markets, but none that relate to a market of markets, as proposed here. Thus, the approach taken here is to consider the rationale for each element, in turn, independently of the other.

In the absence of a specific illustration, the reasons to network in order to achieve that connection, rather than link, are drawn out in Section 9.3.2 in terms of issues arising with linking and the extent to which networking could reduce or avoid them. For the DLT element, in relation to which, on the other hand, use cases are continuing to grow in a dynamic environment, it is necessary not only to distinguish the use case proposed here from the expanding universe of such applications but also to define what that use case is. These considerations are addressed in Section 9.3.3.

9.3.2 *The Reasons to 'Network' Rather Than 'Link'*

9.3.2.1 Political Issues

To determine that it is desirable to connect by linking, jurisdictions need to make a political decision, influenced by factors including perceived environmental stringency/credibility of the overall cap; perceived benefits, such as cost savings; impact on domestic action; distributional impacts; and loss of control.[19] With regard to control, it would seem to be clearly preferable to avoid, as far as possible, compromising the sovereignty of jurisdictions, as part of a process to engage them in a co-operative process. Networking has an advantage in that, first, it requires less compromise of the domestic legal regime for trading, of the institutional structures or of the independence of participating jurisdictions; and second, to the extent that it does involve

18 See generally www.worldbank.org/en/topic/climatechange/brief/globally-networked-carbon-markets accessed 23 January 2018.

19 World Bank and Partnership for Market Readiness (PMR), *Lessons Learned from Linking Emissions Trading Systems: General Principles and Applications* (Technical Note 7, February 2014) 12 www.thepmr.org/system/files/documents/PMR%20Technical%20Note%207.pdf accessed 11 April 2022.

compromise, any such accommodation by jurisdictions participating in the network will be on the basis of equivalence. There would be a level playing field, where the same parameters would be applied equally to all.

Political issues in relation to linking emissions trading schemes (ETSs) flow from the potential impact it may have on jurisdictional sovereignty: for instance, the risk of design features from one jurisdiction's scheme extending to the scheme of the other linked jurisdiction.[20] Conversely, networked jurisdictions' schemes would remain separate, so the potential compromise of environmental objectives and control would not occur. Potential for reduction in an administrator's control over its domestic ETS in a linked system would not arise in a networked arrangement and, similarly, the related issue of harmonisation of ETS design elements would not arise, since the networked schemes remain autonomous and independent.

Linking results from an agreement negotiated by the governments of the respective jurisdictions. These negotiations take time, sometimes a long time: in the case of Switzerland and the European Union (EU), for instance, seven years.[21] Inevitably, also, there will be imbalances between negotiating counterparties. For instance, an economically larger jurisdiction will be likely to have greater influence over the terms on which the parties link.[22] Nevertheless, a smaller jurisdiction may be willing to accept that agreement, even though an unequal negotiating position may put it at a potential disadvantage.[23]

This situation of unequal negotiating positions should not arise in the case of networking. Rather, with networking, acceptance of the parameters by which a jurisdiction's mitigation actions are valued (to give the mitigation value (MV) of

[20] Michael Mehling, 'Legal Frameworks for Linking National Emissions Trading Schemes' in C Carlarne, K Gray and R Tarasofsky (eds), *Oxford Handbook of International Climate Change Law* (OUP 2016) 259 citing J Jaffe and RN Stavins, *Linking Tradable Permit Schemes for Greenhouse Gas Emissions: Implications, and Challenges* (International Emissions Trading Association 2007); also, the challenges raised by linking are largely political in nature: Michael Mehling 'Linking of Emissions Trading Schemes' in David Freestone and Charlotte Streck (eds), *Legal Aspects of Carbon Trading: Kyoto, Copenhagen and Beyond* (OUP 2009).

[21] EC Climate Action announcement on 23 November 2017 that EU and Switzerland had signed an agreement to link their ETSs, noting that negotiations opened in 2010 https://ec.europa.eu/clima/news/eu-and-switzerland-sign-agreement accessed 18 December 2017. Agreement took effect 1 January 2020, ten years after negotiations commenced.

[22] The EU ETS is cited as an example of a unilateral approach under which other carbon markets have to adapt to its architecture, although the California–Quebec negotiation is, on the contrary, collaborative: Dmitry Fedosov, 'Linking Carbon Markets: Development and Implications' [2016] *CCLR* 202. However, both California and Quebec are part of the initial collaboration, the Western Climate Initiative, and their schemes were very similar to begin with: Christiane Beuermann and others, 'Considering the Effects of Linking Emissions Trading Schemes: A Manual on Bilateral Linking of ETS' (German Emissions Trading Authority (DEHSt) on behalf of German Environment, May 2017) 13 www.dehst.de/SharedDocs/downloads/EN/emissions-trading/Linking_manual.pdf?__blob=publicationFile&v=3 accessed 17 July 2017.

[23] The experience to date has been that other schemes linking with the EU ETS need to align themselves with the EU ETS. Switzerland revised its ETS in December 2011, to increase compatibility with the EU ETS; see Angelica P Rutherford, 'Linking Emissions Trading Schemes: Lessons from the EU–Swiss ETSs' [2014] *CCLR* 282.

the jurisdiction's mitigation outcomes) is the compromise to be made by all participants.[24] These parameters would apply on the same basis to all jurisdictions participating in the network. Hence, the compromise would apply equally to all, rather than differentially depending on the relative economic size of counterparties to a particular bilateral or multilateral linking arrangement.

The convergence of prices may have distributional impacts on participants and other stakeholders in linked systems, resulting in substantial capital flows that may affect political support.[25] While it is likely that there would be distributional impacts also in a networked system, networking would afford governments greater flexibility to set the terms for participation by the entities they authorise to trade in the networked market. Networking would also allow greater flexibility for a jurisdiction to opt out altogether were it to determine that trading flows no longer suit its domestic policy objectives.

Another consideration is that linking arrangements can default to the lowest mitigation standard of those jurisdictions participating, thereby affecting jurisdictions whose policies target higher ambition.[26] In a networking arrangement, the aim of the market design is to correlate MV with price, so that the market incentivises continued improvement, in conformity with the Paris Agreement objectives seeking higher ambition.[27] Thus, the aim would be for the market to operate so as to encourage a race to the top, not the bottom.

Linking has been described as being politically complex and this has been suggested as a reason for so few links occurring to date,[28] although there is a divergence of views on the extent to which linking has actually been occurring.[29] Establishing an operational system for trading mitigation outcomes, based on a network between jurisdictions, could also well involve elements of political complexity. All the same, it is posited that many of the issues and obstacles, such

24 Macinante (n 15); see also Justin D Macinante, 'Operationalizing Cooperative Approaches under the Paris Agreement by Valuing Mitigation Outcomes' [2018] *CCLR* 258.

25 Mehling, 'Legal Frameworks' (n 20) 259 citing R Baron and C Philibert, 'Act Locally, Trade Globally Emissions Trading for Climate Policy' (© OECD/IEA 2005) www.iea.org/publications/freepublications/publication/act_locally.pdf accessed 14 May 2017. The nature of impacts will also be a function of the elasticity of demand in certain markets (that is, whether the additional costs can be passed through to consumers) and the extent to which regulated entities are competing in international markets not covered by emission mitigation restrictions; see Mirabelle Muûls and others, 'Evaluating the EU Emissions Trading System: Take It or Leave It? An Assessment of the Data after Ten Years' (Briefing Paper No 21, Imperial College London, Grantham Institute, October 2016) www.imperial.ac.uk/media/imperial-college/grantham-institute/public/publications/briefing-papers/Evaluating-the-EU-emissions-trading-system_Grantham-BP-21_web.pdf accessed 16 March 2017.

26 World Bank and PMR (n 19) 9.

27 For example, arts 2 and 4, para 3, Paris Agreement.

28 Mehling, 'Legal Frameworks' (n 20) 258.

29 World Bank and PMR (n 19), according to which bilateral linking was rare up to the date of that publication. Other authors are more bullish about links up to the date of the Paris Agreement: see Michael A Mehling, Gilbert E Metcalf and Robert N Stavins, 'Linking Heterogeneous Climate Policies (Consistent with the Paris Agreement)' (Discussion Paper ES 2017-6, Harvard Project on Climate Agreements, October 2017).

as those outlined earlier, that complicate, slow or deter attempts to link jurisdictions are not present, or not present to the same extent, in the case of networking, offering a more efficacious way to achieve ITMOs.

9.3.2.2 Legal Issues

That ETSs operate in complex frameworks of rules, principles and procedures under domestic law[30] will be relevant when units are traded across jurisdictions. Just as with linking of ETSs, networking would require agreement between participant jurisdictions. In the case of networking, however, the nature of the agreement is fundamentally different. Rather than an agreement between two (or more) individual jurisdictions, each of which seeks an arrangement on its own terms in order to reduce the degree to which it must compromise its existing system, a networking agreement would be between the jurisdiction seeking to join and the network, that is, the platform on which trading takes place.

Networking arrangements would not need agreement as to the legal alignment of parties' ETSs to ensure that the respective units are fungible; there would not be a need for joint registries, nor would there be a need for joint auctioning, or similarly co-ordinated issuance arrangements. Under networking, the jurisdictions' ETSs would remain independent of each other.[31] There would be no need to harmonise the regulatory systems,[32] institutions, administration or procedures, simplifying the process for jurisdictions to decide whether to participate or not.

This approach relies on the participating jurisdictions accepting the rules, infrastructural arrangements and other measures – such as the mechanism and parameters for determining the value of participating jurisdictions' mitigation actions (the MV) – and adhering to those rules and other requirements. The agreement required of a prospective networking participant would involve, first, acceptance of the same terms on which all other jurisdictions agree to participate; and second, that jurisdiction signifying any limits or conditions it wishes to impose on transactions entered by the legal entities it authorises to trade on the network. The decision of whether to join is either accept and join, or reject and not join. The agreement is not between jurisdictions but rather between the joining jurisdiction and the network (that is, the collective of jurisdictions that have already agreed to the common rules, which rules would be mostly mechanistic in nature). Matters such as

30 Mehling, 'Linking of Emissions Trading Systems' (n 20) 116.

31 This is subject to the qualification that, under the proposal, the ledger (registry) is distributed such that all participating jurisdictions may hold a copy of the ledger for all transactions across the entire network: see Section 9.3.2.3 for further discussion.

32 For instance, art 4 of the California–Quebec linking agreement provides specifically for regulatory harmonisation: see Agreement between California Air Resources Board and the Government of Quebec, Concerning the Harmonisation and Integration of Cap-and-Trade Programs for Reducing Greenhouse Gas Emissions, 27 September 2013 www.arb.ca.gov/cc/capandtrade/linkage/ca_quebec_linking_agreement_english.pdf accessed 6 March 2018.

ETS alignment, registries and issuance do not need to be negotiated, so the relative bargaining position of jurisdictions, as an issue in legal negotiations, would not arise.

9.3.2.3 Practical Issues

In terms of practical application, networking should be administratively more feasible than linking. As proposed, networking would not require the transfer of units from one registry to another, thereby avoiding the legal and administrative complexity that can arise in proposals for linking arrangements. There would still need to be the physical (electronic) infrastructure to give effect to transactions, but, unlike approaches to linking, networking would not require equivalence of the assets – emission allowances – in order to achieve fungibility.

In a networked system, the units may not even need to be the same type of asset, or primarily measured in the same terms (for example, the asset in one scheme might be measured as an absolute value, in the other as a performance standard), provided an assessment can be made of the respective MVs. Thus, subject to agreement being reached on the parameters and methodology for comparative assessments, the actual transaction process should be simpler and more transparent.

It follows that, since there would be no need to move units from the registry of one ETS to the registry of another, accounting and record-keeping in a networked system would be less complicated. Instead, the units the MV of which is to be transferred would be cancelled in their domestic registry. Additionally, once applicable parameters and methodology for comparative assessments have been agreed, networking would not be restricted to ETSs but could include other mitigation actions, provided their outcomes were capable of MV assessment. Hence, networking offers potential scope for a much larger, more flexible market than could occur under linking, which should also be more effective in re-engaging the private sector.

Connecting ETSs, whether by linking or networking, necessarily involves reconciling the differences between schemes. The integral point of difference is the extent of mitigation brought about by the respective schemes. By assessing MV, networking separates this climate element from elements of a more administrative or mechanistic nature. Conversely, linking requires the harmonisation of these elements as part of the process to reconcile climate (mitigation) element differences.[33]

9.3.2.4 Flexibility (Opting In and Out)

It follows that, because there is no need for legal, institutional or administrative integration of systems, it is more flexible for jurisdictions to join or leave the networked market. The network, in this sense, might be viewed as a facility of

[33] In this respect, the line-by-line comparisons of the respective programme regulations carried out by California and Quebec staff spring to mind: see World Bank and PMR (n 19) 15.

which any jurisdiction might avail itself, so long as it sees that there is an advantage for participants in its domestic market, and from which it might remove itself when that advantage no longer continues. While there would be a need for institutional and regulatory frameworks for the network itself and these would require time and resources to establish, their existence and operation should not inhibit the flexibility of jurisdictions seeking to join or leave the network, but rather facilitate it.

Two complementary consequences are, first, the network could continue to operate unaffected when an individual jurisdiction elects to leave it; and second, a jurisdiction that wishes to opt out of the network could do so seamlessly, not only without impacting ongoing network operation but also without affecting the operation of its own ETS. For individual jurisdictions this would mean less of an administrative burden, less cost and the ability to give effect to decisions relatively expeditiously – certainly, much more quickly than the time it would take to negotiate a linking agreement; or the negotiations that may be required in order to de-link.

9.3.3 *DLT*

9.3.3.1 Introduction

The specific type of IT architecture on which the network of carbon markets might operate is DLT. The proposal for the networking of carbon markets across jurisdictions necessarily implies that there must be some form of electronic infrastructure in place to allow such a market to operate by communications between participants. What is proposed, however, is inter-jurisdictional trade in carbon assets and increasingly these are being defined legislatively as financial instruments.[34] Thus, the networked market is proposed as a financial market, implying certain basic essential requirements for its transactional infrastructure, such as security, capacity and reliability. As with any financial market, this infrastructure might be expected to facilitate the accountability, auditability, certainty and accuracy of the transactions it processes, as well as regulatory supervision and the facility to ensure that financial and legal risk management can be addressed, in a time and cost-efficient way.

The context of the proposal recognises that technological developments are occurring that will fundamentally change how financial services are provided and how markets, businesses and governments operate.[35] These include developments in areas

[34] See, for instance, Markets in Financial Instruments Directive 2 (MiFID 2): Directive 2014/65/EU of the European Parliament and of the Council of 15 May 2014 on markets in financial instruments and amending Directive 2002/92/EC and Directive 2011/61/EU, OJ L 173, 12.06.2014, 394–496.

[35] Mark Walport, Chief Scientific Adviser to HM Government, Distributed Ledger Technology: Beyond Block Chain (UK Government Office for Science, GS 16-1, 19 January 2016) www.gov.uk/government/publications/distributed-ledger-technology-blackett-review accessed 30 September 2016.

such as big data;[36] Internet of Things;[37] the platform economy;[38] and in so-called emerging transformative technologies that include biometrics; cloud computing; cognitive computing; DLT, or blockchain; machine learning, or predictive analytics; quantum computing; and robotics.[39]

The focus here is on DLT and blockchain, which has been described as portending 'a new digital revolution',[40] coming after twenty years of scientific research that produced advances in the fields of cryptography and decentralised computer networks.[41] Such claims are supported by the level of attention and related research being applied by intergovernmental bodies, governments and public institutions,[42] global business bodies,[43] the financial sector,[44] lawyers and consultants[45] and market regulators.[46]

Much attention has been applied to the opportunities and potential benefits the technology offers;[47] however, applications such as cryptocurrencies and their uses and

36 Gartner, 'Glossary: Big Data' (2012) www.gartner.com/it-glossary/big-data accessed 8 January 2018.

37 IEEE, 'Towards a Definition of the Internet of Things (IoT)' (Revision 1, 27 May 2015) https://iot.ieee.org/definition.html accessed 8 January 2018.

38 For discussion of definitions and approaches to regulation, see Michèle Finck, 'Digital Co-regulation: Designing a Supranational Legal Framework for the Platform Economy' (2018) 43(1) *Eur L Rev* 47.

39 For how financial services industry transformation has spun off technology innovation over the last fifty years, see World Economic Forum, 'The Future of Financial Infrastructure: An Ambitious Look at How Blockchain Can Reshape Financial Services' (August 2016) 20 www3.weforum.org/docs/WEF_The_future_of_financial_infrastructure.pdf accessed 02 November 2016.

40 Aaron Wright and Primavera De Filippi, 'Decentralized Blockchain Technology and the Rise of Lex Cryptographia' (Background Paper, 12 March 2015); Internet Governance Forum, UN-Department of Economic and Social Affairs, Workshops Descriptions and Reports, 'Bitcoin, Blockchain and Beyond: FLASH HELP!' (Workshop No 239, 2015) 2 www.intgovforum.org/cms/workshops/list-of-published-workshop-proposals accessed 3 November 2016.

41 ibid.

42 For example, Robleh Ali, John Barrdear and Roger Clews, 'Innovations in Payment Technologies and the Emergence of Digital Currencies' (Bank of England Quarterly Bulletin, 2014 Q3) www.bankofengland.co.uk/publications/Documents/quarterlybulletin/2014/qb14q3digitalcurrenciesbitcoin1.pdf accessed 12 January 2017.

43 World Economic Forum (n 39).

44 For example, R3 is a consortium with more than eighty banks, clearing houses, exchanges, market infrastructure providers, asset managers, central banks, conduct regulators, trade associations, professional services firms and technology companies developing commercial applications of DLT for the financial services industry: www.r3cev.com/blog/2016/4/4/introducing-r3-corda-a-distributed-ledger-designed-for-financial-services accessed 12 March 2018.

45 For example, Sigrid Seibold and George Samman, 'Consensus: Immutable Agreement for the Internet of Value' (KPMG, 2016) https://assets.kpmg.com/content/dam/kpmg/pdf/2016/06/kpmg-blockchain-consensus-mechanism.pdf accessed 5 February 2018; Allens Lawyers, 'Blockchain Reaction: Understanding the Opportunities and Navigating the Legal Frameworks of Distributed Ledger Technology and Blockchain' www.the-blockchain.com/docs/blockchainreport-%20legal%20frameworks%20of%20distributed%20ledger.pdf accessed 2 November 2016.

46 For instance, European Securities and Markets Authority (ESMA), 'The Distributed Ledger Technology Applied to Securities Markets' (Discussion Paper, ESMA/2016/773, 2 June 2016); ASTRI Whitepaper On Distributed Ledger Technology (Commissioned by Hong Kong Monetary Authority, 11 November 2016) www.hkma.gov.hk/media/eng/doc/key-functions/finanical-infrastructure/Whitepaper_On_Distributed_Ledger_Technology.pdf accessed 12 January 2017.

47 See, for example, Michèle Finck 'Blockchains: Regulating the Unknown' (2018) 19(4) *German LJ* 665; Julie Maupin, 'Mapping the Global Legal Landscape of Blockchain and Other Distributed Ledger

initial coin offerings (ICOs) are increasingly the focus of lawmakers and regulators.[48] The applications of DLT for business, financial and government services, while growing rapidly, are still nascent, yet already consideration has been given to regulation and this is increasing. Historically it remains largely limited to and directed towards specific applications of the technology, such as cryptocurrencies.[49]

It is noted that there have been issues, previously, with the security of carbon market transactions and the existing carbon market IT.[50] The expectation is that ongoing technological developments can help ensure that recurrence of episodes such as hacking of registry accounts is far less likely, if not impossible.[51] Additionally, these technological developments hold out the promise of better addressing some of the core elements of climate policy incorporated in the Paris Agreement, such as greater transparency, accountability, traceability and security.

9.3.3.2 Use Cases, Especially in Financial Markets

In 2016, the World Economic Forum (WEF) reported that, while there was significant awareness and interest in DLT, hurdles to large-scale implementation (in terms of financial infrastructure), such as an uncertain and unharmonised regulatory environment, nascent collective standardisation efforts and an absence of formal legal frameworks, remained.[52] Some of the potential applications of DLT that have been

Technologies' (Centre for International Governance Innovation, CIGI Papers No 149, October 2017) www.cigionline.org/sites/default/files/documents/Paper%20no.149.pdf accessed 24 January 2018; Benno Ferrarini, Julie Maupin and Marthe Hinojales, 'Distributed Ledger Technologies for Developing Asia' (ADB Economics Working Paper Series, No 533, December 2017) www.adb.org/sites/default/files/publication/388861/ewp-533.pdf accessed 24 January 2018; Angela Walch 'The Path of the Blockchain Lexicon (and the Law)' (2017) 36(2) *Rev Banking & Fin L* 713.

48 Finck (n 47).

49 In the United States, for instance, see Financial Crimes Enforcement Network (FinCEN), US Department of Treasury www.fincen.gov; US Commodities Futures Trading Commission Act 1974 (7 USC §§ 1 et seq) www.cftc.org; New York Department of Financial Services (NYDFS), 'BitLicense' NY Comp Codes R & Regs Tit 23, § 200 (2015) www.govinfo.gov/content/pkg/STATUTE-88/pdf/STATUTE-88-Pg1389.pdf accessed 22 April 2022; Securities and Exchange Commission, Securities Exchange Act of 1934 Release No 81207/25 July 2017 Report of Investigation Pursuant to Section 21(a) of the Securities Exchange Act of 1934: The DAO www.sec.gov/litigation/investreport/34-81207.pdf accessed 21 August 2017.

50 European Court of Auditors, 'The Integrity and Implementation of the EU ETS' (Special Report, 2015) 29–41 www.eca.europa.eu/Lists/ECADocuments/SR15_06/SR15_06_EN.pdf accessed 23 June 2017.

51 There are structural issues as well. For instance, in 2012, the centralised Union registry replaced all national registries in the EU ETS: Commission Regulation (EU) No 389/2013 of 2 May 2013 establishing a Union Registry pursuant to Directive 2003/87/EC of the European Parliament and of the Council, Decisions No 280/2004/EC and No 406/2009/EC of the European Parliament and of the Council and repealing Commission Regulations (EU) No 920/2010 and No 1193/2011 Text with EEA relevance, OJ L 122, 3.5.2013, 1–59; although, the European Court of Auditors report noted that even though the EC operates the EU registry, it has no powers to monitor and supervise transactions (n 50).

52 The World Economic Forum (n 39) reported that at that time more than twenty-four countries were investing in DLT, more than ninety corporations had joined DLT consortia, 80 per cent of banks were

identified include in trade finance, through operational simplification; in compliance automation, by improving regulatory efficiency; in global payment systems, by reducing settlement times; and in asset rehypothecation, thereby enhancing liquidity.[53] Other broader, potential applications being tested or implemented include in relation to record-keeping, such as patient health records, or land property titles; legal inheritance; source traceability for supply chains, including diamonds, or gold production; or other proof of ownership.[54] Some intergovernmental bodies, national and provincial governments have instigated projects to provide services based on DLT.[55] Other application areas that have been reported include decentralised power generation sharing, music streaming royalty payments, and voting in elections.[56]

In terms of potential areas of impact of DLT on financial markets, operational simplification, regulatory efficiency improvement, counterparty risk reduction, clearing and settlement time reduction, liquidity and capital improvement, and fraud minimisation have been identified as value drivers.[57] The claimed 'transformative characteristics' of distributed infrastructure include immutability, which for financial market participants might remove the need for reconciliations; transparency, thereby removing market information asymmetries and increasing regulatory co-operation; and autonomy, disintermediating centralised parties whose roles in bringing trust and reducing counterparty risk will be obviated.[58] Possible benefits of DLT applied, for instance, to the securities market include speeding up clearing and settlement by reducing the number of intermediaries involved; facilitating recording of ownership and safekeeping of assets; facilitating collection, consolidation and sharing of data for reporting, risk management and supervisory purposes; reducing counterparty risk by shortening the transaction settlement cycle; improving the efficient management of collateral; continuous availability; greater security and resilience against attack; and cost reduction.[59] Other possible financial services

predicted to initiate DLT projects by 2017 and, over the preceding three years, more than 2,500 patents had been filed and more than USD 1.4 billion invested.

53 World Economic Forum (n 39) 21.

54 Seibold and Samman (n 45); Maupin (n 47); International Monetary Fund, 'Virtual Currencies and Beyond: Initial Considerations' (Staff Discussion Note SDN/16/03, January 2016).

55 Walch (n 47) 718 n 13; also Walport (n 35) ch 6; Ali, Barrdear and Clews (n 42); Umberto Bacchi, 'U.N. Glimpses into Blockchain Future with Eye Scan Payments for Refugees' (Reuters, 21 June 2017) www.reuters.com/article/us-un-refugees-blockchain/u-n-glimpses-into-blockchain-future-with-eye-scan-payments-for-refugees-idUSKBN19C0BB accessed 28 January 2018; Ferrarini, Maupin and Hinojales (n 47) give examples of digital identity, trade finance, project aid monitoring and results-based disbursements, smart energy and sustainable supply chain management.

56 Finck (n 47) 671–74; Marc Pilkington 'Blockchain Technology: Principles and Applications' in F. Xavier Olleros and Majlinda Zhegu (eds), *Research Handbook on Digital Transformations* (Edward Elgar 2016); Ian Tucker, 'Blockchain: So Much Bigger Than Bitcoin...' *The Guardian* (28 January 2018) www.theguardian.com/technology/2018/jan/28/blockchain-so-much-bigger-than-bitcoin accessed 22 April 2018.

57 World Economic Forum (n 39) 19 et seq.

58 ibid 24; also Allens Lawyers (n 45).

59 ESMA (n 46) 9–13.

applications relate to global payments, trade finance, corporate proxy voting, insurance claims processing, syndicated loans and contingent convertible bond issuances.[60]

Positive sentiment surrounds the applications and benefits to be expected of DLT; however, it is important not to be swept up by the hype of the 'thought leaders'.[61] The perception is that DLT could make networking of carbon markets both feasible and effective, by enabling traceability of the provenance of assets, or their attributes such as MV; by the security dimension it brings; and by the permanence of records it can afford, thereby facilitating accounting and auditability. Thus, it would be promoting the objectives of climate policy, evidenced by the terms of the Paris Agreement, while also facilitating and stimulating an inter-jurisdictional market, so that it would operate efficiently, encourage private sector engagement, promote a stable carbon price and foster the effective application of carbon finance.

9.3.3.3 DLT Terminology

Development of DLT is dynamic and the range of fields in which it might be applied introduces issues of terminology and meaning.[62] For example, the expressions 'DLT' and 'blockchain' are frequently used interchangeably, both in academic and in general literature. Even use of 'distributed' can cause the misperception that, being distributed, a ledger has no overall controlling entity, whereas this is a question of design.[63] Confusion of meaning over the terms used is a risk not only for academics, researchers and business entities designing and building applications in the various different fields but especially for policymakers and regulators overseeing such developments and determining the extent to which their intervention in the use cases is warranted and how that intervention should be carried out.[64]

The technology is populated with particular nomenclature such as 'permissioned' and 'permissionless', 'smart contracts', 'miners' and 'mining', 'tokens', 'cryptocurrencies', 'initial coin offerings' and with a multitude of acronyms. Some expressions even have other parallel expressions (for example, public and private, for permissionless and permissioned), which may have identical meanings, or nuanced differences of meaning.[65]

More concerning, perhaps, is the way in which fundamental characteristics of the technology may be understood, particularly when they are used so broadly and repetitively that they enter the technological/DLT vernacular without scrutiny or

[60] World Economic Forum (n 39) 46–127, setting out 'deep dive analyses of these and other use cases'.
[61] Walch (n 47) 740 n 108.
[62] Walport (n 35) 7 refers to 'the bewildering array of terminology' as a difficulty in communication.
[63] ibid.
[64] Walch (n 47) 728 et seq.
[65] ibid 719–28: Walch has examined this issue in considerable detail, highlighting the particular problems this generates for regulators.

detailed consideration. Walch cites the example of 'immutable', as used to describe the ledger created by blockchain technology, in this respect.[66]

9.3.3.4 DLT Definitions

With changing and uncertain meanings of terminology, formal definitions will not necessarily be universally agreed and, even so, may be superseded relatively quickly.[67] Nonetheless, it is necessary to clearly explain what is meant by the terms and expressions, as employed here, in this particular context.[68]

The infrastructure on which it is proposed to provide networking of carbon markets is, at its most elementary, a series of computers, or nodes, connected with each other in a network, for instance, via the Internet. In this sense, it is no different from other such structures that exist: for example, the connections of computers of legal entities trading in the EU ETS or other markets. The fundamental difference introduced by DLT is that the ledger, or registry – the record of unit holdings of participating entities resulting from the transactions between them – is no longer held only by a trusted, centrally positioned entity (comparable, for instance, to the International Transaction Log (ITL) under the Kyoto Protocol, although the ITL role is also more limited) through which all transactions must be routed in order to be approved, recorded and that record maintained. Rather, the ledger may be held in full and kept up to date on all nodes, that is, on each participating entity's computer (or, alternatively, just on a certain number thereof or, perhaps, only in part – for instance, the most recent transactions). Thus, the ledger is distributed. Another description is as a shared ledger, which has been applied particularly in the context of industry-based (e.g. financial sector) applications.[69]

Further, DLT is considered broadly as consisting of three elements, being the combination of a distributed ledger, with public/private key encryption and decentralised infrastructure.[70] It has also been described as 'a distributed, shared, encrypted database that serves as an irreversible and incorruptible public repository of information', enabling 'unrelated people to reach consensus on the occurrence of a particular transaction or event without the need for a controlling authority'.[71] Another description of DLT is as 'a protocol for building a replicated and shared ledger system', collectively maintained by the participants in that system or network, rather than by one central party.[72]

66 ibid 735–45.
67 See, for instance, ibid 730 in relation to New York's 'BitLicense'.
68 Walport (n 35) 17–19.
69 ibid.
70 For example, see ESMA (n 46) s 2.1; also Wright and De Filippi (n 40) 4, 5.
71 Wright and De Filippi (n 40) 2.
72 ASTRI (n 46).

While DLT is not a huge technological leap, it can be seen as an incremental improvement.[73] In DLT, the ledger can (but need not necessarily) be organised as a chain of blocks of information, each block containing a collection of transactions – new transactions being collected to form a new block that is time-stamped when added to the ledger.[74] Each block thus contains one or more new transactions and the adding of blocks to the chain (hence this implementation is referred to as the 'blockchain') means that the ledger grows cumulatively.[75]

Blockchain is one implementation of a distributed ledger. Records can also just be stored one after the other, on a distributed ledger, in a continuous manner (but not in blocks), being added after the participants reach consensus.[76] There is also a newer type of DLT that transmits and confirms transactions in an asynchronous, as opposed to a chained, way.[77] However, it is not necessary to examine every such form, but simply to note that different technical mechanisms exist for adding to the ledger.

As DLT covers a wide range of potential functionality, it is useful to identify key features that define a DLT system.[78] These are:

- firstly, a decentralised, distributed infrastructure, meaning that the system is composed of multiple entities or nodes, each (or at least a number thereof) holding a copy of the full ledger, obviating the role of the central ledger holder;
- secondly, participants using public/private key encryption to interact with transactions in the system, obviating the role of a trusted central counterparty to intermediate transactions;
- thirdly, a mechanism by which the nodes reach consensus on the valid entries to add to the ledger; and
- fourthly, immutability, meaning that the ledger is accumulative, so that once entries are added to the ledger (theoretically, at least) they cannot be changed or removed.[79] Thus, if it is desired to reverse or unwind a transaction, the transaction will need to be undertaken again, literally, in reverse.[80]

There are also elements of a DLT system that are configurable to suit the desired design and the application to which the system is to be put.[81] The configurable features include permissioning, referring to whether a system is open for anyone to

73 Wright and De Filippi (n 40) 5 n 15. These authors trace the historical development of the individual elements back to the late 1970s. See also World Economic Forum (n 39).

74 Wright and De Filippi (n 40).

75 ibid.

76 Walport (n 35) 18.

77 Ferrarini, Maupin and Hinojales (n 47) 5.

78 Adrian Jackson and others, 'Networked Carbon Markets: Permissionless Innovation with Distributed Ledgers?' (4 July 2017) 7 https://ssrn.com/abstract=2997099 accessed 9 October 2017.

79 ibid table 1.

80 There will, of course, be implications of this if, for example, the counterparties' positions have changed in the interim.

81 Jackson and others (n 78) 8.

join (that is, it is public or permissionless) or is private, or, at least, is set up by a collaboration of parties so that only trusted or vetted participants can partake in the control and maintenance of the system;[82] proof of work, which is a means to achieve consensus in a permissionless system;[83] 'smart contracts', referring to transactional terms and conditions embedded in computer code, which allow automatic execution of the relevant transaction once precise conformity with those terms and conditions has been established;[84] and arrangements for settlement, exchanges or payment systems, which may be required in some shape or form to provide for the actual transfer of money, or settlement of physical assets, between counterparties.[85]

Configuration of all of these elements can add up to very different outcomes.

9.3.3.5 Use Case of the Proposal

In these circumstances, the importance of specifying the configuration of (or, at least, the options for) the use case proposed is evident, for two reasons. First, the way in which the use case is configured will determine whether the perceived benefits of the technology are realisable, or exist only in theory. Second, the design of the technology platform will indicate how the application should be regulated and the institutional framework required.[86]

The specific application of DLT proposed connects the carbon markets (that is, the ETSs) of individual jurisdictions that choose to participate in the network, in order to provide for inter-jurisdictional trading of their carbon assets (the units traded in the respective ETSs). Hence, the aim is to facilitate smart contract-based transactions peer-to-peer, in this case across jurisdictions. For the market system proposed, a primary element is that it will comprise multiple nodes (whether each and every node would need to hold a copy of the full ledger will be a matter of design). There would be encryption, for instance, using public/private keys and there would need to be a consensus mechanism for updating the ledger. If this

82 ibid table 2; also ASTRI (n 46). For a comparison of relative strengths and weaknesses of permissioned, unpermissioned and hybrid blockchains, see (Ferrarini, Maupin and Hinojales (n 47) 2–6. For advantages of private over public blockchains, see Vitalik Buterin, 'Public and Private Blockchains' (Coindesk, 7 August 2015) www.coindesk.com/vitalik-buterin-on-public-and-private-blockchains/ accessed 02 February 2018.

83 As the proposal is for a permissioned system, proof of work is not considered in any detail.

84 Jackson and others (n 78) 8 table 2; also Macinante (n 15) ch 6. The original formulation is:

> A smart contract is a computerized transaction protocol that executes the terms of a contract. The general objectives of smart contract design are to satisfy common contractual conditions (such as payment terms, liens, confidentiality, and even enforcement), minimize exceptions both malicious and accidental, and minimize the need for trusted intermediaries. Related economic goals include lowering fraud loss, arbitration and enforcement costs, and other transaction costs. (Nick Szabo, 'Smart Contracts' (1994) www.fon.hum.uva.nl/rob/Courses/InformationInSpeech/CDROM/Literature/LOTwinterschool2006/szabo.best.vwh.net/smart.contracts.html accessed 26 January 2018)

85 Jackson and others (n 78) table 2.

86 See Macinante (n 15), where these issues are addressed in detail.

updating is accumulative, such that new entries to the ledger follow consecutively on earlier entries (whether in blocks or otherwise being another design question), without changing or altering them, then the four key elements that identify a DLT system (outlined in Section 9.3.3.4) would be present.

As the network would connect the administrators of the respective ETSs, as well as the legal entities participating in each domestic ETS, the participants would all be identified. Thus, the ability for a legal person (presumably corporate, assuming that the criteria applied for participation in their domestic ETS) to participate in cross-jurisdictional trading will depend on their authorisation to participate in their domestic ETS. Accordingly, the distributed ledger would not be anonymous, or public/permissionless, in the sense that anyone at all can participate. Strictly speaking, it would not be private either, in the sense of being closed to all but an exclusive group, since presumably any legal entity satisfying the relevant criteria could be authorised to trade in a domestic ETS. The network may best be described as public but permissioned, since the precondition for participation on the DL network would be that the legal entity was first authorised to trade in a participating domestic ETS.[87]

For Paris Agreement parties, it is assumed that mutual authorisation of each other for the purposes of Article 6 would apply. There is the further consideration of whether participation by a jurisdiction in the DL network would imply that all participants in that jurisdiction's domestic ETS were automatically considered to be authorised, by that jurisdiction's government, to trade inter-jurisdictionally, or if specific authorisation for each individual legal entity to so trade would still be necessary to satisfy the requirement that use of ITMOs to achieve NDCs is voluntary and authorised by participating parties.[88] This will be a matter for each individual jurisdiction to determine.

As a public but permissioned DL, there would need to be a system providing for the type of permissioning granted to nodes, that is, identifying those permitted to view, and those permitted to interact with, the ledger. Legal entities, for example, might have permission to interact with the ledger by submitting transactions for addition to it, as well as being permitted to view that part of the ledger pertaining to their own holdings and transactions. They might not hold a copy of the entire ledger, as this could lead to scalability problems as the ledger grows in size,[89] but might only

87 Also could be described as a hybrid: see Ferrarini, Maupin and Hinojales (n 47) 4–5.

88 UNFCCC: Draft Text on Matters relating to Article 6 of the Paris Agreement: Guidance on cooperative approaches referred to in Article 6, paragraph 2, of the Paris Agreement, Version 3 of 15 December 00:50 hrs, Proposal by the President, Annex para 4(c) https://unfccc.int/resource/cop25/CMA2_11a_DT_Art.6.2.pdf accessed 15 January 2020.

89 There is a discussion of this issue in Ethereum, 'A Next-Generation Smart Contract and Decentralized Application Platform' (White Paper, first published 2014, last updated 2 April 2022) https://github.com/ethereum/wiki/wiki/White-Paper accessed 11 April 2018. Scalability limitations have been identified as a weakness of permissionless DLs: see Ferrarini, Maupin and Hinojales (n 47) 3.

need hold that part relating to their own holdings and transactions.[90] Similarly, ETS administrators might be restrained from interacting with the ledger in the sense of submitting transactions, but might have broader viewing permission rights, for instance, being able to view the accounts of all legal entities in their own ETS and some components of the information held on the overall ledger more generally (although perhaps not, for instance, information pertaining to individual legal entities from other jurisdictions).

Related to this would be the consensus mechanism by which new transactions are entered on the ledger. This might operate on a distributed basis,[91] but only between the administrator nodes. For example, the administrator of the ETS from which a transaction originates would perform the role of validator by confirming that the seller in the transaction is the true owner of the carbon assets being sold. They would then broadcast the information concerning that transaction (and any other transactions originating from its ETS at the same time), as other administrators would also do concerning transactions originating in their respective ETSs at that time. These validating nodes would then agree (by a mechanism they would have determined in advance) which of the transactions – presumably all, if they had all been confirmed as being correct – would be added.

As this proposal concerns the conduct of transactions between jurisdictions, it presumes that there will be contracts setting out the terms and conditions on which those transactions have been agreed. Such terms and conditions could be standardised for all transactions across the network, with provision for variable factors – parties, quantity, price, origin, MV or any other variable characteristics – to be inserted. This will be the function of smart contracts, which would allow automatic execution of the relevant transaction to which they pertain once precise conformity with the terms and conditions had been established. In conjunction with the execution of the smart contract for a transaction, in order to complete the transaction, arrangements for financial settlement co-ordinated with the transfer of the carbon asset will need to be in place.

9.4 CONCLUSION

This chapter introduces proposals for a market between carbon markets, a trading platform connecting and facilitating transactions between individual, separate markets, each of which will continue to operate as an autonomous operation in its own jurisdiction, while participating on the network created by the connection.[92] The

90 Richard Gendal Brown and others, 'Corda: An Introduction' (White Paper, August 2016) https://docs.corda.net/_static/corda-introductory-whitepaper.pdf accessed 12 February 2018; Richard G Brown, 'Introducing R3 Corda™: A Distributed Ledger Designed for Financial Services' (blog post, 5 April 2016) www.r3.com/blog/2016/04/05/introducing-r3-corda-a-distributed-ledger-designed-for-financial-services/ accessed 12 February 2018.

91 ASTRI (n 46) 10–15 provides a description of this process.

92 It draws on and reproduces in part Macinante (n 15) ch 6.

proposed market consists of two distinct elements, being first, the networking of the individual markets across this trading platform, and second, the platform operating on DLT architecture. It aims to facilitate and stimulate an inter-jurisdictional market that will encourage private financial sector engagement, while at the same time promoting the objectives of climate policy evidenced in the Paris Agreement.

Networking is not current practice, presently being only conceptual in nature. The current approach for connecting carbon markets from different jurisdictions is for them to link, which involves the alignment of schemes, policies, laws, processes and so on. This gives rise to political issues, stemming from the perceived impact of system alignment on the sovereignty of the participating jurisdictions. Networking better addresses these issues, as the inherent problem of imbalance of negotiating positions would not arise. Networking also holds out a more time-efficient process by avoiding the need to homogenise laws, systems, registries, policies and other elements of the respective participating jurisdictions' systems. Hence, many legal and practical issues might be avoided, thereby promising a more flexible arrangement.

The global recognition that technological developments are occurring that fundamentally change how financial services are provided, how markets, businesses and governments operate, leads to a conclusion that in proposing a model for networking carbon markets, it is necessary and desirable to propose the technology on which the networked market platform should operate. Application of DLT in this context is not without issues. Some identified with the technology include scalability, interoperability with existing and between systems, need for a way to settle transactions in central bank money, absence of a recourse mechanism for dealing with mistakes, and no scope for margin finance and short selling. Key risks that have been raised include cyber risk, fraud and money laundering, difficulty in identifying anomalies, and how to deal with erroneous coding. However, these can impact on any technological solution and thus are not particular to DLT.

At the same time, DLT offers useful features, including immutability (supporting traceability, auditability and robust accounting); decentralised participants, and so disintermediation of transaction gatekeepers (using smart contracting to facilitate transactions, thus increasing efficiency); distributed information sharing and management (enabling balancing of transparency with privacy, and the permissioning mechanism); and security (based on hash cryptography, and the consensus mechanism). The realisation of these elements and potential benefits, resolution of issues and management of risks, and how the application should be regulated, will be a function of use case design. In the model proposed, all participants would be identified, so the DL would be public but permissioned; and the consensus mechanism, it is proposed, should be based on nodes of the administrators from participating jurisdictional schemes (ETSs).

From a technical perspective, individual features and elements described as part of the DL such as the accumulative nature of the ledger, and cryptographic security, could equally well be incorporated using a centralised database. The question that needs to be considered is whether the distributed architecture adds anything that could not otherwise be achieved using a centralised database currently in use such as, say, the ITL, suitably adapted. The answer proffered is that consideration of the technical arrangements must be set in the broader overall context. Application of the DL, particularly for networking carbon markets, as proposed, affords greater flexibility for jurisdictions to access, or conversely leave, the networked market, according to domestic economic suitability, as well as a level playing field, irrespective of economic size or development. This aligns far more compellingly with the disaggregated, heterogeneous, bottom-up approach evident in the Paris Agreement and related decisions.

10

Conclusions, Recommendations and a Potential Pathway for a Transition to a DLT-Based Governance for Carbon Markets

Michael A. Mehling, Alastair Marke, Fabiano de Andrade Correa and Constantine Markides

The real danger is not that computers will begin to think like men, but that men will begin to think like computers.

Sydney J. Harris (1917–86), late American journalist, *Chicago Daily News*

Decarbonising the global economy by mid-century, as called for under the Paris Agreement and bolstered by a growing number of national, subnational and corporate pledges, raises daunting challenges of policy co-ordination and economic cost. Scalable policy instruments that help reduce the cost of achieving decarbonisation targets and enable co-operation across sectors and jurisdictions are therefore likely to see increased attention in coming decades, favouring continued growth of carbon markets. These can build off an extensive track record of policy implementation, with often difficult experiences resulting in the continuous improvement of system design and governance.

As they expand in scope beyond their traditional starting point in heavy industry and power generation, however, existing approaches to carbon trading face problematic technical limitations. With a growing number of participants, moreover, the administrative burden and transaction costs they impose acquire greater urgency. And with expanding market size and upward pressure on the price of traded carbon units, questions of security and transparency in the market will remain as important as ever. This is the backdrop to the surging interest in the potential role of new technologies – and in particular of distributed ledger technology (DLT) – in improving the implementation and governance of carbon markets.

What the chapters of this book have therefore sought to provide is an overview of promising technologies and their potential application in carbon trading, the legal and regulatory questions that arise from their deployment, as well as a series of case studies discussing their potential roll-out in existing compliance and voluntary carbon markets at the international and regional levels. From this first book-length exploration of the role of emerging technologies and notably DLT in the future evolution of carbon trading, a number of key insights can be inferred for future policy design and implementation. Table 10.1 sets out the key challenges identified in this book and some practical and legal recommendations for tackling these challenges.

Some jurisdictions are already exploring the use of novel technologies such as DLT in their carbon trading systems, and it has also been discussed as a potential

TABLE 10.1 *Summary of major carbon market challenges and DLT-based practical/legal suggestions*

Challenges and legal opportunities	Practical suggestions	Legal suggestions
1. There is an opportunity to combine DLT, AI and IoT to offer solutions to the climate problem. 2. While AI and DLT can foster efficient and intelligent decision-making, IoT allows closer interaction with the physical world, which will improve the quality of real-time data. However, data generated by IoT are only valuable if they are reliable.	To solve the challenges, all devices that are connected must be secured. The data stored on the devices must be protected from external cyber-attacks, for example, through effective firewalls. Further, DLT offers immutability of data and a secure environment. It also ensures data integrity since any change should be verified by most participating nodes in the blockchain network.	Data protection legislation must be watertight to ensure the security of data for all participating actors. A clear legal framework will also be vital, especially in relation to liability among actors (i.e. whether there is strict liability or limited liability) and the remedies available for each network actor.
3. Carbon markets are technically and administratively complex, the traded units intangible and the dynamics in the market entirely dependent on policy decisions. That makes them particularly vulnerable to governance shortfalls.	A robust governance structure can be drafted and agreed by all market participants before they participate. Innovative technologies such as DLT, AI and IoT can meet several governance needs in a more secure and cost-effective manner.	Regulation is critical to ensure the operation of carbon markets, notably with a view to matters of environmental integrity, accounting and transparency, compliance and enforcement, as well as market oversight. Use of innovative technologies raises separate and new regulatory challenges that have to be addressed.
4. A range of public and private actors is involved in the governance of carbon markets, including system administrators, accredited	A DLT-supported system should be piloted with permissioned and permissionless operations that allow testing of the	A clear legal framework will ensure that all parties involved fully appreciate the legal risks involved and are willing to participate on

(continued)

TABLE 10.1 *(continued)*

Challenges and legal opportunities	Practical suggestions	Legal suggestions
verifiers and various market intermediaries such as trading exchanges. This can lead to questions regarding market access or how liability can be attributed between the participants in the event of system breaches.	changed roles of existing carbon market actors and designating of new actors required to operate such a system.	this basis. Clarity as to the penalties to be imposed in the event of any breaches will also be pivotal as parties will be able to make decisions based on their risk-appetite.
5. Application of AI to the following can provide solutions to the climate problem: (a) autonomous and connected electric vehicles; (b) distributed energy grids; (c) smart agriculture and food systems; (d) next-generation weather and climate prediction; (e) smart disaster response; (f) AI-designed intelligent, connected and liveable cities; (g) a transparent, digital Earth; and (h) reinforcement learning for Earth sciences breakthroughs.	An interlinkage among AI, DLT and IoT can ensure that data relating to all the components that contribute to climate change, for example, the atmosphere, atmospheric chemistry, ocean dynamics and ocean chemistry, are factored into their analysis, which could increase the accuracy of climate modelling and simulations.	There will likely need to be an overhaul of the existing separate jurisdictional differences in relation to, for example, intellectual property rights and protection for IoT business-related inventions. Currently, there is no consensus about the patentability of integrated inventions that combine data structures with software data processing and hardware equipment. In such an environment, it might be difficult to obtain judicial protection in case of a cross-border infringement of certain IoT inventions.
6. A DLT-supported ETS would be a DAO composed of several modules and embedded with an intricate web of smart contracts operationalising the crypto-legal structure.	Tracing liability to members of the DAO across jurisdictions may be practically difficult; therefore, clear rules as to whether liability should, in the event of a failure, be apportioned to the developer, promoter or creator of DAO are important. In these circumstances,	A primary legal risk facing a DAO system is the status of the participatory tokens. Given that tokens could represent significant monetary value, with similar attributes to shares or equity, there would have to be a clear legal structure as to the apportionment of liability in the event of a failure of the system.

(continued)

TABLE 10.1 *(continued)*

Challenges and legal opportunities	Practical suggestions	Legal suggestions
	considerations about the legal status of the DAO are also significant (i.e. whether it will be treated as a general partnership, joint venture or incorporated company).	
7. Use of DLT can provide a secured, shared, distributed and transparent register for ETSs. While DLT alone cannot provide real-time data, IoT can be used to accomplish this. The data collected can relate to the specific projects that generate allowances that are traded on the market.	One key recommendation would be to observe the new platforms that have recently emerged that offer DLT-based carbon markets – international organisations could help build technological capacity in the developing world, push for the use of DLT to support programmes such as REDD+ and accept credits that use these technologies in compliance markets.	Data processing and protection legislation can be implemented to cover situations where there is a data leakage from the system. While this is unlikely to happen in practice, a sound legal structure will ensure that data leakages are dealt with effectively.
8. A crypto-legal system could eliminate the possibility of account-operating and transfer-approval failures and security breaches by using the Doorkeeper, KYC and Transaction Modules.	The Doorkeeper Module would provide a shield defending all subscribing servers and accounts from cyber-attacks of virus and malware (such as those that fuelled the EU-ETS attacks in 2010–11). The KYC Module comprises functions of KYC application and processing on-chain and off-chain. The on-chain KYC application function is a permissioned distributed ledger storing identity data of verified companies and traders; identification documents are stored off-chain because foreseeably	The legal governance structure can set out how the Doorkeeper, KYC and Transaction Modules can eliminate the potential issues identified to provide comfort to market participants.

(continued)

TABLE 10.1 *(continued)*

Challenges and legal opportunities	Practical suggestions	Legal suggestions
	the method of processing identity proof might evolve in the future.	
9. Blockchain offers a solution for one of the main challenges regarding the implementation and success of CORSIA, namely, double counting of data. Blockchain achieves this as it is a secured, shared, distributed and decentralised ledger that can be used to achieve data backup in real-time.	A network established between the carbon market registries, offering CORSIA-eligible emissions units, and the CCR will allow collection in near-real-time of information about cancellations of emissions units. Permissioned blockchains can also be used – these are usually privately owned or at least set up by a collaboration of parties so that only trusted or checked participants can participate in control and maintenance.	The crypto-legal framework adopted will need to incorporate ideas such as technological standardisation, proof of ownership of acquired emissions units and ways to ensure identification of ownership.

feature in the governance of co-operative approaches under Article 6 of the Paris Agreement.

Still, as the negotiations on operational rules and guidance for Article 6 have shown, such technological innovations face many questions and political hesitation on account of their complexity and limited track records, at least at the scale that many established carbon markets would entail. As such, a transition from conventional carbon market governance to an architecture that leverages the potential benefits of DLT and other innovations will not be easy. While this book has hopefully shed light on viable pathways towards expanded use of new technologies in carbon trading, many unresolved issues remain and can arguably only be addressed once they are rolled out in practice. That is also where the pilot projects and early actors described in this book become relevant, offering opportunities for policy learning and to demonstrate proof-of-concept at an experimental and more limited scale.

Needless to say, transitioning from existing governance structures to a DLT-supported or based architecture would entail disruptions that merit careful planning and, in some cases, a dedicated policy response. Designed by human beings thinking like a 'computer' of the 1980s as Sydney Harris predicted, administrative capacities currently devoted to operating aspects of market oversight and regulatory enforcement, or intermediaries and service providers facilitating market transactions, could see some of their functions become obsolete, necessitating reassignment of capacities and affecting current revenue streams. Still, just as the idea of carbon trading was first rendered operational through the decisions of public authorities and standard-setting organisations, its governance frameworks have seen continuous evolution, making change a constant and unavoidable dimension of carbon markets in the real world. Disruption, in other words, is not a new feature, and has been managed in the past.

Index

For EU product safety concerns, contact us at Calle de José Abascal, 56–1°,
28003 Madrid, Spain or eugpsr@cambridge.org.

www.ingramcontent.com/pod-product-compliance
Lightning Source LLC
LaVergne TN
LVHW011813200926
848484LV00005B/1183